This book is dedicated to Kendra Lynn,
my partner in life and ministry,
and my favorite model!

The Express Image
How Models Impact Our View of God,
the Trinity, and Everything Else

Printed by Ingram Sparks, November 2025
ISBN: 979-8-9936604-4-8
Published by Scott Lynn
New Hudson, Michigan 48165
Visit our church's website at
www.FamilyApostolic.org

Table of Contents

ACKNOWLEDGEMENTS

As the saying goes, we stand on the shoulders of giants, and I know I have been blessed to have great Bible teachers lay a firm foundation in my Scriptural education. There have been many wonderful influences in my life, but several played key roles in shaping my theology and approach to the Bible. I am incredibly thankful to them and so many others who have poured into my life.

As a young Christian, I first encountered David Bernard's books when I started teaching Junior High and High School Bible classes. I often taught a midweek Bible study in a thriving youth group at Apostolic Faith Church in Ypsilanti, Michigan. Back in the 1990s, I devoured Dr. Bernard's books and compared them to scripture, and the church leaders forgot to tell me I wasn't supposed to teach college-level theology to junior high and high school kids. Two of the teens told me they barely had to study in their first year at Bible college because of those classes. Dr. Bernard continues to be a great influence in my life, both in his books and the careful way he teaches and presents scriptural truth. Thank you, Dr. Bernard.

I was also blessed to be mentored by Scott Sistrunk in the 1990s. We played racquetball weekly for years and discussed the Bible in his office and on road trips. Although I never actually beat him in a single game of racquetball, I think I still won because of all the life lessons and experiences I gained. Scott Sistrunk was the first to encourage me to develop a systematic approach to understanding the Bible, and that started me on a journey that has taken me further in this great book than I ever thought possible. Thank you, Rev. Sistrunk!

I went to Indiana Bible College in 1999 for my 2nd Bachelor's, this one in Theology. I was tremendously blessed by so many professors at IBC. Paul Mooney, Thomas and Terri O'Daniel, O.C. Marler, and Talmadge French all made a significant impact on my theology and approach to ministry. When I left for IBC, I remember my pastor, William Nix, telling me, "I'm not sending you down there to get into foolish arguments about whether Jesus could sin or not... I want you to study the important topics. Learn about the blood of Jesus, faith, and repentance. Things that matter!"

I drove to IBC on a snowy day in January 1999, and I thought about his words and I prayed, "God, I want you to teach me to love the Old Testament." This was an area where I struggled, so I enrolled in Pentateuch when I arrived and met Dr. David Norris that first week in class. Not only did God answer my prayers, but the ministry and example of Dr. Norris profoundly changed my life. I interned at his church in Philadelphia that summer, and I have never met someone who loved the Bible so deeply and intellectually and yet lived ministry with such pragmatism and love for souls. Thank you to both Dr. and Nancy Norris for your profound impact on my life!

Last but far from least, I returned to Michigan and married the love of my life, Kendra. I ended up joining the "family business", as I moved back to help with the church where her dad pastored, Westland United Pentecostal Church. Serving in Ministry with James and Patricia Roberts was an amazing training ground, and I am very appreciative of the mentoring and ministerial experience I gained through the Roberts. I definitely gained in-laws and not out-laws, and James and Patti have become spiritual parents in my life. They have significantly influenced my desire to serve God and pursue ministry.

I have served under and with James Roberts in ministry, including hosting a weekly radio broadcast together for 2 years. We built and delivered an afternoon drive-time call-in program, Radio Bible Answers, broadcast weekly from Lansing, Michigan, on Fridays during the busy commuter timeslot. It was an adventure of many crazy broadcasts and amazing Bible discussions.

Thank you to both James and Patricia Roberts for your influence, love, and opportunities you gave me to grow as a young minister.

Quite a bit of any value found in this book is due to great lives and the influences of those mentioned here and others who poured into me. If there are any deficiencies or shortcomings in this book, those belong 100% to me.

I also want to recognize and appreciate the team of readers who have reviewed this book for content, flow, and grammar during its development. Thank you for your feedback and suggestions.

Dan Fauls	Joseph Ferraiuolo
Amanda Gallaway	Marc Galloway
Pastor Anthony Harper	Pastor Mark Henry
Kelsey Lynn	Kendra Lynn
Meredith Lynn	Tamika McQuiter
Katie McWatty	Pastor James Roberts
Pastor Darren Sistrunk	Pastor Marvin Walker
Reverend Gavin White	

A special thank you for the detailed feedback from James Roberts, Gavin White, Mark Henry, and Joseph Ferraiuolo. Also, Dan Fauls and Katie McWatty each found a gaping flaw that I was able to fix. Thank you!

And a huge thank you to Kelsey Lynn for her help on numerous illustrations and the chapter heading graphics for the 12 Bible patterns in part 2. She created most of the graphics in exchange for purchased books to feed her voracious reading appetite. I don't think I "paid" enough for the quality graphics she created.

A final thank you to my family and church family. Building a church together has been the greatest adventure of my life, and working alongside a wonderful team has only made it more rewarding and successful. Thank you for pursuing and serving Jesus together.

INTRODUCTION

Have you ever found yourself in an unfortunate church argument? Likely it involved some major point of doctrine, Fun... aren't they? Not really. It largely feels like each side is waiting for the other to pause long enough to jam in their next point, and one or both sides often stop hearing what the other is even saying.

This even leads to one of the most troubling questions in the modern Christian[1] world. Most understand why Catholics have different beliefs from the rest of Christianity, since they openly declare the right of the Pope and Church Councils to add and change doctrine over time, but what about all the other churches? Almost all claim their beliefs are from the Bible alone, yet there are dozens of different groups that disagree on baptism methods, salvation details, or on the identity of Christ, speaking in tongues, pre-destination, the age of the Earth, the Endtime, and even attending church on Saturday or how we should administer communion.

When an outsider considers Christianity, I feel their confusion when they ask, "Well... which group is right? How can I know?". More realistically, many conclude that no one can figure it out, so they might give up on the

---

[1] In this book, I'm using the word Christian in the general sense of anyone who identifies themselves as following Christ. I'm not interested in labeling who is a true Christian and who is not. It's above my pay grade.

whole endeavor or just pick a church because they like the music and snacks, and the preacher doesn't annoy them.

Most assume that the Bible is the issue. Each side of a given debate has its "favorite verses", and in many cases, the same side might have a list of verses that they conveniently don't talk about a lot or largely ignore. We want to assume that our group is the right one in each debate, but if we are ignoring even one verse, are we really putting God's Word in charge of our beliefs?

I didn't know about any of these church fights when I became a Christian at 17. I grew up basically Agnostic, only going to church with my mom for a few Mother's Day services. I didn't care for it. When my brother "found Jesus" in college, I was intrigued and amused at the news. I later visited Him and went to a youth service. Seeing teens truly worship, I believe I really felt God's presence for the first time in my life and wanted more. I was hungry, and looking back, I see God's hand reaching for me.

I gave my life to Christ and powerfully received God's Spirit in my first Pentecostal service on February 16, 1992. I was baptized that night in the wonderful name of Jesus and began the long and rewarding pursuit of living for God. I stayed ignorant of a lot of the doctrinal drama in the Christian world in the early years.

I met my first Jehovah's Witness, and when I learned that groups did exist that had their own special Bible or put some other authority above scripture, I immediately concluded they were ignorant and misguided to put anything above God's Word. After decades of striving to live for God, I still struggle to understand why someone would trust God to preserve His Word, then believe something else somehow outranks the Bible.

When I first learned about the Trinity, I dismissed it as a Catholic doctrine. I have never been mad at Catholics, the Pope, or the Church Councils that made their historic declarations, I just didn't care. Admittedly, I have a rebellious streak in me that automatically views traditions with skepticism. Once I learned it wasn't directly declared in the Bible, I thought that should be enough for any serious Christian to not take it seriously.

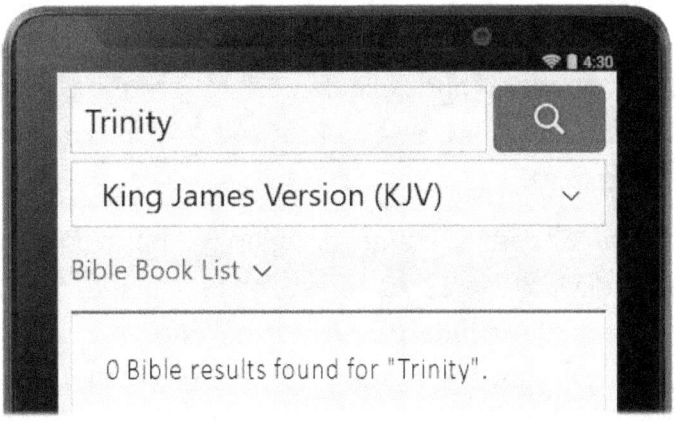

My friends in church persuaded me that this was a really big deal for many Christians, and the more I met other believers, the more I discovered that not believing in the Trinity is quite shocking to the larger Christian world.

With over 30 years of talking to people, teaching Bible studies, and bumping into doctrinal differences in different church groups, I have learned that most assume the Trinity is obviously Biblical, and daring to suggest it isn't scriptural is like suggesting we should tear one of the Gospels out of the Bible. They might know the word Trinity isn't in there. Most don't seem to know that every single one of the key words and phrases of the Trinity are missing as well. We find nothing about a "Triune God" or "co-equal, co-eternal, and co-existent". The Bible clearly teaches that Jesus is not just human but also divine, and He is plainly declared as God manifested in the flesh. The Bible never calls Jesus, "God the Son", or the second person of three. He is called both Son of Man and Son of God, but we don't find a single declaration that God is multiple persons or a single place where God is declared to be three.

Trinitarian Christians mainly bring up the baptism of Jesus and Matthew 28:19 and seem unwilling to look at verses that sound different than the Trinitarian perspective. They see multiple other verses that appear to mention different titles or roles of God (as our Father, in the Son, and through His Spirit), and they see this as clear evidence for different persons. They are rarely interested in considering an alternative perspective.

I can understand how a Trinitarian reads verses like 2nd Corinthians 13:14 and others and then struggles to believe that any other Christian doesn't see what they see.

2nd Corinthians 13:14 NKJV
The grace of the Lord Jesus Christ, and the love of God, and the communion of the Holy Spirit be with you all. Amen.

You might even be called a heretic or worse for disagreeing. This seems quite bizarre for the Apostolic who is trying to use only Biblical language and scriptural statements to describe God. If you talk any further, you can end up in another doctrinal debate that doesn't seem to get very far.

This book attempts to change this debate and actually some other doctrinal fights into a hopefully more positive perspective where both sides might actually learn something about themselves and the Bible. I am dangerously making the claim that these arguments are not over Bible translations or about whether certain words or verses should be present in the Scriptures. We agree on the Bible and are usually comfortable using any major recognized translation and all the verses in it. I believe almost everyone is on board with that point. I propose it isn't even about a favorite verse list on each side. Not just for Oneness versus Trinity, but most church debates come from a deeper divide that one or both sides likely do not recognize.

I want to recognize the divide for what it truly is. Humans use models to fit complicated pictures into simpler categories with labels that feel easier to understand. We do this all the time to make sense of our world. The shocking part comes if you realize that we use these models constantly, yet we often don't realize that models control so much of our thinking.

You will find that models are common and even directly used in Scripture. Even God does this to make His Word more understandable. Both models in the Bible and models outside God's Word serve a role in understanding ideas. But we must use them correctly!

The trouble comes when our models collide or have flaws, or we forget we are using them. Then, people arguing don't realize that their disagreement is often more about models than about Bible verses. One or both sides charge forward often completely ignorant that they have a model.

Not only do we forget we have a model, correct or possibly flawed, but we rarely understand much about the other side's model. Then, especially in matters of faith, when you question someone's model, in their ears, it sounds like you are questioning the validity of God's Word. We could make real progress if we could step back and look at our models and how different models affect how you and I view scripture.

And no… I am not saying both sides are right, but I do think we could do a lot better if we made the journey to understand a little how models control and frame our thinking. Not just in theology, but this affects most of our disagreements. Disconnected arguments and pointless debates don't get far, and moving these debates online has only further isolated groups into echo chambers. It is easier than ever to accuse the "other side" and throw cheap labels around.

In the Christian world, we dismiss the "heretic" or even pull out the big guns and label someone as being in a "cult". Maybe they are, but very few even know the characteristics of a cult. Someone being different or living differently than your beliefs is not an indicator that they are in a Christian cult – even if they like the taste of Kool-Aid®. In the political arena, we play the same games, labeling people as Fascist, Racist, or Socialist just for supporting a candidate we don't like. At least for Christians, shouldn't we show some patience and love for people who don't view the world exactly as we do?

I think self-awareness and humility help a lot here. We would do well to listen to the stern words of Jesus. He was the master at attracting followers and demanding the most from them, while pouring out grace and understanding at the same time. We have too many so sure of their beliefs and views, so arrogant in their understanding, and so quick to judge others who don't see the world the same way.

Matthew 7:3-5 NKJV

And why do you look at the speck in your brother's eye, but do not consider the plank in your own eye? ⁴ Or how can you say to your brother, 'Let me remove the speck from your eye'; and look, a plank is in your own eye? ⁵ Hypocrite! First, remove the plank from your own eye, and then you will see clearly to remove the speck from your brother's eye.

I believe it is great and appropriate to stand firm on clear scriptures for Salvation, the deity of Christ, the rejection of sin, and the authority of the Bible, while showing some grace and humility on other areas where your "models" are playing a bigger role in your thinking than we might realize. I have seen Christians go "on the attack" about their view of the rapture, or the age of the Earth, or even how to serve communion properly. They speak with the same zeal and confidence they have that Jesus is God incarnate.

I have seen people accused of not being saved or being heretics for not agreeing with the attacker's viewpoint (or model). I have been accused of being an idol-worshipper or being in a cult for wanting to just stick to Biblical language to describe Jesus. And the attacker often does not know that they even have a model.

We can do so much better. Some are likely not capable of changing their thinking, but I hope and pray you are up for it, and I hope and pray that I am too.

1st Thessalonians 5:21 NKJV
Test all things; hold fast what is good.

This book attempts to test my thinking and yours. I have a lot of stories and fun examples of good and bad thinking to make this clear. Then we can embrace Paul's instruction to the Thessalonians and hold on to the good thinking.

You made it this far in the intro, so I suspect that you and I share something in common: we both want to know the truth more than we want to win a debate. Maybe you disagree with one of the models I intentionally or accidentally have for how I view the world and God. I hope you do. I hope we can meet and talk about it. Maybe I can learn something about myself, learn where one of my models has one or more flaws, and I can take another step closer to knowing more truth. Maybe you can learn a little too, and we both can grow.

Thank you for attempting this journey with me.

Part 1

UNDERSTANDING MODELS

"I love the concept. Love the layout... but take out the arches."

Models are so universal to human thinking that talking about them might be like fish talking about what water feels like. We categorize people, observations, and ideas into models and boxes so we can make sense of a really complicated world.

"That's a stranger, keep your distance."

"Things that slither or have 8 legs go in the creepy, crawly category."

We build more complicated models to handle deeper human relationships. If you had a stable home with loving parents, your model of family and home might be one of security and warmth and love. Many have a very different upbringing, and so another model of "home" and "family" might be jagged and broken. It might cause anxiety instead of peace.

We continue to build models about school and teachers, about history, and our society. I entered high school in the late 1980s. In my public-school education, I learned that our society had a Judeo-Christian, Greco-Roman heritage and foundation. None of my teachers taught or ever encouraged us to have faith in God, but we were presented with the bedrock principles of Western Civilization. We learned about the ideas of John Locke, Voltaire, Jefferson, and others. We read the works of Christians and Atheists and talked about their ideas.

My high school history teacher, Mr. Clauser, talked openly about the greatness of America and the flaws in its past. We learned about both the Declaration of Independence as well as the stain of slavery and the sacrifices this country made to free the slaves. We read papers and books by W. E. B. Du Bois and Frederick Douglass, and we argued about their positions in class. I am thankful for an education that taught me to love the greatness of this country while not being blinded to our shortcomings.

That's one model. Maybe you would say I was indoctrinated into it, but I believe I was never forced into a worldview. My teachers taught us how to think and how to question the very things they were teaching us. I would be hard-pressed to guess the political affiliation of most of my public-school teachers. I am sure there were Republicans and Democrats in the mix. I bet some of them hated Ronald Reagan and others despised Bill Clinton, but it felt like it would have been wrong for them to tell us who to vote for even as we entered our first real election year as new adults in 1992.

Numerous online videos demonstrate modern teachers abandoning this kind of neutrality. They rarely teach about the greatness and success of Western Civilization and the American Dream. Instead, we see a generation of young people often raised to be ashamed of America. They often view the freedoms, prosperity, and values of the West as toxic and racist and one of the great evils in the world today. Teachers today seem very vocal about their political leanings and openly share their hatred for the opposition political candidates. You might agree with some or all of these views.

I am not asking you to switch to my worldview (at least not in this chapter...). I am asking you to recognize that this is a very different model through which to view the world.

WHAT DO I MEAN BY MODELS?

At the simplest level, a model is an idea box with a label, and inside the box, you find the details of the idea along with any rules and assumptions on using it.

Label Goes Here

It might be a simple idea, such as basic math through addition, or a complicated one like Capitalism or Monotheism. Models should allow you to understand the idea, sometimes to visualize it, and easily refer to that idea in conversation. They can also be like an architectural preview used to show how a building or design would look and function or fit into the neighborhood.

"It's just a model, but hopefully you get the idea..."

Some models can be incredibly complicated and difficult to build or even learn. It took scientists millions of hours over many years to identify all the elements and their properties and build the Periodic Table of Elements, but this model forms the foundation of modern chemistry.

H																	He
Li	Be											B	C	N	O	F	Ne
Na	Mg											Al	Si	P	S	Cl	Ar
K	Ca	Sc	Ti	V	Cr	Mn	Fe	Co	Ni	Cu	Zn	Ga	Ge	As	Se	Br	Kr
Rb	Sr	Y	Zr	Nb	Mo	Tc	Ru	Rh	Pd	Ag	Cd	In	Sn	Sb	Te	I	Xe
Cs	Ba	Hf	Ta	W	Re	Os	Ir	Pt	Au	Hg	Pb	Tl	Bi	Po	At	Rn
Fr	Ra	Rf	Db	Sg	Bh	Hs	Mt	Ds	Rg	Cn	Nh	Fl	Mc	Lv	Ts	Og

Once you mostly understand the box and know its label, you can refer to it by name instead of describing the entire thing each time you need it or use it.

When students learn how to solve parts of a triangle, they likely learn the famous triangle formula, the Pythagorean Theorem:

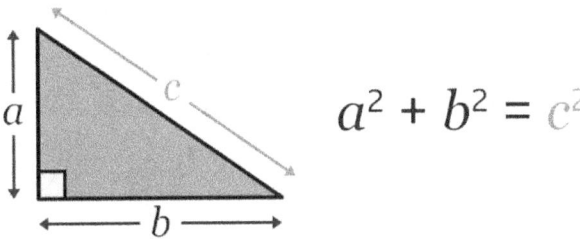

$$a^2 + b^2 = c^2$$

My teacher in high school, Mr. Kuhnert, pulled a nasty trick on us when we were learning this "model". For two years of Algebra and Calculus, he taught us the "Path-a-gor-ee-an Theorem", with the wrong pronunciation on purpose. Sometime in my senior year, someone corrected him, "My dad says you're saying it wrong." He explained that someday in college, or later in life, we would remember his special pronunciation, and get embarrassed, but later laugh and remember him.

I doubt this is great educational theory, but I did just that in my Calculus classes in college, and I looked stupid. I still smile when I remember my favorite high-school math teacher. He taught us some amazing models and idea boxes, even if he messed up the label on one of them.

Many models have little to do with math. Socialism is a model, but what's in the box with this label depends on which Socialism model you were taught.

If your teacher looked or smelled a bit like a hippie, or if their hair was green, violet, or indigo, they might have taught the paradise version of Socialism. This magical idea promises everyone's going to share the wealth, tax the rich, and live happy lives free from the oppression of the factory owners. Just because it failed every single time they tried it, doesn't mean it won't fail this time. Just vote for this group that wants your trust. They will deliver Utopia if you give them all the political power. This is one version of the model that wears the label of Socialism.

The other version, wherever Socialism's been tried, is an authoritarian regime where everyone's equal. They're equally miserable, equally poor, and equally enslaved to the power of the state. Yet somehow, the ruling political class still enjoys mansions and special food and freedom and privileges. They then extend some of those perks to their family and supporters who keep them in power. This is also Socialism, but it has only occurred in 100% of the cases where it has been tried on Earth. Maybe the other version is the real Socialism...

I mention this, not because I hate Socialism (I do hate it, because it represses freedom and blocks people from worshipping God and sharing the Gospel). I mention it because this disagreement on models, even with the same label, remains part of the problem in our arguing.

When we talk about God, we might not realize that our "God" box might not be the same box. For the atheist, their box might have Zeus and Thor and other limited, pagan deities in them. They think of the Christian God as petty, limited, and similar to these flawed examples.

For the Christian, our idea of God doesn't come from Mount Olympus but transcends the rules of space and time in this universe. So it helps to pay special attention to how some models are used and what you or I might mean when we mention a label. Often, people disagree on what ideas are in a box with the same name.

I promise we'll discuss more about what your God box might look like, but it's critical to realize that these models influence so many areas.

POLITICAL MODELS

In the past few elections, tens of millions voted for one candidate while tens of millions voted for the other. Even if we don't count all the dead people that might have voted, that's still a lot of votes for two very different directions for this country. We've reached the point where both candidates openly and regularly claim that voting for the other might be dangerous to the future of Democracy.

What astounds me is not the hatred and vitriol. Humans are broken and sinful, and we see the worst extremes in politics. I'm more amazed when I think about how little most voters actually disagree on what they want. The majority of our voters, while voting for two very different parties, really want a lot of the same things. Most of us want to live our lives, build a future, find someone to love, start a home, raise our kids, and live in safe communities. We hope to see affordable groceries on the shelves, go on a vacation now and then, and have enough money left over to maybe relax a little and avoid eating cat food in our retirement years. Most Americans in both political parties want a safe and prosperous country. We just fundamentally disagree on how to get there.

We disagree about models; some want more Capitalism, and others want more government regulation, and we need to stop labeling those who vote differently as evil.

This is getting way too controversial and heated... maybe we can switch to a topic with less tension and emotion... How about Israel and Palestine? The question of whether the Jews should have the right to a homeland in the Middle East easily tops the charts for strong emotions. Arguments are filled with incredible claims of violence and hatred on both sides. Jews are not asking for the right to a homeland. They are demanding their right to defend their country. I see their position as moral and justified, even if some of their actions are not perfect. This is one model.

If you attempt to talk to many Muslims, their perspective is often bizarre and rooted in a very different model that (for me) feels disconnected from reality. They claim the Jews are taught at a young age to hate Arabs, and they seem unwilling to consider any evidence to the contrary. They claim Israel is committing genocide against the Palestinian people. Could this be true? Less than 200,000 Arabs were living in Israel at the end of the Arab-Israel war in 1948. There are more than 1.5 million Arabs in Israel today. I am not sure they understand what the word Genocide means. Where are the Jews in Libya, Egypt, Iran, Syria, and other countries? Their "disappearance" feels a lot more genocidal than the growing Arab population living around and in Israel.

Maybe you cannot agree with me that the Jews are treating Palestinians much better than Arabs in general treat Jews, but can we agree that this whole conflict is rooted in two very different models about how to view a Jewish nation and their right to a homeland?

So our culture and politics, even world politics, have models. I know I have yet to be specific on those models, and this book is largely focused on models in Christian doctrine, but you must understand that the modeling problem is a human one, and it can touch every area of human interaction. If we can get people to talk about the models and the basis for their models, maybe we can enact real change in the world.

I was talking to a young Arab man, I believe from Tunisia, about the Palestine-Israeli conflict. He was the most recent, for me, to claim that Jewish children are taught to hate Arabs in school. I disagreed, because I have seen no evidence of this... at all... anywhere. The Jews, as far as I can tell, just want to peacefully live in their homeland, and I mentioned that many Arabs love living in Israel, and some even serve voluntarily in the Israeli Defense Force. He rejected the claim and adamantly declared it was not true. Yet there are multiple videos on YouTube by different media groups with the life stories of these soldiers. Watching those videos might be the first step towards seeing huge flaws in the model he has been taught. He appeared completely uninterested and unwilling to watch a single video.

I believe the very idea that his model might be wrong, was just unacceptable... or inconceivable. It was easier to refuse to look at anything[2] that might disagree with his worldview. The Arab-Israeli conflict is simple. Many Muslims want the Jews dead, and the Jews are not cooperating with their efforts. Getting a Western Muslim growing up in America to see this is often not simple. I don't know what it takes to get someone living in Syria or Iran to see this.

Hopefully, I haven't distracted you with these diverse examples. I included them to show how universal and difficult it is to get people to think about their models. It takes courage to consider that YOU or I might be wrong and need to change our view of the world. It takes a little courage and a lot of effort just to make the journey to see the world through the eyes of a different model. You must ask questions and contemplate ideas that feel

---

[2] YouTube® video titled "*Arab, Israeli, & Proud*", published Nov 8, 2021 on the channel: PragerU.

foreign and strange to your mind. Judging others is easier and often more fun.

We would hope that these same complications won't be found among Christians. After all, we know we're supposed to love each other and even our enemies. Add to that the strong Biblical language against judging too quickly.

Unfortunately, Christians are still human, sinful, and flawed, and so the same tendencies of the world creep into the church. We're not perfect and far from it.

Then we add religious fervor to the mix. It's not just our worldview that we naturally want to defend. Now we have a desire to protect things that we believe are sacred. As a result, church fights can cut deeper than even political divides. We're not just defending our models; we believe we're defending God and His Word.

THE POSITIVE CASE FOR MODELS

You made it this far. Congratulations. I wrestled with the question of including cultural and political models in the book, but I believe it's essential to recognize that this problem is not fundamentally a church problem but something hard-wired into humanity. Maybe it's just a sin problem.

And models are NOT the problem. They're incredibly useful in almost any field where you want to build upon prior knowledge. Have you ever wondered why they wanted us to learn Algebra and Geometry in school? One Dad once said, "Are they still looking for X? They were looking for that when I was your age..."

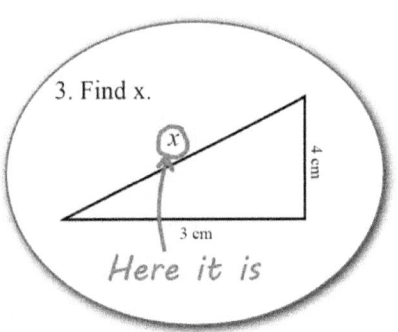

3. Find x.

x

4 cm

3 cm

Here it is

But Algebra plays a role in the ability to develop higher reasoning and abstraction skills. If your life goal is to run the deep fryer basket at a fast-food chain, then maybe you can skip Algebra, but if you want to dive deeper into any branch of higher reasoning, including science, medicine, engineering, computers, or even theology, then get used to using fundamental blocks of knowledge through models that you learn to trust and build upon.

We have a model for Logic, and we then take Algebra, Geometry, and what we learned in Logic, and build a new layer on top of that called Calculus. This opens a door to deeper understanding. Now we can solve more challenging problems, including advancements, especially in Physics and Engineering, but also in Biology and Medicine.

Even many in the skilled trades, such as Carpenters, Plumbers, and Electricians, benefit from deeper knowledge. What goes on inside the pipes, across the wires, and where beams connect leads to better buildings, better flushing toilets, and even that phone you have been staring at too much this week.

You don't need to find X to live a great and fulfilling life. You don't need to find X if you want to love God or even to figure out why so many Muslims and Jews don't get along very well. But you really want your pilot, your surgeon, and the engineer who designed your anti-lock brakes to be someone who was able to find X. Then they went on to solve a bunch of harder problems afterwards.

Algebra is one example. Knowing models can yield even greater fruit in many fields. Linguists use models to understand how languages form and change over time. Historians use models to explain how societies shift and change. Colonialism is a model. Nationalism, Capitalism, and Socialism are models that can be adopted or abandoned and should at least be understood.

Then they can be argued on their own merits. They should be argued if you want to understand what kind of world we should live in. Models are everywhere and form the basis of higher reasoning and progress. It remains essential and useful to recognize models and know how they work.

How do we analyze a model? When should I adopt a model, tweak a model, or even abandon it?

THE MODEL FOR THIS BOOK

This book attempts to get into your head and get you to think about your models and how accurate they might be. I fear some meandering is necessary, as we explore different examples of models and how they affect us. We've done some wandering already, and we have more to cover. Perhaps a roadmap, or even a model for this book, can help you on the journey?

I'm approaching this topic in two parts. The first half makes the case for how models work. I've already claimed that most disagreements are rooted in their models, and not necessarily individual facts, but also that models might influence which facts we're willing to examine. We will shortly explore some models found directly in the Bible, including an example of a model not directly declared in scripture, but agreed upon by almost all Christians (the Dual-Nature of Christ). Then we explore a few models that cause common church fights.

We finish the first half by looking at what makes a great model and then comparing that to a poor model for God.

In the second half of this book, we dive deeper into our models, specifically for God, and why they matter. We will compare two models for the Incarnation against the major themes found in the Bible. We conclude by asking a simple but sublime question: "What does God look like, according to His Word?"

To revisit an earlier point, our models matter, and we need models (God even gave us models) as a means to think more complicated and deeper thoughts about Life and the Universe. I am pro-model and believe that it is an essential building block for higher learning and progress. Without these good "idea boxes" and labels, we remain stuck in the shallow end of the pool of learning.

Genius in 1969

"We did it. We put a man on the moon!!!"

Genius Today

"I rebooted your phone, it works now"

LIFE WITHOUT MODELS: FLAT-EARTHERS

If you want to see what life is like without models, the Flat-Earth community might be a great start. There are a few brave souls in this odd group who are trying to build limited models for their pizza-shaped world, but the "movement" as a whole is a group who have not excelled much at math or higher education. They have then concluded that everyone else has bought into a lie that would seemingly benefit no one. It's a conspiracy that makes no sense, but most of these people are not joking.

Flat-Earthers, all over the globe, reject the very idea that any ball model of our Earth should define our perception of reality. Go ahead and give it a try and attempt to explain the sheer size of the planet to these open-minded geniuses. Tell them how difficult it might be to detect rotation or see the curvature while standing on the surface of such a huge world. They will mock your silly spinning-ball model. They walk outside, and look around, and it looks flat enough to them!

Then they want to shock you with sentences they have memorized that do sound strange when you first hear them. "How could we be moving 1,000 mph sideways on a spinning ball?" "Why can't we detect all that motion and change?" Then they show you a picture of a tranquil lake. They say things like "water seeks its own level". You will likely be asked to prove the Earth is round, without using NASA's help, and you may be shocked that it's harder than you think. When you ask why you cannot use pictures from NASA or the moon missions, you learn that they're supposedly all faked. NASA is in on the conspiracy, hiding the truth of Earth's flatness to maintain the globe deception. No tinfoil hats here...

The Flat-Earther feels vindicated when most people struggle to provide a single proof of Earth's curvature. Most of us have a very limited science education, and we haven't used it in a meaningful way in years. Most people haven't invested[3] hundreds or thousands of hours committed to a conspiracy that doesn't seem to accomplish anything.

How far can they go to reject models? Most Flat-Earthers don't believe humans ever went to space, and that landing on the moon was faked. Most don't even believe in gravity. But they're not willing to step off a roof to prove it. It is common for them to believe that we live on

---

[3] wasted...

a disc surrounded by a giant ice wall and covered by a dome. Humans are "not allowed" to visit Antarctica, and the sun and moon are much smaller and closer and circling overhead.

If you ask for details or math formulas, you can forget about it. They won't talk about the details. The Flat-Earth "model" is very limited. It really is a rejection of models.

Flat-Earthers mention things like density and buoyancy as the cause for stuff falling. They don't understand that density is not a force. They often don't understand forces or how pressure works, and they especially struggle with perspective and math in three dimensions. Their entire set of proofs is very simple experiments often done on a kitchen table or in the backyard.

For some reason, many believe that taking a bubble level on a plane proves our world is flat. They apparently think that flying over a gigantic and gently curving ball should feel like riding a roller-coaster over the crest of a hill. I am thankful it is not.

My favorite example is when a group raised the funds to purchase a ring-laser gyroscope for $20,000 to prove that there is no rotation on Earth. This incredibly sensitive instrument can detect rotation, which they say isn't happening here. They also filmed what they found, and (to their credit) they shared the results online. The fancy gyroscope detected a 15° change per hour sitting still on a table. You can find the video of their experiment on YouTube. In an amazing coincidence, if you consider the 360° rotation of the Earth every day and divide it by 24 hours... well... you will find X, and it looks like X is on a very round ball. Our world actually shifts 15° every hour as it rotates. So, their own experiment proved we live on a globe, but they are so against the idea of a "globe model" that they rejected the evidence in front of them.

That's why Flat-Earth might be the best and worst example of the rejection of models. They are determined to find truth through simple experiments, and when you ask for a model of how the sun and moon move above us, or how tides work, or why long airline flights work in the southern hemisphere, they struggle or refuse.

Why do they believe this? I believe their root issue is not math, but a perception of a world that feels broken to them and a profound disconnect between what they want to believe and what they see around them. The conspiracy is their model. Then a bunch of weird observations fall into the mix. They see a political world that doesn't represent common people, and a media empire that feels like indoctrination. They are not wrong about some of those issues. Heap other disconnects and frustrations on top of that, and the conspiracy monster starts whispering in their ears. They don't really want to dive into deeper abstractions and math. It looks really hard, because it often is. Math is tricky, and Physics using math even more so[4]. They want to look outside, see how flat it often looks, and do simple experiments and insist this is the path to the "truth".

For the rest of us, the reasonable person should not reject models outright, but should test them and weigh them, and view them as potential building blocks of learning. It helps to know that models can have limits, even ones that are absolutely believed to be valid and trusted.

We should not hate or despise models. They are tools to be used to gain knowledge and solve problems. As we dive next into models found in the Bible, we can learn about the natural limits of even the models we know that we know are true[5].

---

[4] And yes, we live on a giant spinning ball. If you live near the equator, you are moving sideways about 1,000 mph. Just because you cannot feel the movement, doesn't mean you are standing still. Go on a cruise, on one of the really large ships, and you can enjoy experiencing movement you cannot feel or detect on multiple days.

[5] Remember, this is a book by a Christian for Christians.

SCOTT'S FIRST RULE OF MODELS

You are NOT your models. Your identity can remain separate from models, even from models you agree with as true and trusted.

You are free to "identify" with a model if it aligns with your values, but allowing a model to control your thinking without being aware of it is dangerous and the very definition of ignorance.

For instance, I think Capitalism is the best model for voluntary human interaction, but I do NOT identify as a Capitalist. It works better than the other options and is the most moral, but it is not part of my core identity.

I do identify as a Christian and an Apostolic, but I don't demand that you accept or affirm my labels and models to be my friend. You can reject my models without rejecting me. You can even reject my favorite models.

I can disagree with or reject your models and ideas without rejecting you.

MODELS IN THE BIBLE

This section is not the same as Biblical models. I believe Christians have come up with multiple true models to make it easier to understand the Bible. Those would be "Biblical models". Unfortunately, we have other models believed by Christians but incompatible with the Bible, or at least not supported by scripture. How do you know which ones are true? Well, obviously, the ones you believe are correct, and all the others are wrong[6]...

Let's first look at some models that God has given us and declared as models for us. One clear difference is that the models God directly provides should be accepted and understood with much greater confidence than models we have created to "better understand God's Word".

If you are like me, then you know that God's Word IS TRUE, but any models we have added to explain God's Word should not be defended with the same confidence and commitment. By the way, this understanding of God's Word is also a model – I think a very valid one.

Let's consider three models found directly in the Bible that are metaphoric. They are absolutely true but have limits in their application.

---

[6] Please don't make me clarify that this is a joke...

MODEL #1 – JESUS OUR PASSOVER LAMB

Exodus 12:3-13 NKJV

...every man shall take for himself a lamb... Your lamb shall be without blemish, a male of the first year... Then the whole assembly of the congregation of Israel shall kill it at twilight. ⁷ And they shall take some of the blood and put it on the two doorposts and on the lintel of the houses where they eat it. ⁸ Then they shall eat the flesh on that night; roasted in fire, with unleavened bread and with bitter herbs they shall eat it... So you shall eat it in haste. It is the Lord's Passover.

Now the blood shall be a sign for you on the houses where you are. And when I see the blood, I will pass over you.

John 1:29 NKJV

The next day John saw Jesus coming toward him, and said, "Behold! The Lamb of God who takes away the sin of the world!"

Christians marvel at the word pictures in scripture, and few move us as much as the knowledge that Jesus Christ took our punishment so we don't have to pay a penalty we cannot afford. The picture of Jesus as our Passover Lamb powerfully evokes that we need this blood applied to our lives for God to pass over us at the time of judgment.

Even in the last supper (a Passover meal) and also in remembrance at communion, we recognize and celebrate this symbolism when we eat the bread (often made without leaven) and drink the wine and consume Christ metaphorically, connecting us with a teaching that begins in Exodus 12:8 and continues in the church today.

For the unbeliever, the cross and the sacrifice of Christ are a stumbling block or foolishness. But for me, and hopefully for you, it is the power and wisdom and love of God on display through this model.

Jesus is truly our Passover lamb, but this model is metaphoric and there are limitations, because Jesus is also the great I Am, and so it would be wrong to limit the identity, role, and scope of Jesus to just this sacrifice.

He is absolutely the lamb that takes away the sins of the world, but He is also and obviously, much more than a lamb. It would be b-a-a-a-a-a-d to attempt to limit our thinking of Jesus in terms of sheep. This is God in Christ reconciling the world to Himself, and the word picture God gives us is Biblical, but metaphoric and limited.

Jesus is also the King of Kings, the Alpha and Omega, He is God manifest in the flesh, as well as the great I Am. Jesus is the Son of God and also the Son of Man. Isaiah tells us that His name is called Wonderful, Counselor, Mighty God, Everlasting Father, and Prince of Peace. He occupies and fulfills multiple titles and roles in the lives of His followers. If you are keeping score, some of the titles above are metaphoric and some are not.

MODEL #2 – TAKE UP YOUR CROSS

Matthew 16:24-25 NKJV
Then Jesus said to His disciples, "If anyone desires to come after Me, let him deny himself, and take up his cross, and follow Me. ²⁵ For whoever desires to save his life will lose it, but whoever loses his life for My sake will find it."

Calvary represents the burden of Christ and the burden each Christian must carry, and the cross represents losing your life and gaining Christ in return.

In this model, and in the Passover Lamb, we see the first clear examples that these models have limits. They should be understood this way if we want to pursue and fulfill their meaning.

Jesus is much more than a lamb, and his ministry and teaching clearly encompass all of that. Understanding that He is our Passover Lamb should not detract from His miracles, His ministry, and His message.

In the same way, we should understand that this cross for us is not physical in nature, but symbolic and spiritual. It should be a real thing in our lives, but not necessarily made of poplar or perpendicular wooden pieces. It could be a burden to win souls, or support your church, or to use your musical talents for the kingdom of God instead of worldly gain.

We see the broken version of this metaphor where a few odd Christians in the past intentionally hit themselves with boards and whips to suffer on purpose. Others built and climbed atop pillars and lived there for years to demonstrate their desire for holiness and piety.

Really... a pillar? Where everyone can see you and you are clearly "above" the rest of us? That's not taking up your cross. It could only be more obnoxious if they had social media, and they posted updates about their own special #PillarLife spiritual journey.

These are false, man-made replacements for what God would ask from each of us. They draw people's attention away from God to the glory of public suffering.

I have a cross to bear, and it might take a lifetime to fully determine what it is. I gladly give that lifetime to Christ in pursuit of this knowledge, and I'm honored to commit to this great calling. I don't need to proclaim the details to anyone else, and neither do you. We just need to pursue Christ. But this model is, again, metaphoric, and best understood and applied this way.

MODEL #3 – THE CHURCH IS THE BRIDE

Revelation 19:7-8 NKJV

Let us be glad and rejoice and give Him glory, for the marriage of the Lamb has come, and His wife has made herself ready. ⁸ And to her it was granted to be arrayed in fine linen, clean and bright, for the fine linen is the righteous acts of the saints.

Ephesians 5:25-27 NKJV

Husbands, love your wives, just as Christ also loved the church and gave Himself for her, ²⁶ that He might sanctify and cleanse her with the washing of water by the word, ²⁷ that He might present her to Himself a glorious church, not having spot or wrinkle or any such thing, but that she should be holy and without blemish.

This model, to me, might be the most sublime and wonderful in all of Scripture. Marriage is not just about love and commitment, but God intended this union to point to a deeper, eternal relationship. This teaching is utterly lost on the modern Christian world. We focus too much on feelings, love, and gratification, and many avoid being politically incorrect, while we are attacked for our supposed intolerance.

Marriage is a model of an eternal relationship between two creatures, very much NOT THE SAME. Marriage points to a model of Christ and His church, and it does this through the man and the woman. In our God-given genders, we are very different in physiology and temperament, in capabilities and talents, and yet we can join together and build something more beautiful than either could construct alone.

This is another metaphoric model that clearly comes with limits. The wife can only be "like the church" in certain ways, and we know the husband has a challenge to strive to be like Jesus. This is why Biblical marriage is between one man and one woman. When we realize we can pursue the call of God and honor sacred things in how we live, it is thrilling to be in a Christian marriage and to strive to live God's way!

The Biblical model makes marriage more significant and gives us a reason to celebrate weddings, protect marriage, and honor this great institution. As our society has abandoned its Biblical underpinnings, it is no wonder that the quality and endurance of marriage have sharply declined in the past half-century. Secular America gave up on the Bible, lost the model, and is now losing the benefits of the nuclear family that helped make our nation so great.

I love the model of the church as the bride, even if I am a man, and I don't look all that great in white, but the metaphor of belonging to God intimately and being so highly valued should speak volumes to a world that values human life so poorly.

I have one last critical observation about metaphoric models, and once you see it, it may be hard to unsee this amazing pattern in scripture. Consider the Passover Lamb, or the model of marriage, or take up your cross, or any other model with a type and shadow. If you think about it at all, you will realize that in Biblical models, specifically in the metaphoric models, the type and its fulfillment are always connected, but always fundamentally different in their nature.

✓ The Red Sea crossing was a baptism –
   but they didn't get wet...

✓ Christ is the Rock that provided drink in the desert –
   but He isn't actually a rock...

✓ The priest had to wash before serving in the Temple –
   but that physical washing was only symbolic of the
   spiritual cleansing that comes from faith.

✓ Then Jesus had to be baptized before beginning His
   ministry, but His washing wasn't even spiritually
   necessary, but was to fulfill the pattern.

✓ Jesus is our Passover lamb – but more than a lamb.

✓ Jesus is our shepherd – but we're not really sheep.

✓ We are to take up our cross to follow –
   but not a physical wooden cross.

✓ Marriage symbolizes Christ and the church –
   but it is fulfilled through one man and one woman.

✓ Baptism represents a burial –
   I am glad they don't keep you under for long...

When considering the Biblical models, especially the ones that are metaphors, look carefully at the ones where we understand more about their fulfillment. In the case of types and shadows, the hint or promise is always different in some way from the thing that it points towards.

This last point isn't central to the message of this book, so no extra charge for including it. As a nugget of wisdom, it's just too good to leave out:

SCOTT'S SECOND RULE OF MODELS

Biblical models and their fulfillment are almost always different in kind and nature.

OTHER CHRISTIAN MODELS

Let's examine a model that is very scriptural but not directly declared in scripture, like the ones listed before.

MODEL #4 – THE HYPOSTATIC UNION

Colossians 2:9 NKJV
For in Him [Christ] dwells all the fullness of the Godhead bodily.

Philippians 2:5-7 NKJV
Let this mind be in you which was also in Christ Jesus, [6] who, being in the form of God, did not consider it robbery to be equal with God, [7] but made Himself of no reputation, taking the form of a bondservant, and coming in the likeness of men.

Revelation 22:16 NKJV
I, Jesus, have sent My angel to testify to you these things in the churches. I am the Root and the Offspring of David, the Bright and Morning Star.

The Bible clearly teaches the full humanity and full divinity of Christ, but past that, how these interact is not fully explained. Yet this doctrine of the Dual-Nature of Christ is one of the most agreed upon in the Christian world. Jesus was fully God and fully man. He acted and spoke sometimes in His divinity and other times He acted and spoke under the limitations of a real human man.

This is affirmed by multiple verses. It is also held by the Roman Catholic church and multiple church councils, along with the Orthodox churches and Protestant church groups. Apostolics do not consider any of these extra-Biblical sources as authoritative or binding, but the doctrine of the Dual-Nature of Christ is also recognized and affirmed by Apostolics (i.e. Oneness Pentecostals).

We can agree and hopefully do agree that this is a great Biblical model. This is an excellent example of a declarative and ontological model that requires more than one verse to clearly demonstrate it, yet is clearly scriptural. We explore this model in greater depth in the second half of this book as we consider the full deity and humanity of Christ.

Ontology – the study of the nature of being or what exists. Ontology explores fundamental categories and the structure of reality. Ontological statements define what a thing is, or how it must operate.

If you don't believe in the Dual-Nature of Christ, then you either have not studied the Bible much, or you have some other external model that is controlling your thinking and blinding you to the basic Biblical presentation of Jesus.

This model enjoys widespread agreement in Christianity. Unfortunately, the next Christian models are where more common and famous church debates begin...

Models #5, 6, 7 – The Rapture Models

Pre-Trib Rapture

✓ Defines all 7 years of Daniel's 70th week as the Tribulation.

✓ Absolutely convinced that the church is not appointed to receive or experience the wrath of God in Revelation.

✓ Believes the return of Christ is imminent (can happen at any time), and it is wrong to believe that any event could be required to happen first.

Post-Trib Rapture

✓ Only the last three and ½ years are called the Great Tribulation.

✓ Points to examples of believers facing the mark of the beast and other evidence that we are going to go through some Tribulation.

✓ Believes that the rapture happens at the end of the Trib week, perhaps in Revelation 14.

Pan-Trib Rapture

✓ Fairly tired of all the rapture debate, and this group just believes in Jesus, and that it will all pan-out at the end!

It's amazing to think about how 2 positions could come from the same book and be any different. In this case, it makes more sense when you realize that the primary timeline used as a framework for understanding the Endtime comes from Daniel 9. Yet none of the major events in this 7-year timeline are mentioned even once directly in the book of Revelation. We find no clear mention of a treaty, or the breaking of the treaty, or even the Abomination of Desolation event. We have no direct reference in Revelation to when the 7 years clearly start or when they end. Yes, there are references to time that add up to three and ½ years, but that still is one step removed from the "1 week equals 7 years" model.

Please don't misunderstand me. I know that at least one person reading this, and obsessed with the Endtime, is incredulous and frustrated with the idea that I might not believe in the rapture.

That is wrong. I do believe in the rapture as a literal and vertical gathering of the church to meet Jesus in the air. I also believe that each "week" in Daniel 9 is 7 years long, and there is a final 7-year "week" coming. I believe most of Revelation is still future. I still believe for numerous scriptural reasons that the Daniel 9 timeline of "70 weeks" contains an Endtime fulfillment. You can calm down now and continue reading...

I am only daring to suggest that the connection between Daniel 9 and Revelation is a lot more indirect than many Endtime scholars recognize. The lack of clear references to Daniel, in the book of Revelation, causes some of the tension and debate.

Most of the rapture disagreement is a model fight, and the lack of communication on the different sides tends to exhaust the rest of us.

I struggle with this one, because I see Biblical truth from both sides. I agree with the Pre-Trib model that the church will not be present for God's wrath. The scriptures on this seem very clear[7]. I also agree with some claims of the Post-Trib model, especially where it looks like some Christians are here for at least the 5th seal. Other verses, including Matthew 24:31 and 2nd Thessalonians 2:1-4, seem to put a "vertical gathering" at least after the Abomination of Desolation. Can these be reconciled? Not in this book... But at least I succeeded in annoying both sides by bringing it up.

I made the mildly dangerous decision to include the Rapture models in this book because they are clear examples of models where their advocates sometimes make very little effort to understand the position and reasoning of the opposite side.

I do wish that both camps were more aware that these are models, and we need to show some humility in these disagreements. If we could talk about our models and their common ground and differences, both sides and the rest of us might learn something.

---

[7] 1st Thes 5:9, Rev 3:10, Probably Luke 17:26-36

MODEL #8 – CALVINIST PRE-DESTINATION

Calvinism

- ✓ Points to the verses that specifically mention pre-destination and the elect as proof for the tenets of Calvinism.

- ✓ Concludes that humans play zero role in their own salvation. God picked a few and damned the rest, no matter what people do.

The Rest of Us, Provisionalists and Arminianists

- ✓ Points to numerous verses that mention human choices, describing them as real choices made by real people with real free will.

- ✓ Humans play a direct role in accepting or rejecting God's offer of salvation, and this in no way earns salvation. It is a gift of God, and we are given a real choice. This choice to live for God is a significant theme of the Bible.

Again, it's amazing to think about how 2 positions could come from the same book and be any more different... but that is the problem with bad models.

Again, this is a model fight, and not really a Bible verse fight, but in this case, it is bizarrely difficult to get a Calvinist to even realize they have a model. They don't even struggle to dismiss the Free-Will position, largely because they see predestination as clearly scriptural, and their side is viewed as a beautifully integrated philosophical system they believe comes from the Bible. Any opposition to this system is just the result of a fallen and sinful man attempting to understand God's beautiful system. Contemplating any alternatives appears ridiculous, and dismissing the verses that don't sound or feel Calvinist becomes second nature.

If you have never heard of Calvinism, this position likely begins as a reaction and opposition to the rampant corruption and works-based salvation of the Catholic Church. Martin Luther concluded that humans play basically zero role in their salvation. John Calvin took this starting point to its worst conclusion – that God doesn't really love everyone, and he made some to be saved, and others were designed by God to go to hell.

The acronym TULIP is often used to describe Calvinism. Although it was developed centuries later, it remains accurate in describing their core beliefs. Most Calvinists use this acronym to describe their system.

T – Total Depravity – We are so enslaved to the service of sin, and we are utterly unable to choose to follow God, refrain from evil, or accept the gift of salvation as it is offered. We don't choose God. He chooses us, and only some of us, according to His purposes.

U – Unconditional Election – Before God created the world, he chose to save some people according to his own purposes. Saving grace is given by God. You do nothing to activate, accept, or receive it.

L – Limited Atonement – Jesus did not die for everyone, but only for the predestined elect of God. His death and the atonement are limited to just those predestined to salvation. Even many Calvinists struggle to believe in Limited Atonement because of Bible verses like John 3:16 that directly contradict this odd teaching.

I – Irresistible Grace – Those who obtain salvation do so, not by their own free will, but because of the sovereign grace of God. People do not choose God and cannot refuse God. Their free will is an illusion. If God chooses you, you cannot resist His grace. This one amazes me, because the longer I live, the more I see that humans seem to be experts at resisting the grace of God.

P – Perseverance of the Saints (Once Saved Always Saved) – Once someone is truly born of God, nothing in heaven or earth shall be able to separate them from the love of God, including their own free will. You didn't decide to be saved, and you cannot refuse salvation if you change your mind. Your choices don't lead to salvation and won't ruin it either.

This is a case of models at their very worst. The Calvinist worldview is in charge, and the Bible is pushed to the back seat. The resolution isn't obvious, because Calvinist thinking and definitions dominate the conversation.

They just dismiss the promises of scripture, including John 3:16, which says God loves everyone, and Titus 2:11's declaration that God's grace is for everyone.

Titus 2:11 NKJV
For the grace of God that brings salvation has appeared to all men.

Predestination is in the Bible. God's Word declares that He has predestined numerous things. Revelation 13:8 declares that the Lamb was slain from the beginning of creation. Genesis 3 reveals that the offspring of Eve is predestined to wound the head of the serpent. One last example: God declares that He will bless the whole world through Abraham in Genesis 12. Calvinism goes much further than specific declarations of scripture to require God to predestine everything, including every individual decision, and the Bible doesn't back them on this.

Besides basically reading the Bible and seeing a constant theme that human choices matter to God, the simplest proof against Calvinism is found in 1st John 4:8 and 1st Corinthians 13:5. The Bible says that God is love and...

1st Corinthians 13:5 NLT
...[Love] does not demand its own way.

As the NKJV puts it, love "does not seek its own", so we can know that God, in His core attribute of love, will not force His will on us, but in love gives us a true choice.

Once you abandon the non-Biblical idea that God pre-determined every specific detail and decision ever, you can examine the parts that are actually pre-destined, and you might see that God has pre-destined the church corporately, but the verses on individual choices are also real, clear, and true. This only works if the Calvinist can suspend belief in their model long enough to really let God's Word back into the driver's seat. This is a huge ask, and requires humility, something that appears to be rare for many, but the starting point is to recognize that there is a difference between your model and the Bible.

This book is not about refuting Calvinism. Other works were predestined for that task. I just need to get you to think about models and how they affect your thinking. If you want to learn more about this specific model, I highly recommend Dr. Leighton Flowers' YouTube channel, Soteriology 101.

My goal in presenting these different models is to firmly establish that we have multiple model fights in the church, and really throughout humanity, and that the models are the primary source for disagreement and disconnect. It's not the "facts" or different "Bible verses" that cause the conflicts. The models divide us.

I am risking offending and annoying quite a few readers by bringing up examples like this, but I badly need you to realize how much the models influence our thinking. Therefore, thinking about the models really matters.

I have been too controversial in my examples. Let's look at one last model that probably won't offend anyone...

MODEL #9 – BIBLICAL SALVATION

The Just-Believe Model

✓ The emphasis is on simple belief in Jesus and the acceptance of Jesus as personal Lord and Savior.

✓ There is a general belief that you must be born again, but few details about what that means.

✓ Bible passages that emphasize being born of the water and/or Spirit as part of salvation are rejected as NOT necessary to avoid anything that looks like "works salvation". They are either accepted as bonus experiences or rejected and dismissed as not for today. Definitely not part of salvation.

✓ Baptism is taught as an outward sign of an inward confession.

You Must Be Born of Water and Spirit Model

✓ Emphasis is on fulfilling and obeying plain and simple verses in the Bible (John 3:5, Acts 2:38).

✓ "You must be born again", "of the water and Spirit", "He that believes and is baptized shall be saved", "repent and be baptized in the name of Jesus Christ for the forgiveness of sins, and you shall receive the gift of the Holy Spirit."

Apostolics differ with the larger Christian world in three significant areas:

1. We point to the Biblical language about God and the deity of Christ over the historical language of the Trinity added centuries later.

2. We recognize the Biblical commands about salvation and obeying the gospel over the commonly accepted language of just believing on Jesus as your Lord to be saved.

3. We honor and follow the Biblical language and commands to strive to live a holy life and to apply the plain Biblical principles for modesty, separation, and Christian conduct over the popular message that God loves you just the way you are, and you don't have to change to be a Christian.

Apostolic Pentecostals are criticized, sometimes harshly, over all three areas of difference. I do see an interesting pattern in this second area, specifically with salvation doctrine. The disagreement of models for salvation feels very different than the Oneness vs Trinity debate. In both cases, Apostolics are attempting to emphasize Biblical language while believing our critics are emphasizing church traditions over the Bible.

In the Trinitarian debate, our model is the "simpler" one. We just believe God is one and honor the emphasis on the Oneness of God in scripture. Then we see that

God is in Jesus, and Jesus is the image of God. Jesus acted both in His divinity and His humanity, and this one explanation answers most scriptural challenges.

Since Trinitarians also believe in the Dual-Nature of Christ, on a fundamental level, both sides agree with these core doctrines. The Trinitarians then add multiple details and language not taught in scripture, making the Trinitarian picture of God more complicated than the Oneness model.

When we consider our differences in Salvation, the situation flips in a strange way. The Apostolics now have the "more complicated" model. Evangelical Christians hold to the "simpler" view that you just need to "believe on Jesus" and you are saved.

Romans 10:9 NKJV
That if you confess with your mouth the Lord Jesus and believe in your heart that God has raised Him from the dead, you will be saved.

Apostolics have been accused of requiring more than simple belief. Of course, we believe that Romans 10:9 is a true and wonderful promise, but we do not believe this verse is comprehensive in describing salvation. For instance, this verse does not mention faith, but most agree that faith is required for salvation. This verse, in context, is not about the methodology of salvation but about the critical need of Jews to accept and confess the identity and authority of Jesus.

In a broader sense, acknowledging Jesus is part of anyone's salvation, but the focus in Romans chapters 9 through 11 is on Israel and their rejection of the Messiah. Paul is reminding Jewish believers of the critical need to acknowledge Jesus as Lord as part of God's plan for us.

Apostolic Pentecostals get accused of legalism for looking at and including other verses in the larger answer of "what must I do to be saved?". For instance, Romans 10:9 mentions nothing about repentance. Do you have to repent of your sins to be saved? Most of the Just-Believe-on-Jesus Christians would agree that a sinner still needs to repent of their sins. So, Romans 10:9 is true, but not a comprehensive description of salvation.

Apostolics believe salvation includes the following:

- ✓ **Faith in Christ** – a belief that drives a person to real actions to live for God (Ephesians 2:8-9, Romans 5:1-2, Hebrews 11:1).

- ✓ **Repentance** – intentionally turning away from sin and towards God (Luke 13:3, Luke 24:47, Acts 2:38, 2nd Peter 3:9).

- ✓ **Being born of the water** – through baptism by immersion in the name of Jesus for the forgiveness of sins (John 3:3-5, Mark 16:16, Acts 2:38, Acts 10:48).

✓ **Being born of the Spirit** – by receiving God's Holy Spirit as a distinct supernatural experience (John 3:3-5, John 7:39, Acts 2:38, Acts 8:14-17, Romans 8:9).

✓ **Living a Spirit-led life** - Christians should pursue an ongoing desire to be connected to God and His plan. This is not a one-time fire-insurance experience, but salvation is the start of a vibrant relationship of living for God as a born-again, Spirit-led believer (Matt 22:37, Gal 5:18, Romans 12:1-2, 1st Peter 1:3-9).

You might very well agree with several items on this list. Even if you come from the Just-Believe-on-Jesus model, you likely think that faith and repentance are part of salvation, but that is not why I mention salvation models here. Perhaps this will lead to another book. I mention the disagreements here because of how the Apostolic model is "more complicated" than how most Evangelical Christians view salvation.

Our Oneness view of God is "simpler" than the Trinitarian model, while our salvation model is the more "complicated" one. It involves more steps than simply believing on Jesus. Why do we have these differences?

Apostolics point to the scriptures as our basis for both areas of difference. We hope and believe that our model in both cases comes directly from Scripture instead of man-made traditions and church history.

For the Apostolic, we see the Trinitarian model attempting to add to and change the scriptural word picture. The Bible simply declares that Jesus is the image of God (Colossians 1:15). The Trinity says, "No, that is not what God looks like. God is three persons, and Jesus is actually the 2nd person of a Triune God that includes the three but are somehow one substance."

Which picture is true? Which is described in the Bible? For the Apostolic, the Trinitarian statements seem to harshly and directly contradict the simple picture given in Colossians 1:15 and numerous other verses.

When we consider salvation differences, the Evangelical Christian model seems to ignore multiple verses that plainly ask people to do more than just simply believe on Jesus. It feels like multiple passages in Acts are downplayed or dismissed, as well as numerous statements and commands in the Gospels and Epistles.

The larger Christian world seems far too comfortable adding to the Word of God to reach the Trinity and then taking away from the Word of God to simplify salvation.

I believe this should seriously bother any Bible-believing Christian, but most don't seem to care.

Apostolics enjoy a much simpler approach. It does require you to abandon the authority of Catholic church councils and Protestant confessional statements. We see these as extra-Biblical and non-binding. Once you move away from the influences of broken church history, you can pursue the true Sola Scriptura approach that many Protestants claim to follow.

Apostolics are trying to genuinely speak where the Bible speaks and be silent where the Bible is silent. We are likely not perfect; I certainly am not in my theology, but our approach and mindset appear much more defensible and consistent compared to all the differences between the various Protestant groups, as well as the Catholic Church.

I believe the starting point is found in choosing the Bible above church traditions.

SCOTT'S THIRD RULE OF MODELS

Always remember the difference between your models and the Bible, and whenever you must decide between the Bible and a model, always pick the Bible over the model.

But be careful that you are actually picking the Bible over a model, not one group's interpretation of the Bible over another group's interpretation.

THE KEYS TO GREAT MODELS

A good model should fit like a good piece of clothing. There are some data points (or Bible verses) that might fit carefully, and there is nothing wrong with that.

In woodworking, some joints are very tricky to form, and even need to be tapped gently into place, but they fit perfectly when the pieces slide together.

A great model should fit all the data points well, or at least there should be valid and reasonable explanations where the model fails to fit. A poor model will fit the "favorite verses" but runs roughshod over multiple other verses.

Calvinism was predestined as a great example of a poor model. It can fit verses that mention pre-destination, and some verses about God choosing us, but it ignores all the verses that present human choice as a real and pertinent part of reality. It fits some verses well, and can stretch to fit some other verses, then it ignores a bunch of verses that violate almost every element of their model. They just ignore or explain away all the awkward passages that point in another direction.

For serious Bible-believing Christians, we need to do better in our model fitting, and we need to understand the two major kinds of Biblical models, and you will find that the fit requirements are different for each.

Metaphoric models teach us something about how we should live or think. These models are meant as a pattern or a lesson, but not declarations of reality. "Take up your cross and follow me" uses metaphoric language. It's not a declaration about the need to consider logistics in crucifix transportation. These models have inherent limits in their application and will not fit every part of the Christian experience.

Biblical metaphors are true, but do not apply universally. There are other places where the metaphor will break down. Jesus is the good shepherd, and we are His sheep. Although we have a lot of sheep-like qualities I'm not proud of, there are still numerous theological applications where the sheep model doesn't work as well. For instance, when you are building a tower and counting the cost (Luke 14:28), I hope you are not as sheep-like in this context. You need to think like an engineer and an accountant while building that tower, and Luke 14:28 is also metaphoric. Christianity is not about literal "tower-building".

As a Christian, you are absolutely commanded to take up your cross and follow Jesus, but then we might spend a lifetime learning exactly what that means. If you find yourself arguing over oak crosses versus mahogany or white pine, you have missed the point of this model and beautiful command. Metaphoric models have limits and should be understood and pursued as such.

Declarative or Ontological Models are very different. This second kind of model, in the Bible, states truth about existence and reality. These models are not limited in their fit and application. They should fit all, YES ALL, related verses. The Dual-Nature of Christ is an ontological model. It explains profound truths about the nature of Jesus and makes it easier to understand scripture. No verse in the Bible violates the plain doctrine that Jesus was fully God and fully man. All the verses fit this declarative and ontological truth.

Ontology – the study of the nature of being or what exists. Ontology explores fundamental categories and the structure of reality.

Ontological statements define what a thing is, or how it must operate. "A triangle has three sides" is ontologically true, but if you describe someone as a "married bachelor", it is false and impossible, because each word invalidates the meaning of the other.

The doctrine of Absolute Monotheism is declarative and ontological. It is plainly taught and reinforced by multiple verses in scripture, and it fits all the verses in the Bible – every single one. There is one and only one God, and all other proclaimed gods are false deities and poor impersonations of the Almighty. This model fits lots of verses easily (i.e. Isaiah 43:10, Isaiah 44:6-8) where scriptures declare there is only one God and no other besides Him. Other verses mention various gods

(Exodus 20:3, Exodus 23:13), but these do not invalidate Strict Monotheism. They fit with the understanding that all other gods are false gods and empty idols and not real, according to the Bible.

1st Corinthians 8:4 NKJV
Therefore concerning the eating of things offered to idols, we know that an idol is nothing in the world, and that there is no other God but one.

Human agency and free will demonstrate another declarative model. From Genesis to Revelation, the Bible paints a story of human choices. These choices abound in scripture. Which tree will you eat from? Will you build an ark or travel to the land I will show you? Will you give the right sacrifice? Will you answer the call of God?

Joshua 24:15 NKJV
"...Choose for yourselves this day whom you will serve... But as for me and my house, we will serve the Lord."

In the New Testament, we are asked if we will repent, take up our cross, and follow Jesus. Will we be led by the Spirit and demonstrate faithfulness? These real questions are answered by our choices.

If Calvinism were true, our decisions would all be illusions, and God, in Calvinist sovereignty, already determined all choices. The verses about making choices, and enduring till the end, do not matter.

The Bible presents our choices as real, and so human free will is real, and our models must allow for it. I just wasn't predestined to prove it in this book.

Any declarative or ontological model, if it is a Biblical model, must fit every and all related verses well; otherwise, it is not Biblical and therefore a false model.

Let's consider the options for how a model fits verses:

Model Fitting Options
✓ *Easy Fit* – *The model fits directly and nicely, and the language of the verse and its plain intent matches the spirit and language of the model.*
✓ *Careful Fit* – *The verses can fit the model without violence to the text but must be nuanced and interpreted in a certain way for the model to fit. Lots of careful fits may indicate a flawed model.*
✗ *Stretch Fit* – *The verses can "barely fit" the model, but the "interpretation" is forced, and there is a partial or total disconnect. For ontological models, stretch fits are plainly unacceptable. All relevant verses should fit easily or carefully.*
✗ *Nope* – *The plain language of one or more Bible verses violates a basic tenet of the model, and so these verses are dismissed or ignored by a model holder.*

A BAD MODEL – THE WATCHTOWER SOCIETY

Maybe another example of a flawed ontological model would make this clearer. Let's pick a model that all Bible-believing Christians would agree is wrong, and yet it claims to be compatible with the Bible or even claims that it came from the Bible.

Charles Russell had some interesting ideas about Hell and the Endtime. Influenced by the incredibly inaccurate prophecies of William Miller, Russell taught that Jesus had already returned invisibly to Earth in 1874. He started publishing his views, and his company eventually took the name of the Watchtower Bible and Tract Society. Its followers are known as Jehovah's Witnesses.

Although Charles had to revise some of his Endtime predictions, the Jehovah's Witnesses have continued to teach some unique and strange ideas. Their most notable doctrine is that Jesus is NOT God Almighty in the flesh. They teach that Jesus is a created god or angelic being separate from Jehovah. They claim and pretend to be monotheistic while embracing the idea that there are multiple entities called gods in the Bible.

They explain their interesting model by saying things like, "Yes, there is only one capital-G God, but there are many little-g gods." There is only one God Almighty, and others are called gods. This is part of their unique model, and then they go hunting for scriptures to support it. You can find verses where men are called gods and then ignore any verses where Jesus is called the Everlasting Father (Isaiah 9:6) or the I Am (John 8:58). Instead, they focus on other verses where Jesus is recognized as distinct in some way from the Father and still divine (such as Hebrews 1:8-9).

The Jehovah's Witness model is a great example where it can fit some passages and observations in scripture, but it absolutely violates so many other scriptural declarations, including the Strict Monotheism of the Bible, the Dual-Nature of Jesus, the supremacy of the name of Jesus, the messianic prophecies, as well as other statements by Jesus, and later, the Apostles.

I hate to repeat a point, but you must step outside your own model of God long enough to grasp what I am saying here. The Jehovah's Witness model for Jesus fits Hebrews 1:8-9 just fine. It works here. It works great... at least here.

Hebrews 1:8-9 NKJV
But to the Son He says: "Your throne, O God, is forever and ever; A scepter of righteousness is the scepter of Your kingdom.

⁹ You have loved righteousness and hated lawlessness; Therefore God, Your God, has anointed You with the oil of gladness more than Your companions."

It is really difficult for people to empathize with a model they don't agree with. If you are a Bible-believing

Christian, you likely struggle to understand how a Jehovah's Witness could read that Jesus is God and yet think this is different than the one true God.

But can you read just the verses in Hebrews 1:8-9 and see how that fits the model that Charles Russell invented? There are, quite clearly, two entities in the verses, and both are called God. Take your shoes off if you need help counting. There are two in this passage. That is more than one. Their model makes sense here.

The rest of Christianity reads this verse and understands it as God speaking to Himself in the Son. The Son is a real and created person, a man, in whom God fully dwells and manifests Himself to us. Maybe the Jehovah's Witness scoffs at that explanation, but it strikes most Christians as very reasonable and a 100% valid way to read this beautiful passage. This is a great example of a careful fit. It does not bother me. I don't know if it bothers you.

God is allowed to show Himself as He wants to. God is allowed to speak to Himself as He wants to. I have no problem here and would be reluctant to tell God what He can and cannot do. The Strict Monotheistic reading of this verse (a careful fit) also lines up with all the other plain, declarative verses that teach there is only one God, and also that Jesus is fully God in the flesh.

If a Jehovah's Witness is reading this book, they won't be at all impressed with my short explanation.

I have not convinced them of anything, and they would dismiss my claims. That's not the point of this example. I am speaking to the broader world of Bible-believing Christians, and we universally agree on both the Strict Monotheism of scripture and the clear Biblical teaching of the deity of Jesus. Jesus is not a second-class deity.

Yet here is a group that has a different model, and Jehovah's Witnesses definitely make declarative and ontological statements about Jesus. These teachings also violate declarative and ontological statements in scripture that plainly show Jesus is God Almighty in the flesh — such as John 8:58, Isaiah 9:6, John 10:30, 1st Timothy 3:16, Colossians 2:8-9, John 14:9, Revelation 1:8-13, Zechariah 12:10, Acts 20:28... sorry, I got carried away...

But their model reigns supreme in their thinking, and they have figured out how to twist or dismiss any verses that don't fit their worldview. That is why they are a great example of how declarative and ontological statements and models must be evaluated differently from metaphors.

As a Christian, whatever models you believe and follow should fit all the relevant scriptures well. If you are twisting scriptures, or dismissing and ignoring awkward verses, that's a good sign that your model might be flawed. Whether you are willing to deal with a flawed model honestly remains the greater challenge.

The easy road is to stick your head in the sand and ignore the verses that don't fit well. Maybe just focus on the scripture passages you like, the ones that your group emphasizes and celebrates.

I have coined a name for this disease. I call it Selectaversitis, and I believe it is running rampant among Christians in how they treat the Bible. They cherry-pick verses that match their beliefs and avoid the "awkward verses" that challenge them.

For the serious Christian, the Bible does not leave us this option. The Bible instructs us to do the hard work, to study the scriptures, and apply them to our lives and our thinking. That means all of them, and sometimes, the verses we don't like are the most important to figure out.

2ⁿᵈ Timothy 3:16-17 NKJV
All Scripture is given by inspiration of God, and is profitable for doctrine, for reproof, for correction, for instruction in righteousness, ¹⁷ that the man of God may be complete, thoroughly equipped for every good work.

2ⁿᵈ Timothy 2:15 NKJV
Be diligent to present yourself approved to God, a worker who does not need to be ashamed, rightly dividing the word of truth.

THE MOST IMPORTANT MODEL

At the risk of invalidating everything written so far, here is one of my favorite quotes from American humorist, P. J. O'Rourke, on the political identity of God, and also Santa Claus...

"I have only one firm belief about the American political system, and that is this: God is a Republican and Santa Claus is a Democrat.

God is an elderly, or at any rate, middle-aged, male. A stern fellow, patriarchal rather than paternal, and a great believer in rules and regulations. He holds man strictly accountable for their actions. He has little apparent concern for the material well-being of others. He is politically connected, socially powerful, and holds the mortgage on everything in the world. God is difficult. God is unsentimental. It is very hard to get into God's heavenly country club.

Santa Claus is another matter. He's cute. He's non-threatening. He's always cheerful. He loves animals. He knows who's been naughty and nice, but never does anything about it. He gives everyone everything they want, without a thought of quid pro quo. He works hard for charity and is famously generous to the poor.

Santa Claus is preferable to God in every way but one: there is no such thing as Santa Claus."

- P. J. O'Rourke

How we perceive God, and especially God in Christ, will have a profound impact on our view of Scripture, each other, salvation, and the world we live in. Therefore, your model of God is the most important framework, because it can reach into every nook and cranny of your mind. It influences all the other models in our lives.

I have some obvious theological issues with P. J. O'Rourke's definition of God, but this witty perspective captures a certain truth. Remember my premise: how you view God affects everything.

People on the political right often believe in the Christian God, and therefore, the natural sinfulness of humanity. Most of the right-leaning people don't think that the institutions of our world are the primary problem. Conservatives often identify sin as the problem, and the solution is often individual responsibility and action. Solving problems through more powerful institutions often makes us more vulnerable to tyranny and oppression. This country was founded on a worldview of limited government with separate branches specifically to set the egos of sinful humans against each other. An intentional power struggle hopefully limits the tyranny. This country started with a specific view of God and mankind that shaped our entire political framework.

Even where our nation fell short, such as slavery in our southern states, our fundamental view of God and mankind made it inevitable that America would right the wrong of slavery and even influence the rest of the world to follow our belief that all humans matter; all humans deserve freedom and dignity.

Our view of God and God's creation not only created America but also led to great prosperity here and freedom for everyone. This includes the descendants of African slaves brought here by force. This view of God affects everything in a very positive way!

Those on the political left tend to focus less on the role of God and typically believe people are naturally good inside. They often view the institutions as the primary problem, and if we only replace broken institutions with better ones, the natural goodness of people will rise to the occasion. That's why many Leftists think Socialism works if done correctly, and why they lean towards government solutions to solve problems.

Each side's view of God and God's creation, or lack of one, drives so much of their thinking that you can almost tell how they will vote just by knowing their religious beliefs. A. W. Tozer said it in a different way when he wrote about how your theology about God reveals your theology about man. It really affects everything.

> *"What comes into our minds when we think about God is the most important thing about us."* — A. W. Tozer

From the Biblical perspective, truly knowing God is the most important thing...

Jeremiah 9:23-24 NKJV

Thus says the Lord: "Let not the wise man glory in his wisdom. Let not the mighty man glory in his might, nor let the rich man glory in his riches;

24 But let him who glories glory in this, that he understands and knows Me. That I am the Lord, exercising lovingkindness, judgment, and righteousness in the Earth. For in these I delight," says the Lord.

This seems so clear, but then it requires that we be very careful when we use models to describe God's character, His nature, and His revelation in scripture. We are safer to use scriptural models if we are reasonable in their application, so calling Jesus our Passover lamb or our Rock works well.

The farther we stray from Biblical models and language, the more likely we are to mess this thing up and introduce external errors and corruptions. In the centuries that followed the book of Acts church, competing models arose in debates about the identity and nature of Jesus Christ. I genuinely believe these debates began over legitimate questions and scriptural observations.

These are the same questions new Christians often encounter as they study the Bible and learn about Jesus:

- ✓ If Jesus was God, why did He pray?
- ✓ Why did He say, "not my will but thine be done"?
- ✓ Why did He make statements identifying Himself with the Father and speak other times about the Father or God's Spirit as separate from Himself?
- ✓ What did Jesus and the New Testament authors mean by the word picture of the Son sitting down at the right hand of God?

These questions all pertain to how we understand the deity and humanity of Jesus – an area of belief often called Christology. The questions above and scriptural patterns around them make up several of the twelve Scriptural observations and patterns that I believe any Christological model should fit well. These patterns make up most of the second half of this book.

There have been multiple attempts to explain the above questions, but there are two Christological Models (two ways to understand the incarnation) that seem most relevant to me today. I admit I am biased, in that I hold to one of the models, and the other one is the most popular model in modern Christianity. We will explore the historical reasons at the end of this book, but I want to focus first on scriptural observations and let the Biblical patterns drive the debate.

THE TRINITY MODEL

In a sparring match, hopefully a friendly one, it helps to introduce the two opponents. In one corner, we have the defending champion, the heavyweight fighter that dominates in Christian circles, the Trinity. In this model, God is described as one being who is also three persons. Let's consider the definition given by Dr. James White from Alpha and Omega Ministries[8]:

... The doctrine of the Trinity is simply that there is one eternal being of God – indivisible, infinite. This one being of God is shared by three co-equal, co-eternal persons, the Father, the Son, and the Spirit... The three Biblical doctrines that flow directly into the river that is the Trinity are as follows:

1) There is one and only one God, eternal, immutable.

2) There are three eternal Persons described in Scripture – the Father, the Son, and the Spirit. These Persons are never identified with one another – that is, they are carefully differentiated as Persons.

3) The Father, the Son, and the Spirit are identified as being fully deity—that is, the Bible teaches the Deity of Christ and the Deity of the Holy Spirit.

---

[8] The full article is included in the appendix along with source URL.

Many educated Trinitarians are aware that the word Trinity and the key definitional phrases of the Trinity are not found in scripture, but they do believe that the Trinity Model reflects, honors, and agrees with scriptural statements.

There is profound disagreement among Trinitarians about how and when a Trinitarian understanding developed. Many Christians believe that the Apostles were very much Trinitarian; they just failed to use the specific words and language of the Trinity in the Bible.

Some with more education in Church History are aware that the language and definitions of the Trinity took several hundred years to develop. Multiple key people and controversies played a role as the historic church wrestled with questions of Jesus' identity, deity, and humanity. It took about 350 years for the Catholic Church to settle on a final definition of the Trinity and another 300 years to agree on the Dual-Nature of Christ as fully God and fully human.

Trinitarians are typically consistent on the basic formula of "One God in Three Persons" and the belief that the Son and Holy Spirit are Eternal Persons, co-equal with the Father.

Different triangle-shaped diagrams are often used to explain how each person of the Trinity is God, and that each person of the Trinity IS NOT the same as another person of the Trinity. "The Father is not the Son... The Son is not the Holy Spirit..."

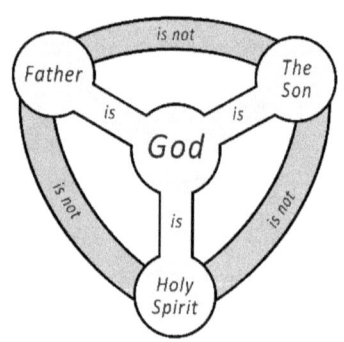

Trinitarians also commonly describe God as "One What and Three Who's". God is one substance (homoousios) yet three persons (hypostasis). As part of this doctrine, it is strongly held that God the Son is the 2nd person, and as such, the Son is eternally begotten by the Father.

It is generally believed that the Holy Spirit proceeds from both the Father and the Son, but this development came later and is not held by all Trinitarians. The Eastern Orthodox church holds to the earlier Nicene view that the Spirit proceeds from the Father alone.

In recent years, it has become increasingly popular to find hints of the Trinity in the Old Testament, claiming that Gen 1:26 and other verses indicate a plurality in God from the very beginning. It is also popular to appeal to philosophical necessity to explain the Trinity. Since God is love, according to 1st John 4:8, God must have had someone to love, and therefore the persons of the Triune God could love one another in eternity past.

THE ONENESS APOSTOLIC MODEL

In the other corner, we have a challenger, the Oneness Pentecostal view, also called the Apostolic view. This position is held by many millions of believers around the world but is a minority belief among Christians at large.

This is often called the Apostolic view by its followers, because we are attempting to stick closely to the language, ideas, and statements made by the Apostles and directly found in the Bible.

The Oneness view focuses on Jesus so much that it is sometimes labeled "Jesus Only", but this leaves out the profound belief by Oneness adherents that Jesus is the Father and that the Spirit of Jesus is the Holy Spirit. This view contends that God is one, and emphasized as one in scripture, and that God can reveal Himself in multiple ways, including His full revelation of Himself in the Son, in the man Christ Jesus, who is fully God and fully man.

Because so much Oneness language comes directly from scripture, we share quite a few ideas and dogmas in common with Trinitarian believers. Oneness Pentecostals enjoy a lot of overlap, and Trinitarians find the initial presentation of Oneness Christology often very agreeable.

Trinitarians and the Apostolic Oneness position typically agree on the following five core Christian ideas:

- ✓ There is one, and only one, God[9].

- ✓ God was manifest in the flesh in Jesus Christ, called both Son of God and Son of man[10].

- ✓ Jesus was fully God and fully man[11].

- ✓ Jesus sometimes acted and spoke in His divinity, for instance, when He forgave sins or declared Himself as the I Am[12].

- ✓ Jesus sometimes acted and spoke in His humanity, when he was tired, or struggled, or declared His own knowledge as limited, or even when He prayed in the garden, "not My will…" [13].

Some might want to disagree on the last point or believe that Trinitarians do not view the prayers of Jesus this way, but it is easy to find examples supporting Jesus praying in His humanity. The dual nature of Jesus Christ is also well established as an orthodox doctrine held by all Christians. For instance, look at a comment from the

---

[9] Deut 6:4, Isaiah 43:10-11, Isaiah 44:6 and 8, 1st Corinthians 8:4

[10] John 1:1 and 14, 1st Timothy 3:16, 2nd Corinthians 5:19

[11] John 8:58, John 20:27-28, John 1:14, 1st Timothy 2:5

[12] Matthew 9:2-7, John 8:58, Mark 4:35-41

[13] Luke 2:52, John 5:30, Luke 22:41-44, Mark 13:32

Trinitarian website, GotQuestions.org[14], on why Jesus specifically prayed, "not My will but Your's be done":

> *Worse than the thought of death, Jesus, in His humanity, must have dreaded the thought of bearing the sins of the world... the Lord fell to the ground... and offered God this desperate cry of His soul.*

The Apostolic Oneness model goes beyond these 5 points to assert additional claims that Trinitarians would likely find problematic, except that the language used comes directly from scriptural statements.

✓ The fullness of deity dwelt bodily in Christ. He is the image of the invisible God. The Son is the express image of God's person (or hypostasis)[15].

✓ The Son is a real person. As a genuine human man, He is separate and distinct from the Father. This is how and why Jesus can pray and genuinely speak about God to us. He can also act in divine authority and power at other times. He does not "turn His humanity and divinity on and off like a light switch". He is fully God and fully man as one person. This is the true and valid mystery of the incarnation[16].

---

[14] *Not My Will, but Yours Bed Done*, Article on GotQuestions.org, https://www.gotquestions.org/not-my-will-but-yours-be-done.html

[15] Colossians 2:8-9, Colossians 1:15, Hebrews 1:1-3

[16] 1st Timothy 3:16

✓ Jesus is the supreme name of God in the New Testament, and the only name used to fulfill the Great Commission in every Baptism recorded with details. This is the name we should use to baptize people today. Jesus is the name of the Father, the Son, and the Holy Spirit, and there is no other name given among men whereby we might be saved[17].

✓ It is the humanity of Christ, the man Christ Jesus, and the sacrifice He made at Calvary in the flesh, which mediates the sins of mankind to God. The emphasis is on His flesh and His body as a man, as our legitimate high priest, who fulfilled the law and reconciled us to God[18].

✓ When the Bible describes Jesus at the right hand of God, the language chosen in the inspired Scriptures makes it clear that this is a metaphoric picture of the humanity of Jesus resting adjacent to God. It is not God sitting next to God. It is not God the Son sitting next to God the Father. The Son of Man, Jesus, specifically as our High Priest, sits next to God. This is figurative language and best understood in this way. It's a powerful word picture of the humanity in

---

[17] Isaiah 9:6, Matthew 28:19, Luke 24:47, Acts 2:38, Acts 8:16, Acts 10:48, Acts 19:5, Acts 22:16, Acts 4:12

[18] 1st Timothy 2:5, Ephesians 2:14-16, Romans 8:3, Colossians 1:21-22, Hebrews 10:11-12

completion of the mission[19]. As Luke 22:69 so beautifully puts it, *"Hereafter the Son of Man will sit on the right hand of the power of God".*

✓ There is only one God and one Spirit that is of God. The Holy Spirit is the Spirit of God, also called the Spirit of Christ and also the Spirit of the Son. Jesus declared He will come to us as that Spirit[20].

✓ The Incarnation was planned from the beginning of the world, but the Son was made when the time was right, made of a woman, made under the law. He was made by the overshadowing of the Holy Spirit over Mary. For this reason, He is called the Son of God. God came in the flesh through the Son that we might be reconciled and have eternal life[21].

✓ The Son had a beginning. Although the Deity in the Son is the Deity of our eternal God, the humanity had a beginning. This is why the Bible calls the Son begotten and firstborn. Those words are real words and mean something[22].

---

[19] Mark 16:19, Luke 22:67-69, 1st Peter 3:21-22, Acts 7:55-56, Hebrews 8:1, Hebrews 10:11-12

[20] Ephesians 4:4-6, Romans 8:9, John 4:24, Galatians 4:4-7, John 14:16-18

[21] John 1:1-14, 1st Peter 1:19-20, Rev 13:8, Gal 4:4, Luke 3:36-38

[22] Luke 1:35, Micah 5:2, John 3:16, Colossians 1:15

✓ The Bible plainly declares that God the Father is greater than the Son of God, and that the Son at times is limited in what He can do or what He knows. We understand these limitations as due to Christ acting in His humanity, not as divine limitations[23].

I do recognize that I included numerous Bible references in the Oneness summary. I included no scriptures in the Trinitarian definition. That is not my fault, but a common theme in Trinitarian explanations. They rarely mention verses, and in Dr. White's description, he mentions none. If that bothers you, join the club. It bothers me too.

The Trinitarian descriptions usually focus on analogies or philosophical presentations about God as a triangle or God needing to be plural inside Himself so He has someone to love. Then, they might offer a couple of Bible verses that sound Trinitarian, but since their model is not declared directly in scripture, Trinitarians largely argue outside of the Bible to explain and prove the Trinity.

So we have 2 models, two contenders in the ring...

The defending champ, the Trinity, and the underdog, the Oneness Apostolic model. At this point, it would be common and popular to just start throwing jabs and attempting to block hits and see if my side can score some points while not taking any blows.

---

[23] John 14:28, John 5:30, Mark 13:32

I want to try something different, something I haven't seen done before. Instead of defending my model, or attacking the other one, I would rather attempt to set the models aside as much as possible and look at scriptural patterns and observations. Can we examine Bible themes independently of the two models?

I recognize I am biased, and I suspect you are as well. So it isn't easy to set aside one's bias and try to look at the Bible with fresh eyes, but it might trigger a new perspective and understanding.

Can we identify easily established Biblical observations about God and the Incarnation and Christology, and then try... objectively... to look at the two models in light of the Scriptural patterns?

Then I can evaluate or adjust my model in light of these Bible verses, and perhaps you can too. The difficulty comes from trying to set aside our own models, but the reward comes from putting God's Word first and letting the Bible direct our understanding, if we can pull it off.

Part 2

EXAMINING OUR MODELS

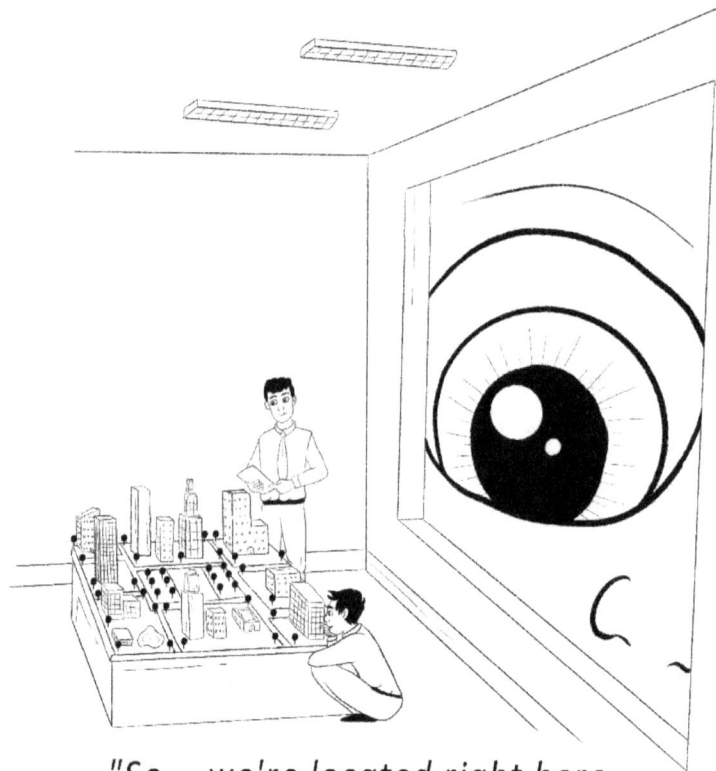

*"So... we're located right here,
in the corner of this building?"*

LET'S TEST THE MODELS

We have at least twelve patterns or observations in scripture that pertain to the nature of God and the incarnation. I believe I am recognizing major themes, patterns, and threads of thought found throughout the Bible. Hopefully, I am not cherry picking my favorites, but it falls to you to decide how objective I have been.

Ask yourself, am I showing symptoms of Selectaversitis, or am I putting God's Word in charge?

Let's look at each area and strive to let Scripture speak as the primary voice and not our favorite model to know and understand God's nature. Each pattern receives its own chapter, with commentary and comparison to the models, but let's save the final grading of the models until after considering all the patterns.

I tried my best to be objective but admit I am biased here. Please think about what grade you would give each model as fairly as possible. How well does the Trinity model fit these verses? How well does the Apostolic Oneness model fit? You will be prompted to grade the models before seeing my grades near the end.

If you don't agree with my grades or analysis, that is your right, but ask yourself why? And remember, we're not criticizing Scripture but analyzing models about Scripture. Disagreement is a symptom of healthy analysis. Hopefully, you are engaged in the process of separating the model from the Scriptures and, hopefully, letting the Bible be in charge.

When we are describing God, please remember we are not focused on metaphors, but this discussion is rooted in **declarative, ontological models.** These models attempt to declare truth about God's nature, which must be true all the time, for all verses, if the model is correct.

We must also be aware that some scriptures about God might not be ontological in nature. Some of the passages we'll consider will be figurative or include metaphoric language, but we can note those as we encounter them.

Psalm 18:15 NKJV
"Then the channels of the sea were seen, the foundations of the world were uncovered at Your rebuke, O Lord, at the blast of the breath of Your nostrils."

Most of us are quite content to agree that word pictures like this psalm are figurative and not ontological in nature. God did not physically use His giant nose and nostrils to stop the flood and provide deliverance in this evocative psalm of provision and answered prayer.

We also have zero interest in going to our favorite verses and ignoring any list of verses that might be awkward for our model. Instead, we intentionally look for all the verses that speak to the topic at hand. Ideally, we want to examine passages that best demonstrate the Biblical pattern, and especially any verses for a given pattern that might challenge one of our models in question.

Remember our four options when comparing a declarative and ontological model against the Bible:

Model Fitting Options

✓ *Easy Fit* – *The model fits directly and nicely, and the language of the verse and its plain intent matches the spirit and language of the model.*

✓ *Careful Fit* – *The verses can fit the model without violence to the text but must be nuanced and interpreted in a certain way for the model to fit.*

There is nothing wrong with a careful fit, but lots of careful fits may indicate a flawed model.

✗ *Stretch Fit* – *The verses can "barely fit" the model, but the "interpretation" is forced, and there is a partial or total disconnect. For ontological models, stretch fits are plainly unacceptable, and the model should be dismissed as invalid. All relevant verses should fit easily or carefully.*

✗ *Nope* – *The plain language of one or more Bible verses violates a basic tenet of the model, and so these verses are dismissed or ignored by a model holder. The model should be dismissed as invalid.*

A summary of the patterns and observations to follow:

Observation	Short Description and Examples
#1 – Strong Commitment to Monotheism	The emphasis on 1 and only 1 God. Duet 6:4, Isa 44:6-8, 1 Cor 8:4
#2 – The Deity of Jesus Christ	He is the fullness of Deity bodily, God in the flesh, the manifestation of God. Col 2:9, 1st Tim 3:16, John 8:58
#3 - Dual-Nature of Christ	Jesus Christ is described in the Bible as God incarnate, fully God and fully man. John 8:58, Heb 10:12, Rev 22:16
#4 - Adjacency Language	Jesus prayed to the Father, along with many references to Father, Son, Spirit. Luke 22:42, Matt 28:19, 2nd Cor 13:14
#5 - Subordination in Scripture	Is the Father greater than the Son? John 14:28, Mark 13:32, John 5:30
#6 - Eternity References to the Son	References to the Son that predate Bethlehem and point to eternity. John 1:1, Micah 5:2, John 17:5,24
#7 - Firstborn, Begotten & the Logos	The Bible uses different language to describe this connection between the Father and the Son. Col 1:15-17, John 3:16, John 1:1, Gal 4:4

Observation	Short Description and Examples
#8 - The Supremacy of the Name	The name of Jesus is emphasized as supreme. Isa 9:6, Matt 28:19, Acts 2:38, Col 3:17
#9 – The Right Hand of God	Multiple verses show Jesus in Heaven at God's right hand. Luke 22:69, Romans 8:34, Heb 8:1
#10 - Overlapping Activity	Multiple references where the roles of Father, Son, and Holy Spirit overlap or are interchangeable. John 14, Rom 8:9, Matt 28:19, Acts 2:38
#11 - Biblical Emphasis on Mediation	Mediation verses emphasize humanity. Rom 8:3, Col 1:22, 1st Tim 2:5, Heb 10:12
#12 - Baptism Instruction and Fulfillment	If Jesus is not the name of the Father, of the Son and of the Spirit, then why did the Apostles baptize in this name? Matt 28:19, Acts 2:38, Acts 8:16, Acts 10:48

Whatever model we use to describe God must fit ALL OF THESE PATTERNS! It is ontological and declarative and must fit all related scriptures.

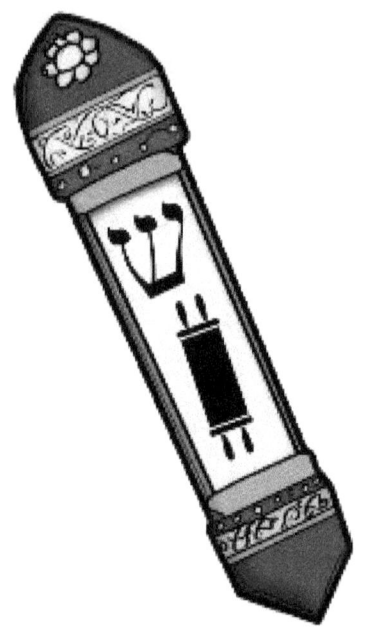

This is a Mezuzah, traditionally containing the verses from Deuteronomy 6:4-9 and other scriptures. It would be affixed to a doorpost in obedience to the Torah.

#1 – STRONG COMMITMENT TO MONOTHEISM

Israel uniquely stands as the only nation from antiquity that exists today with its original language, culture, religion, and ethnic identity intact. Almost everyone else has abandoned or changed their foundational religion or identity. Most have changed so much in their culture that modern citizens in these lands visit their own archeological sites the same way foreign nationals do, as tourists.

Modern Jews are possibly more connected to the pyramids than modern Egyptians. What is left of the original Chinese religion is effectively outlawed in China today. The Greeks still light cheese on fire, but don't have an operational Parthenon for Athena. The Hindu people of India are likely the next best case for claiming their ancient roots, but Hinduism has survived by radically changing with the times, from polytheism to monotheistic ideas to a triad of primary gods. Hinduism continues to be syncretic, incorporating other religious practices while attempting to maintain its roots. Other ancient empires just don't exist anymore. The Hittites, the Babylonians, and the Persians, along with the Mayans and Aztecs, are all gone. The Jews are still here.

Israel not only remains, but this tiny nation throughout history has only 1 major export. Not known for their technology or military might, or enduring wealth, or educational system, the Jews' only major export was

Strict Monotheism, and it successfully spread and influenced over half the planet today. Christian Monotheism obviously comes from the Jews. Islamic Monotheism is also directly inspired by the Jews, and the Muslims claim their faith also arrived through Abraham.

The Jewish cry for one God is best captured in the famous declaration of Deuteronomy 6:4. This verse is nicknamed "the Shema", which is the word "Hear" in Hebrew and the first word in a verse often regarded as the most important verse in the Jewish scriptures.

Deuteronomy 6:4 NKJV
"Hear, O Israel: The Lord our God, the Lord is one!"

Modern Christians struggle to understand the rarity of Monotheism when Abraham accepted the call of God to leave his country. He travelled to a new land to follow only one God. We're so distant from an ancient and polytheistic culture that it might feel more like science fiction if you haven't experienced it first-hand.

When Abraham would visit his neighbors, the customs of hospitality dictated that they would show off their idols and possessions as a demonstration of their wealth and power. Maybe this was some kind of caste system to make sure everyone understood their rank and place in the neighborhood. It is an Eastern idea that still happens today throughout the Southern Mediterranean region, all the way to India.

I have been fortunate to experience this tradition first-hand, at least twice. In my younger and foolish college days, I backpacked in Morocco for 10 days after spending much of the Summer learning French. I took the ferry across from Spain and headed South, starting in Tangier, Morocco. I found out quickly, I was largely unprepared for the bumpiness of travelling in a very foreign country. I don't recommend this adventure, but I learned a lot.

I met a young man on the train, named Jahlil, and he invited me to visit his family for the weekend. I was hesitant but prayed and felt strongly impressed that it was safe to go, so we got off the train and boarded a bus and travelled into the Moroccan countryside. It feels foolish now to write that I didn't even know the name of

the town I visited, but I believed I was safe, and I met his family and stayed in their three-room, modest house for a couple of days. I was the first American,

I was told, to visit their town. Their hospitality impressed me in a profound way.

I only share this story here because, as Jahlil brought me around to meet friends, I had my first encounter with this custom of displaying wealth. Jahlil introduced me to a family that appeared to have the wealthiest home in town, and the son took me on a tour and showed me not just the rooms, but their collection of silver dinnerware and such. I knew to nod and give compliments in my limited French, but I found it odd to look over a stranger's wealth like this. This happened in several homes as Jahlil showed me around.

Fast forward quite a few years, and I met a family from India who moved to America and lived near us in Michigan. The grandfather was Christian, but the rest of the family and decorations in the home looked Hindu to me. They were new to America, and the son and his wife spoke English. They were the ones with visas to work here. All other conversations were translated. When I visited their home, the son took me on a tour of the house and showed me every room, even multiple closets. I recognized this was the same "eastern" concept I experienced in Morocco. I smiled, nodded, and complimented them on the beauty of their home.

I am sure this "tour" is not universal to all people in this large stretch of cultures, but I've read enough to know it is common in many. In my studies of the Pentateuch, I learned this experience of the home tour as part of hospitality would have been familiar to Abraham, even four thousand years ago. It reminds me of the Berbers I had met when I crossed the Atlas Mountains and made it out to the Sahara Desert. They were nomads who travelled with a camel caravan, apparently maintaining some part of their history. It was bizarre for me to see actual tent-living out in a desert. If you could ignore the moped parked next to one tent, it felt like I stepped into history.

My Sahara Desert adventures might put me in a unique place as an American imagining Nomadic life in Canaan.

Four thousand years ago, Abraham arrived in what we call Israel today and travelled in that foreign land looking for a fresh start for his family. He would have visited many neighbors, and they likely showed off their wealth. Maybe they had a special chest in the middle of the tent, or likely an altar area with one or more spots dedicated to their gods. They might have one or two idols carved and polished in something pricey, such as ivory, if they had the wealth. They might also have a small idol cast from bronze metal. Other lesser statues might be polished wood, or perhaps only wooden idols revealed the limits of the family's resources. These were considered the treasured possessions of the home.

I admit we're left with limited data on what Abraham believed about idols. We know he followed the one true God. We don't know how quickly he gave up idolatry. The Bible doesn't say, but Idols are consistently connected with ungodly thinking, even in Genesis. Jacob's Father-in-Law, Laban, had idols, but Genesis portrays him as a flawed cousin who deceived and manipulated. Abraham's kids weren't much better.

Genesis, surprisingly, speaks little of idols. We do see household gods as common when Jacob flees from Laban in Genesis 31.

Genesis 31:17-20 NKJV

Then Jacob rose and set his sons and his wives on camels. [18] *And he carried away all his livestock and all his possessions which he had gained, his acquired livestock which he had gained in Padan Aram, to go to his father Isaac in the land of Canaan.*

[19] *Now Laban had gone to shear his sheep, and Rachel had stolen the household idols that were her father's.* [20] *And Jacob stole away, unknown to Laban the Syrian, in that he did not tell him that he intended to flee.*

Abraham and his descendants would have easily understood what household gods meant. We generally understand that Abraham not only gave up all other gods but likely idolatry as well.

When Abraham's neighbors came to visit him, his faith and worship of only one God would have been utterly foreign to them. Not just foreign, it was likely viewed as pathetic and embarrassing. When they visited, they would wonder or even ask where his household gods might be, and he likely explained, over and over again, that he only served the one true God. Not only that, he had no idols to explain what his God looked like. The gossip about this stranger would likely spread quickly through the valleys he visited.

> *"Have you met Abraham from Ur? He has lots of sheep, but he's still so broke he cannot afford even a single idol in his house..."*

> *"He only has one God... Wow.... Maybe we can loan him a few of our lesser idols until he gets on his feet a little better..."*

As his descendants went to Egypt and eventually returned to the wilderness and Canaan, the stories of this people would have spread throughout the lands.

> *"Have you heard of the descendants of Jacob? They're so poor, they have only one God and no idols..."*

From the faithful stubbornness of Abraham through the descendants of the twelve tribes of Jacob, this Strict Monotheism remains central to the identity of God's chosen nation and His self-revelation to humanity. It was worn as a badge of faith, not a mark of shame or poverty.

Codified into the first two laws given at Sinai, these words are familiar to us today, but many in the West cannot easily relate to how foreign it was to believe in that time in only one God and no idols.

Exodus 20:2-5 NKJV
"I am the Lord your God, who brought you out of the land of Egypt, out of the house of bondage. ³ You shall have no other gods before Me.

⁴ You shall not make for yourself a carved image—any likeness of anything that is in heaven above, or that is in the earth beneath, or that is in the water under the earth; ⁵ you shall not bow down to them nor serve them..."

Strict Monotheism dominates as a theme throughout the Old Testament. God identifies Himself as one, with a single personality and single will. He presents Himself in scripture consistently as a single mind with one consciousness and a total ban on idol-making.

Isaiah contains a majestic series of pronouncements from God. Chapter 40 begins with stunning, poetic word pictures of His power and His willingness to protect, provide, and save His people.

These passages[25] alternate with mocking contrasts of

---

[25] See Isaiah 40:1-17

man-made idols[26]. In the midst, we find messianic pronouncements that even hint that the LORD Himself is coming[27], and we see a continued presentation of God emphasizing Himself as one all-powerful being. He is God, and there is no other.

Isaiah 43:10-11 NKJV
"You are My witnesses," says the Lord, "And My servant whom I have chosen, that you may know and believe Me, and understand that I am He. Before Me there was no God formed, nor shall there be after Me. [11] I, even I, am the Lord, and besides Me there is no savior."

Every word for God in Hebrew (El, Elohim, Eloah) plays a role in these chapters to absolutely declare there is one God, and He is God alone!

Isaiah 44:6, 8 NKJV
"Thus says the Lord, the King of Israel, and his Redeemer, the Lord of hosts: 'I am the First and I am the Last; besides Me there is no God... [8] Do not fear, nor be afraid; Have I not told you from that time, and declared it? You are My witnesses. Is there a God besides Me? Indeed there is no other Rock; I know not one.'"

God even uses hyperbolic language to mock the notion of any other deity: "before me there was no god

---

[26] Isaiah 40:18-20, Isaiah 41:5-7, Isaiah 44:9-20

[27] See Isaiah 40:3-5

formed", "is there a god beside me?" and "I know not one". This pattern is reinforced repeatedly through the scriptures and cannot be overemphasized.

Psalm 86:10 NKJV
For You are great, and do wondrous things;
You alone are God.

Malachi 2:10 NKJV
Have we not all one Father?
Has not one God created us?...

Deuteronomy 4:39 NKJV
Therefore know this day, and consider it in your heart,
that the Lord Himself is God in heaven above and on the
earth beneath; there is no other.

This theme continues in the New Testament, with the same strong declaration that there is only one God.

1st Corinthians 8:4 NKJV
Therefore concerning the eating of things offered to
idols, we know that an idol is nothing in the world, and
that there is no other God but one.

God in the Bible is not a cloud or a mystical energy field like "the force" in Star Wars. God is personable and identified in scripture repeatedly and consistently in the singular. God is one, and you can know Him, pray to Him, and He hears your prayers.

Jesus confirms this pattern and theme of Strict Monotheism in the Gospels. He reiterates the Shema three times, but it likely happened at two different points in His ministry. Mark's gospel gives one account:

Mark 12:28-31 NKJV

Then one of the scribes came, and having heard them reasoning together, perceiving that He had answered them well, asked Him, "Which is the first commandment of all?"

[29] Jesus answered him, "The first of all the commandments is: 'Hear, O Israel, the Lord our God, the Lord is one. [30] And you shall love the Lord your God with all your heart, with all your soul, with all your mind, and with all your strength.' This is the first commandment. [31] And the second, like it, is this: 'You shall love your neighbor as yourself.' There is no other commandment greater than these."

Both the Old and New Testament emphasize Strict Monotheism, and the only number in scripture connected to God's nature is "one". Absolutely not three or any other numeric value. Any attempt to introduce another number as an attribute of God is just plainly not supported by declarative statements in the Bible[28].

---

[28] If you are thinking of the references to "seven spirits" of God, in Isaiah and Revelation, then I applaud you for prioritizing scriptural language. These references are not ontological but have strong figurative overtones. Isaiah 11 describes God's Spirit 7 ways. Rev 3:1 compares this to 7 stars, Rev 4:5 draws a picture of 7 lamps, and Rev 5:6 describes 7 horns and 7 eyes. No sane Bible scholar believes these are literal.

Trinitarians claim that the baptism of Jesus is a clear presentation and revelation of the Trinity, but there is nothing in the text that indicates anyone present understood anything new was being revealed about God's nature. God clearly demonstrated His approval of Jesus, and He does that through two means: through His voice and a manifestation to John of God's Spirit.

> **Matthew 3:16-17 NKJV**
> *When He had been baptized, Jesus came up immediately from the water; and behold, the heavens were opened to Him, and He saw the Spirit of God descending like a dove and alighting upon Him. [17] And suddenly a voice came from heaven, saying, "This is My beloved Son, in whom I am well pleased."*

No Jew present, based on scripture, would shift away from established Strict Monotheism and find a new doctrine from this baptismal account. The basis for finding a Trinity here is really quite odd. Since the Bible never declares God to be three, apparently the methodology is to find the place in the Bible where God is doing the most things simultaneously, and count what God is doing, and that's how many Persons God is in His nature.

"Oy vey, there's three!"

I understand that a Trinitarian has likely never thought that this is the technique, but without a declarative and ontological statement about God being three, there is no other way to arrive at this number.

Another suggested support for the Trinity is found in the commissioning of the church in Matthew 28:19, but that faces an even greater challenge as a support for the Trinitarian model. We cover that in pattern #12 later in this book. We'll address other aspects of what it means to be the Son of God in other sections as well. In this first pattern, we observe in the Bible, we're focusing on the powerful theme of Strict Monotheism.

The Apostolic answer is to simply accept the clear Biblical emphasis on one and only one God and to embrace and celebrate what the Bible emphasizes. At the baptism of Jesus, we see God's approval of God's Son. God shows His approval in two distinct ways. God is allowed to multitask as He wishes.

This is one way in which the Apostolic model may not agree with some presentations of Modalism. Modalism sometimes teaches that God somehow switches modes or roles in a way that the Bible never explains or declares. Modalists have described God as switching from the Father to the Son and back, or putting on a mask for a role and taking it off and returning to the other role. This idea is not declared in scripture. The Apostolic position might be similar to Modalism, but we don't see any clear language in the Bible to justify the idea that God switches modes or somehow stops being the Father just because God is also in the Son. Apostolics see no reason to believe that God has these limits when multitasking. Instead, let's focus on the declarations of scripture over any non-Biblical ideas or rules.

I believe God can clearly multitask. I hope and suspect you do as well. When you consider how many millions of prayers reach Him all the time, this seems self-evident to most Christians. This shouldn't be an Apostolic or Trinitarian question. Does anyone believe that God is limited in His multitasking by the number of persons in His nature? Is He limited to doing three things at once? I highly doubt it. We see nothing in the Baptism of Jesus that declares or demands that God must be somehow three eternal entities, and nothing here takes away from the scriptural emphasis that God remains one.

Trinitarians do declare belief in One God, and I believe Apostolics are sometimes in error when they accuse Trinitarians of Polytheism. I understand the accusation, since some Trinitarians talk about God in a way that seems identical to three separate beings cooperating on a committee. If there is no operational difference between the Trinity and three gods on the same team, then the Polytheistic accusation becomes valid. Most Trinitarians are committed to Monotheism, they just struggle to explain the difference between the Trinity and three deities in full cooperation. That's polytheism.

Many Christians sound a lot like Apostolics or Modalists in how they describe God in operation. They struggle to explain the Trinity and resort to calling it a mystery when challenged with Bible verses they can't explain. The Trinitarian scholar, Dr. James White, plainly describes his concerns and frustrations with these Christians. He sees a disconnect with what he believes is a fundamental Christian doctrine[29].

> *"And the fact that there's so much Modalism in the church. I think a large portion (I'll speak for American Christians), if I were to give a test, on a Sunday morning, in almost any large, conservative, Bible-believing church, I am quite concerned that over-a-majority of the attendees would test out as Modalists."*

I don't think Dr. White is saying they don't believe in the Trinity, just that many Christians have little idea what the Trinity means or how it would work. On a basic level, they just believe that God has shown Himself in different ways, but God is one numerically. An Apostolic or Modalistic model actually fits their thinking better.

I agree that most Trinitarians don't functionally believe in the Trinity and struggle to understand it or explain it. In 30 years of talking to Christians from all walks of life,

---

[29] YouTube® video titled "*James White concerned most Christians are Oneness, Modalists!*", published June 12, 2020 on the channel: Focus on the Kingdom.

I've found that most enjoy and prefer Biblical language to describe God, and they know that Jesus is God in the flesh, that He is the Son of God. They just struggle to understand what that means. If you press them with questions, they often resort to, "It's a mystery."

When it comes to the model of the Trinity, many believe there is something about this special "T-word" that they are supposed to acknowledge, and if you don't also acknowledge it, it really bothers some, even to the point of questioning your faith and doctrine for not acknowledging a word not remotely found in the Bible.

In fact, it seems like you can say almost anything you want about the nature of God and sound 99% Apostolic. As long as you say the magic "T-word", you will be accepted. Or you can sound like a raging Polytheist, treating God as a committee of three beings in cooperation, and as long as you also say the magic "T-word", everything is fine.

But if you dare to suggest that this word, Trinity, and the ideas behind it are somehow not Biblical, oh boy... trouble is a brewin'. This is where "model thinking" has taken over, and where awareness of our models would help everyone to know more and understand each other better.

It would help a lot to know that when someone questions your model, they are not necessarily challenging your belief in the Word of God.

If we can practice separating our models from the Bible, we can learn more about ourselves, others, and even the Bible.

It would be better not to get bogged down in semantic differences, and the best means to do this is to stick to Biblical language and declarations to describe God's nature. If the Bible is our final authority, then whatever the Bible emphasizes should be our emphasis. Our models should come second to the Word and should bend to the Word or be abandoned if they don't match the Bible.

In the analysis of Strict Monotheism, we find a clear Biblical doctrine and pattern. It is declared and ontological, and there is nothing in scripture that should distract from this simple truth in God's Word. The Bible emphasizes clearly, plainly, and consistently that God is one. This is the only number declared to describe His character, and the Apostolic model for God aligns beautifully with this Biblical pattern.

To say that God is somehow also three in His nature distracts from the plain declarations of scripture and takes away from the Biblical pattern and emphasis. It adds confusion instead of clarity. Since the Bible never declares that God is three, why should we believe it or defend it? Why are so many comfortable with making a statement that the Bible does not make?

The language of the Trinity, specifically the words and phrases the Catholic Church added, along with the emphasis on the word "three" instead of "one", makes the Trinity model feel very disconnected from the Strict Monotheism of scripture. For this reason, the New Schaff-Herzog Encyclopedia, in its introduction to the Trinity[30], describes the Trinity as "a modification of Christian monotheism". Apostolics reject this modification.

Apostolics would find the description[31] of the Trinity in the Encyclopedia Britannica to accurately reflect the disconnect between the Bible and this doctrine, which developed several centuries later.

"Neither the word Trinity, nor the explicit doctrine appears in the New Testament, nor did Jesus and his followers intend to contradict the Shema in the Old Testament: 'Hear, O Israel, The Lord our God is one Lord' (Deuteronomy 6:4)."

---

[30] Article on *The Doctrine of the Trinity*, The New Schaff-Herzog Encyclopedia of Religious Knowledge, 1969, Volume 12, p.18.

[31] Article on *The Trinity*, The New Encyclopedia Britannica, 1993 Edition, Volume 11 Micropedia, p.928.

#2 – THE DEITY OF JESUS CHRIST

This observation from scripture should not trouble either of our models. Both Apostolics and Trinitarians believe strongly in the Deity of Jesus Christ. Its inclusion in the book and this list comes from clear Biblical declarations.

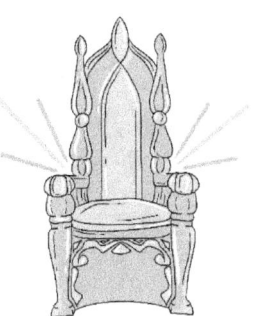

Any summary of the New Testament themes regarding God's nature and the Incarnation would remain grossly incomplete without it. The Bible declares that Jesus is more than a man, more than a prophet. This is God Himself, manifest in the flesh.

1st Timothy 3:16 NKJV
And without controversy great is the mystery of godliness: God was manifested in the flesh, Justified in the Spirit, Seen by angels, Preached among the Gentiles, Believed on in the world, Received up in glory.

2nd Corinthians 5:19 NKJV
...God was in Christ reconciling the world to Himself, not imputing their trespasses to them, and has committed to us the word of reconciliation.

With plenty of scriptural support, this claim is easily demonstrated, but it's worth noting that we want to prove this with the correct scriptures. Just saying that Jesus was "sent from God" is not enough to establish deity. God might send a prophet, and the prophets in the Old Testament would speak with the words and authority of God, as if God were speaking through them.

So, having the words of God does not demonstrate a specifically divine nature or claim to deity.

Deuteronomy 18:18 NKJV
I will raise up for them a Prophet like you from among their brethren, and will put My words in His mouth, and He shall speak to them all that I command Him.

The name itself, "Jesus", also doesn't qualify one as deity. American Christians are sometimes surprised to learn that this name, as spelled and pronounced in Hebrew, was common for men in the first century. It is spelled and pronounced by Jews almost identically to the Old Testament name "Joshua". This is the same Joshua who succeeded Moses and the name of the 6th book of the Bible. Spanish-speaking Christians are more familiar with non-Messiahs bearing the name of Jesus. There are many sons in Latin-American countries, as well as in Spain, called "Jesus", but of course, in Spanish.

Even the title "Son of God" does not directly identify deity. I might cause trouble bringing this up, but Sonship in scripture is more nuanced than that. Sonship in the Bible often indicates a direct Father-Son relationship, but also more generally points to the source, lineage, or nature of the bearer. We see this in the other sonship references connected to Jesus. Jesus is called the Son of

Man and also the Son of God. He is also called, in scripture, the Son of David. How does all this work?

Matthew 9:27 NKJV
When Jesus departed from there, two blind men followed Him, crying out and saying, "Son of David, have mercy on us!"

The blind men call Him Son of David because King David belongs in His legitimate lineage as a source. By the same reasoning, Jesus is called Son of Man. He does not have a specific "man" as His direct human parent, but He is genuinely human, with a human nature and will, and so His sonship to humanity is celebrated in that title as well.

The title Son of God does not uniquely prove deity, as it can be used in scripture to more broadly indicate where someone comes from. Luke 1:35 tells us why Jesus is called the Son of God, because He came from God. Two chapters later, in the same book, the Bible provides a legal genealogy for Jesus that ends with another Son of God reference.

Luke 3:23-38 NKJV
Now Jesus Himself began His ministry at about thirty years of age, being (as was supposed) the son of Joseph, the son of Heli, [24] the son of Matthat, the son of Levi... the son of David, [32] the son of Jesse...

[38] the son of Enosh, the son of Seth, the son of Adam, the son of God.

Adam, in scripture, is clearly also called the son of God. Except for silly Mormon theology, no one believes Adam could be a deity. This careful analysis might seem outside of the scope of this book, but it's central to the idea of how models influence your thinking. Most Christians have a "Son of God" model in their head, and they get this from their religious background, sometimes more than scripture. I want to do the work to test all our models and put Scripture in charge where possible.

To be very clear, I am NOT saying that Jesus is the Son of God in the same way that Adam is called a Son of God. Jesus is the Son of God because of His unique origin, identity, and nature. He is the only begotten of the Father. No one else is remotely like Jesus. The title, Son of God, is not what makes Him unique. Others have been described with this title and were not deity manifested in flesh. **The title doesn't make Him divine. The title is part of His unique list of attributes because of His divinity**, and most Christians do not understand that difference.

According to the pattern of scripture, Jesus is not divine because He is the Son of God. **Jesus is the Son of God because He is divine.** You may need to read this box more than once to understand the difference.

The above distinction will remain difficult for a Trinitarian to understand because their model for "Son of God" comes from the Catholic church and not directly from the Bible. For many Trinitarians, Son of God is a name of a separate eternal being, not an attribute, and they might even call Jesus, God the Son, a title never found in scripture.

But if scripture is your sole authority, then these insertions should bother you and be discarded.
I encourage you to remain consistent and careful. We should prioritize Biblical usage above church traditions. Jesus and Adam were both described as the Son of God, even if their fulfillments were different in nature. Your model for God should have room (or make room) for this clear Biblical observation.

Let's get to some verses that clearly declare the deity of Jesus Christ. We will explore this further in the chapter on the Dual-Nature of Jesus, but a few are worth examining and might even trigger an out-loud Hallelujah, circumstances permitting...

> **John 8:56-58 NKJV**
> *"Your father Abraham rejoiced to see My day, and he saw it and was glad." [57] Then the Jews said to Him, "You are not yet fifty years old, and have You seen Abraham?" [58] Jesus said to them, "Most assuredly, I say to you, before Abraham was, I AM."*

No declaration in scripture matches this claim of self-existence. Jesus is more than just a man and identifies Himself as one outside of time and space. He used a similar expression to the one spoken by God Almighty to

Moses from the burning bush[32]. God described Himself as the "I Am", and Jesus applies this same profound label to Himself when addressing these Jewish leaders. They understood the claim, but rejected it, attempting to stone Him for this clear claim of divinity.

The disciples may not have fully recognized His deity until after the resurrection. They clearly understood that Jesus was sent from God and had supernatural power, but seemingly didn't understand Jesus' claims at times, even at the Last Supper.

John 14:6-10 NKJV

Jesus said to him, "I am the way, the truth, and the life. No one comes to the Father except through Me. [7] If you had known Me, you would have known My Father also; and from now on you know Him and have seen Him."

[8] Philip said to Him, "Lord, show us the Father, and it is sufficient for us."

[9] Jesus said to him, "Have I been with you so long, and yet you have not known Me, Philip? He who has seen Me has seen the Father; so how can you say, 'Show us the Father'? [10] Do you not believe that I am in the Father, and the Father in Me? The words that I speak to you I do not speak on My own authority; but the Father who dwells in Me does the works."

---

[32] Exodus 3:14

Jesus plainly declares and explains that the Father is revealed through the Son. If you know the Son, you know the Father. If you see the Son, you see the Father.

After the resurrection, we see Thomas declare the deity of Jesus, fully and without reservation.

John 20:27-28 NKJV
Then He said to Thomas, "Reach your finger here, and look at My hands; and reach your hand here, and put it into My side. Do not be unbelieving, but believing."

28 And Thomas answered and said to Him, "My Lord and my God!"

Why do we call him Doubting Thomas? None of the other disciples believed reports that Jesus had risen. They even doubted His identity when He stood in front of them in Luke 24 and Mark 16. Jesus had to eat to prove He wasn't a ghost. Then John 20 reveals that Thomas shared their doubts but finally gets to see Jesus.

Nothing in the text demands that he had to actually touch him once Jesus showed up. He just plainly confesses the lordship and deity of Christ. I prefer to call him "Believing Thomas".

This is the first truly unqualified declaration of the full divinity of Jesus by a disciple.

1ˢᵗ Timothy 3:16 NKJV
And without controversy great is the mystery of godliness: God was manifested in the flesh, Justified in the Spirit, Seen by angels, Preached among the Gentiles, Believed on in the world, Received up in glory.

The New Testament Epistles use numerous phrases and word pictures to declare Christ's deity, including the "Image of the invisible God" and "God was in Christ".

Multiple Old Testament prophecies also declare the divinity of the coming Messiah. Isaiah 9:6 tells us the Son, who is coming, also has the titles Mighty God and Everlasting Father. Micah 5:2 declares His origin as "from everlasting", and Zechariah 12:10, with the LORD speaking, even declares that Yahweh Himself would be pierced. Israel still would not realize what they had done until God's Spirit is poured out – a beautiful picture of both Pentecost and the deity of Jesus.

In our model-fitting discussion, most of these verses are easy fits for both the Oneness and Trinity models. The only question might be how some Trinitarians react and interpret word usage in these verses. For instance, I have seen Trinitarians struggle with the clear words of scripture declaring God was in Christ, when they really believe that one person of the three persons of God was in Christ. In fairness, this shortcoming applies to some, not all, Trinitarian believers.

One Catholic priest asked me why I didn't believe in the Trinity, and I replied that when I read the Bible, I see that the fullness of the Godhead is in Jesus. Not knowing I was quoting scripture, he told me I was wrong.

Colossians 2:8-9 NKJV
Beware lest anyone cheat you through philosophy and empty deceit, according to the tradition of men, according to the basic principles of the world, and not according to Christ. [9] For in Him dwells all the fullness of the Godhead bodily.

I pointed out the verse in Colossians 2:9, and he said I was reading it wrong. I don't think he was misrepresenting his model. The Trinity just directly disagrees with the specific words of Colossians 2:9 and other verses.

Either the fullness of deity is in Jesus, or just the Second Person of the Trinity is in Jesus. Let's frame this another way to help some see the question. Are all three Persons of God in Jesus? Or is it just the Second Person in Jesus? Is the Godhead in Jesus, or is Jesus in the Godhead?

The Bible uses different language and expressions to indicate it is all of God, the fullness of God, in Christ. Apostolics believe this directly contradicts the Trinity model. You need to look at the verses and decide for yourself. We can discuss what the word Godhead means, but at a minimum, the Bible declares that the fullness of the Godhead dwells bodily in Christ.

I believe it is becoming common for Trinitarians in recent years to affirm Colossians 2:9. I have heard multiple Trinitarians say that all three Persons of God were in Christ. This would better match the description in Colossians 2. I don't think most realize that they are rejecting Orthodox Trinitarian thought that has remained consistent for 1,500 years when they make this change.

Fundamentally, all these verses are central to any New Testament analysis of the Incarnation and Christology. The Bible clearly declares the full deity of Jesus Christ. These declarations are consistent and ontological, and all Bible-believing Christians recognize this.

The Oneness Apostolic model and the Trinity model both teach that Jesus is absolutely divine. Other than specific semantic issues for some Trinitarians, this Biblical pattern does fit both models.

God was in Christ. Creator stepped into creation to demonstrate His love and our value. This truth remains one of the most sublime and marvelous declarations ever revealed.

Hallelujah!

#3 – THE DUAL-NATURE OF JESUS CHRIST

Much like the deity of Christ, this observation from scripture should not trouble either of our models. Both Apostolics and Trinitarians believe strongly in this doctrine of the Dual-Nature of Jesus Christ. This does get more interesting in the details, however, since Trinitarians typically believe this doctrine, they're just reluctant to allow it to explain too many Bible questions. Let's first define and demonstrate this teaching from scripture, and then analyze its impact on our models.

John chapter 1 powerfully introduces this idea through the vivid word picture of the Logos or Word of God.

> **John 1:1, 14 NKJV**
> *In the beginning was the Word, and the Word was with God, and the Word was God…*
>
> *14 And the Word became flesh and dwelt among us, and we beheld His glory, the glory as of the only begotten of the Father, full of grace and truth.*

In the section on Firstborn, Begotten, and Logos, we will explore the exact meaning of this Logos. For now, we recognize that the Word of God was God, and the Word became flesh, became human, and dwelt among us.

This Word is Jesus Christ, revealed as the Son of God, and scripture declares His full divinity and full humanity.

1ˢᵗ Timothy 3:16 NKJV
And without controversy great is the mystery of godliness: God was manifested in the flesh, Justified in the Spirit, Seen by angels, Preached among the Gentiles, Believed on in the world, Received up in glory.

Colossians 2:9 NKJV
For in [Christ] dwells all the fullness of the Godhead bodily.

Hebrews 10:11-14 NKJV
And every priest stands ministering daily and offering repeatedly the same sacrifices, which can never take away sins. ¹² But this Man, after He had offered one sacrifice for sins forever, sat down at the right hand of God, ¹³ from that time waiting till His enemies are made His footstool. ¹⁴ For by one offering He has perfected forever those who are being sanctified.

This doctrine may not be fully expressed by any single passage of scripture, yet it is widely held by all Bible-believing Christians. I don't know of another doctrine so uniformly agreed upon that isn't expressed in a single summarizing passage. I suspect its universality comes from the overwhelming body of Bible verses to support it. Lots of verses teach that Jesus is God, and lots of verses teach that He is a genuine human man. Both of these statements are Biblical, wonderful, and true.

If you want to try a summary of the Dual-Nature of Christ from a Trinitarian website, look at the description from this article[33] on GotQuestions.org:

> *"According to the New Testament, Jesus really is a man, born into the human race, yet He is also fully God. John 1:1 states that the Word is God and then in verse 14 we see that the Word John is speaking of is Jesus who took on human flesh and "tabernacled" among us. Matthew and Luke both tell of Jesus' birth of the Virgin Mary and give His human lineage. It is difficult to understand and explain, but that is what the New Testament teaches. Jesus is God who entered the human race as a man."*

I agree with quite a bit of this description, and it's worth noting that Oneness and Trinitarian believers agree on a decent number of doctrinal points concerning Jesus Christ. We both believe in His divinity and humanity. We largely agree on His role and earthly mission and its fulfillment. Modern Trinitarians also increasingly believe that when you receive God's Holy Spirit, you are receiving Jesus Christ. I don't think they realize that this is a fairly recent change. This also modifies the orthodox Trinitarian position held by Catholics and most Protestant groups. I applaud any efforts by Christians to prefer the Bible above church traditions.

---

[33] *Does Christ have Two Natures?*, Article on GotQuestions.org, https://www.gotquestions.org/Christ-two-natures.html

If you are curious about the graphic at the start of this chapter, it comes from one of the strangest declarations of the Dual-Nature of Christ. My daughter, Kelsey, created most of the illustrations in this book, but you might not imagine the difficulty in coming up with drawings to describe abstract things like "Dual-Nature", "Subordination", and "Eternity". It wasn't easy. This one comes from a verse in the last chapter of the Bible. If you look closely, you will see Jesus' name on one of the branches and also on the roots of the tree, because in scripture, Jesus is both.

Revelation 22:16 NKJV
"I, Jesus, have sent My angel to testify to you these things in the churches. I am the Root and the Offspring of David, the Bright and Morning Star."

The Bible declares that Jesus is both the one who made David and also the one who came from David. How can this be? Because in His Dual-Nature, He is both God and man, Creator and created. He is eternal, and He had a beginning. This one verse, as mysterious as it might be, could be the best example of Jesus' Dual-Nature in a single Scriptural statement.

The Dual-Nature gets more interesting when you consider the explanatory power of this doctrine.

Apostolics contend that this Biblical teaching can be key to understanding many of the challenging questions asked about Jesus Christ.

- ✓ If Jesus was God, why did He pray?

- ✓ Why did He say, "not my will but thine be done"?

- ✓ Why did He make statements identifying Himself with the Father and speak other times about the Father or God's Spirit as separate from Himself?

- ✓ Why did Jesus say the Father was greater than He?

Each of these questions and others can largely be understood as an expression of Jesus acting within the limitations of His genuine human nature or acting in full divine power. He prayed and struggled with the agony of Calvary, as a man, and then submitted to God's plan of redemption, as a man. He spoke about God and to God as a man. He also spoke at times as God, forgiving sin and taking authority over nature. He did both, a lot and repeatedly, in His earthly ministry.

I want to be careful to not claim that Jesus switched His humanity or divinity on and off like a mode or a light switch. The Bible presents Jesus as fully God and fully man at all times. He ultimately spoke as a singular being. I am not sure exactly where the limitations of humanity ended and where any self-imposed or necessary limitations of Divinity began. Only that Jesus operated in both capacities throughout His earthly ministry.

I believe the Dual-Nature of Christ would play a larger role in Trinitarian explanations if it weren't for the strange series of events that made up the development and acceptance of the Trinity.

WARNING… RAPID CHURCH HISTORY DOWNLOAD…

The doctrine of the Trinity evolved over several centuries, with the Father and Son first being split into two divine beings in the mid-100s. Another 60 years passed before anyone proposed that there might be three persons in one God, and it was still not widely accepted. The Son of God, even for Tertullian, was considered subordinate and a created being, and Tertullian was the first to call God a Trinity (or Trinitas in Latin). He also described belief in one person in God as "the majority of believers" in his day. It was Origen in his work, *On the Principles*, that leveled up the three persons to the idea of co-equality. Origen described the teaching that God was a single person as still held by "the great multitude of those who are counted believers".

Nicaea, in 325 A.D., was the first council to adopt the idea of an Eternally Begotten Son. Then, around Constantinople in 381 A.D., the formal idea of "One God in Three Persons" was finalized and adopted as the official doctrine of the church.

This history will be better documented at the end of the book with lots of sources, but for the purposes of the Dual-Nature, the Catholic church still had questions.

In 451 ^A.D.^, at the Council of Chalcedon, they affirmed that Christ had two natures, human and divine. Then a century passed, and they met again in 553 ^A.D.^ at the Second Council of Constantinople and agreed that Christ had two natures but was only one person. They met again in 680 ^A.D.^ in Constantinople, this time to decide that Christ had two wills, one human and one divine.

It took about 350 years to fully develop and agree on the language of the Trinity and another 300 years to fully agree on the Dual-Nature of Jesus Christ.

From the Apostolic perspective, they got it half-right.

DOWNLOAD COMPLETE...
BACK TO THE BOOK...

I apologize for a couple paragraphs of church history, but the download is minimally necessary to note the following. The Catholic church, over several centuries, settled on the Trinity as the best explanation of why Jesus prayed, talked about God, and also identified Himself as deity.

Ironically, had they settled on the Dual-Nature of Christ first, they could have skipped the Trinity part, because once you identify Jesus as fully God and fully man, that includes the explanatory power to know why He prayed and talked about the Father.

In other words, they came up with the Trinity to explain why Jesus prayed, with Jesus originally as a second divine person, subordinate and created. Then they leveled up the members of the Trinity to make them all equal. But now they have created a new problem. If Jesus is equal with the Father, then why did He pray?

Then they came up with the Dual-Nature of Christ and explained that Jesus sometimes acted and spoke from His human nature and will.

If you are paying attention, you might notice that they changed the Trinity into something that doesn't explain anything. Then they discovered why Jesus prayed in a way that makes the Trinity optional and useless.

For those with a bit more education or interest in this topic, go research the history of the Economic Trinity versus the Ontological Trinity to learn more. For the rest of you, please pretend the previous sentence didn't make it into the book. I know I'm a nerd, but I don't want you to realize how big a Bible and theology nerd I really might be ☺.

In terms of the Dual-Nature of Christ, this doctrine is widely accepted by Christians, both by Apostolics and Trinitarians. The Apostolics lean on it much more for its amazing explanatory power.

Apostolics also take the doctrine further than most Trinitarians in both directions – in both the deity of Christ and in recognizing the role of His humanity.

John 14:6-10 NKJV

Jesus said to him, "I am the way, the truth, and the life. No one comes to the Father except through Me. [7] If you had known Me, you <u>would have known My Father also; and from now on you know Him and have seen Him</u>."

[8] Philip said to Him, "Lord, show us the Father, and it is sufficient for us."

[9] Jesus said to him, "<u>Have I been with you so long, and yet you have not known Me, Philip? He who has seen Me has seen the Father</u>; so how can you say, 'Show us the Father'? [10] Do you not believe that I am in the Father, and the Father in Me? The words that I speak to you I do not speak on My own authority; but the Father who dwells in Me does the works.

John 14:16-18 NKJV

And I will pray the Father, and He will give you another Helper, that He may abide with you forever— [17] <u>the Spirit of truth</u>, whom the world cannot receive, because it neither sees Him nor knows Him; but <u>you know Him, for He dwells with you and will be in you</u>. [18] <u>I will not leave you orphans; I will come to you</u>.

In the direction of deity, Apostolics recognize the declared truth in scripture that the Father is in Jesus, and that when you see Jesus, you see the Father. When you have Jesus, you have the Father. In the same way, the scriptures make it clear that the Spirit of Jesus is the Holy Spirit, and that the same Jesus who dwelt WITH them will shortly dwell IN them. So Apostolics take the deity part of the Dual-Nature, and based on many Bible verses, go further than most Trinitarians would dare.

Apostolics, based on multiple Bible verses, also take the humanity of Jesus further than most Trinitarians. We see the man, Christ Jesus, as our High Priest and mediator, and we recognize that His humanity better explains why Jesus prayed and even how we can understand the instruction in Philippians 2 to think like Jesus.

1st Timothy 2:5 NKJV
For there is one God and one Mediator between God and men, the Man Christ Jesus.

Luke 22:41-42 NKJV
...He knelt down and prayed, 42 saying, "Father, if it is Your will, take this cup away from Me; nevertheless not My will, but Yours, be done."

Philippians 2:5-7 NKJV
Let this mind be in you which was also in Christ Jesus, 6 who, being in the form of God, did not consider it robbery to be equal with God, 7 but made Himself of no reputation, taking the form of a bondservant, and coming in the likeness of men.

The Bible states that Jesus, as a man, mediated our sins. It makes more sense to understand that He prayed in His humanity, and the only reasonable way to fulfill Philippians 2 and have the same mental attitude, is to pursue the mindset he took as a true human servant.

When considering the majesty of the Dual-Nature of Christ, I sometimes think of a word picture I heard from one of my favorite preachers, the late Dr. Johnny James. He was often called the walking Bible, because He quoted scripture so frequently. His explanation of the Dual Nature of Jesus Christ went something like this:

1. *Jesus Christ was natural on His mother's side, but He was supernatural on His Father's side.*

2. *He was the seed of Abraham on His mother's side, but He's before Abraham on His Father's side.*

3. *He was the seed of David on His mother's side, but He's the root of David on His Father's side.*

4. *He was finite on His mother's side, but He's infinite on His Father's side.*

5. *He was physical on His mother's side, but He was spiritual on His Father's side.*

6. *He was temporal on His mother's side, but He is Eternal on His Father's side.*

7. *He was created on His mother's side, but He created everything on His Father's side.*

8. *He was maybe 6 feet tall on His mother's side, but He filled all space on His Father's side.*

9. *He preached the word on His mother's side, but He WAS THE WORD on His Father's side.*

10. *He walked by the sea on His mother's side, but He walked on the sea on His Father's side.*

11. *He was 33 years old on His mother's side,*
    but He was the Ancient of Days on His Father's side.

12. *He got hungry on His mother's side,*
    but He fed 5,000 on His Father's side.

13. *He got tired on His mother's side,*
    but He gives us rest on His Father's side.

14. *He prayed in the garden on His mother's side,*
    but He answers our prayers on His Father's side.

15. *He died on the cross on His mother's side,*
    but He kept on living on His Father's side.

16. *He got His body from His mother's side,*
    but He got His blood from His Father's side.

17. *He's the Son of Man on His mother's side,*
    but He's the Son of God on His Father's side.

You might struggle with the idea that Jesus can be two things simultaneously in one person, both deity and man, Creator and created, but this amazing mystery is plainly declared and supported throughout God's Word!

1st Timothy 3:16 NKJV
And without controversy great is the mystery of godliness: God was manifested in the flesh, Justified in the Spirit, Seen by angels, Preached among the Gentiles, Believed on in the world, Received up in glory.

Revelation 22:16 NKJV
"I, Jesus, have sent My angel to testify to you these things in the churches. I am the Root and the Offspring of David, the Bright and Morning Star."

#4 – THE LANGUAGE OF ADJACENCY

You made it. In many ways, this chapter is the main event of the book. I hope you are enjoying the journey so far. This book, *The Express Image*, really started with two ideas that kept swirling in my head. The first was how models affect our thinking, especially how they cause most of the disagreements between Christians. Models even cause most of the fruitless arguing in secular circles.

Then, when it came to the Oneness vs Trinity debate, I kept encountering a gap in understanding when talking with both Trinitarian believers and even some Apostolics. I started working on a different way to have the conversation. Since we agree on the validity of the Bible verses, can we talk about this as a model disagreement?

The Trinitarians don't understand why the Apostolics cannot see the obvious language of the Trinity in the Bible. *"Look over there, a verse about the Father... And here is a verse about the Son. Here are a couple of verses that mention all three together, such as the baptism of Jesus. What is wrong with you people? Can't you count to three? It isn't hard to see the Trinity in scripture..."* Trinitarians see their model throughout scripture and wonder why Apostolics don't or can't...

Although I play hard for Team Apostolic and clearly see no support for the Trinitarian model, I do see why they have one and cling to it so fiercely.

When I talk to Apostolics, I sometimes run into a completely different mindset where they hardly see a single verse in the Bible that even remotely sounds like the Trinity. Even more surprising, when I talk about God being in any way separate from the Son of God, I have noticed that some Apostolics squirm over this. That smells, to me, like a case of Selectaversitis. To be clear, there are Apostolics who frankly act like the Son of God is not a real and separate thing and seemingly ignore many of these references in scripture.

I don't see the same attitude and behavior in Apostolic leadership. This idea of ignoring the Son is not found in published works by respected Apostolic authors. And I admit I am judging my own side much more harshly than the Trinitarian side. I have scripture for that...

Matthew 7:3 NKJV
"And why do you look at the speck in your brother's eye, but do not consider the plank in your own eye?"

My comparison is unfair, and maybe I have not travelled enough and been to enough Apostolic churches. I have taught and preached in many churches in half a dozen states. I have 20 years of ministerial experience, interacting with thousands of Apostolics of many different backgrounds. At least here, I am comparing what average Apostolics often say, including some ministers, to the published works and official positions I have encountered from educated Trinitarian sources.

As you might guess, this situation would reverse pretty quickly if I compared average Trinitarians to the published and polished Apostolic sources. The average Christian attending Trinitarian churches often has no idea how to explain the Trinity. (A lot of their ministers also struggle here.) They frequently sound like a Modalist or Apostolic when asked questions about why Jesus prayed and such. You might remember the James White quote from the Strict Monotheism chapter.

But I am happy to stack the deck against Team Apostolic, because I want the truth more than I want to be right, at least I hope I do. If the Apostolic model is correct, then this framing will endure the small load I place upon it. I'm a firm believer in the "test all things" mentality.

1ˢᵗ Thessalonians 5:21 NKJV
Test all things; hold fast what is good.

For the purposes of this book, I am attempting to judge Team Apostolic more harshly, and I suspect I might get some negative feedback from my fellow ministers for that. I welcome it, because I believe the Apostolic model can easily endure some criticism.

I do want to introduce a new word to describe a pattern clearly found throughout the New Testament. This pattern is one that both the Trinity model and the Apostolic model should explain. This is original to me, so if this is a terrible idea, I guess I am fully to blame.

The Bible clearly and consistently describes Jesus Christ as the Son of God and Son of Man. How many verses describe Jesus as begotten, sent from God, apart from the Father, talking about the Father, praying to the Father, and talking about God's Spirit?

With dozens of verses, this is clearly a Bible thing, and something that all serious Trinitarians, as well as all respected Apostolics, recognize and believe in. This is Bible. This is ridiculously Biblical.

John 3:16-17 NKJV
For God so loved the world that He gave His only begotten Son, that whoever believes in Him should not perish but have everlasting life. [17] For God did not send His Son into the world to condemn the world, but that the world through Him might be saved.

Matthew 3:16-17 NKJV
When He had been baptized, Jesus came up immediately from the water; and behold, the heavens were opened to Him, and He saw the Spirit of God descending like a dove and alighting upon Him.

[17] And suddenly a voice came from heaven, saying, "This is My beloved Son, in whom I am well pleased."

God sent His begotten Son into the world, and God shows His approval for this Son majestically at His baptism. These scriptures are astounding and beautiful to all believers.

This separation between Father and Son happens in both directions. God sent the Son and speaks about the Son, and the Son points to God, and speaks about and prays to God.

John 14:1-2 NKJV
"Let not your heart be troubled; you believe in God, believe also in Me. ² In My Father's house are many mansions; if it were not so, I would have told you. I go to prepare a place for you.

Matthew 27:46 NKJV
And about the ninth hour Jesus cried out with a loud voice, saying, "Eli, Eli, lama sabachthani?" that is, "My God, My God, why have You forsaken Me?"

I came up with a word to describe this, and I'll explain why shortly. I call this pattern **Adjacency**, which unfortunately has four syllables and sounds more academic than I want, but I believe you are smart enough to understand that something can be adjacent or next to something else.

Adjacency – means near or next to, and also requires that there is more than one "entity" in question. If you have a box adjacent to another box, that is two boxes.

In the case of the scriptures, the Son of God is clearly separate in some way from God. This is the word picture we see in the Right-Hand of God passages in Heaven. It is even more visible in the Gospels and the earthly ministry of Jesus Christ. The Son is separate and adjacent somehow to the Father. The Son prayed to the Father. The Son spoke repeatedly and often about the Father. In a few cases, Jesus also spoke about the Holy Spirit as separate.

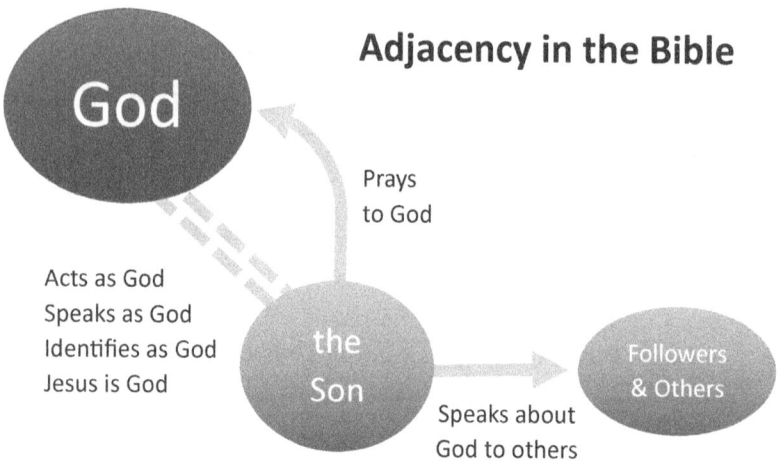

Adjacency in the Bible

God

the Son

Followers & Others

Prays to God

Acts as God
Speaks as God
Identifies as God
Jesus is God

Speaks about God to others

This feels separate, because somehow it is separate. Jesus, as the Son, also spoke about Himself at times as the Father. He spoke as God with the authority and identity of God. And Jesus also said He would come to us in the Holy Spirit. All of this is clearly scriptural and included in the idea of Adjacency. The idea of adjacency is not up for debate in scripture. The word "adjacency" comes from my head, so that could be debated, but the idea behind it is very Biblical and clearly present in the New Testament.

Why do we need a new word? I fear I sound like one of these progressives who has to redefine everything and throw out our foundations. I assure you I am not. I love our foundations, and we don't need the word "Adjacency" to understand the Bible. Apostolics can continue to be Apostolic without this idea and preach the Bible and see God change lives. Trinitarians can continue being Trinitarian without this word just fine.

But we have a gap between these two groups, and both sides struggle to understand why the other even exists. I am attempting a bridge-building maneuver. It might fail spectacularly, but I believe we can understand each other, and maybe even the Bible better, if we are willing to make the journey.

If you remember my earlier chapter about how models work, you might recognize that I have created a new box, a new idea model with a label on it - Adjacency. That box describes a bunch of Bible verses that clearly show Jesus as separate in some way from the Father. Other times, He spoke as God, and Jesus identified Himself as the Father. "I and my Father are one." "If you've seen Me, you've seen the Father." "Before Abraham was, I am." This is also in the Adjacency box.

Apostolics and Trinitarians should be able to agree that Adjacency is in the Bible, even if you don't like the label.

The Trinitarian sees Adjacency and believes it proves the Trinity, but Adjacency is not the Trinity. Adjacency in scripture is consistently connected to humanity, to the Incarnation, and our created world. It is clearly scriptural.

The Trinity model concludes that Adjacency in the Bible shows something about the eternal nature of God that is never declared in scripture. Then wherever they see Adjacency, they believe they see support for the Trinity.

When the Trinitarian encounters the Oneness position, they see how Apostolics hold scripture in high regard. From numerous conversations, I have seen how certain verses do challenge the Trinitarian view, and they often see the issues on their side. Many Trinitarians know that Isaiah 9:6 doesn't fit their model. Neither does Colossians 2:9, nor all those awkward scriptures in Acts about baptism in Jesus' name.

Isaiah 9:6 NKJV
For unto us a Child is born, unto us a Son is given; And the government will be upon His shoulder. And His name will be called Wonderful, Counselor, Mighty God, Everlasting Father, Prince of Peace.

Colossians 2:9 NKJV
For in [Christ] dwells all the fullness of the Godhead bodily.

I believe most Trinitarians don't like that the basic language of the Trinity is completely missing from the Bible and feels very different than many verses.

They likely grew up hearing this language of "One God in Three persons", and they believe in their hearts that part of their model is Biblical. I am convinced most struggling Trinitarians think they have to give up and ignore all the Adjacency verses if they give up the Trinity. They just cannot ignore so many verses. I appreciate and agree with that instinctive reaction. Ignoring Bible verses only causes Selectaversitis. Never ignore scripture!

What they don't understand is that the Trinity is not the same thing as Adjacency. Adjacency is a clear Biblical pattern abundant with scriptural support. The Adjacency verses and especially all the verses about the full deity and humanity of Jesus Christ, declare and explain the depth of God's love for us. This is the richness of God's plan for humanity. Deity stepped into His own creation in the Son, to show His love and pay the ultimate price.

The Trinity is an external model that attempts to explain the pattern of Adjacency and other verses. You can abandon the Trinity and embrace all these beautiful verses, and you lose nothing of value. You don't need the Catholic language of multiple eternal persons in a Triune God to explain and understand the Bible.

For the Trinitarian, they struggle to realize that everything found in scripture can be explained just as well or even better without the complication of inserting Catholic definitions of multiple persons into God's eternal nature.

For instance, let's look at a Trinitarian description of the "Biblical Foundation" from The Gospel Coalition website[34]:

> "The Person of Christ in his incarnation logically and ontologically precedes his work as prophet, priest, and king. The eternal person of the Son of God, uncreated, infinite, sharing equally the essence of deity with the Father and the Holy Spirit, by means of an inexplicable miracle embraced the nature of humanity into his person.
>
> Thus, the eternal existed simultaneously as the temporal, the uncreated as the created, the infinite as the finite, the immutable as one who would increase in 'wisdom, stature, and favor with God and man' (Luke 2:52). In short, Jesus was Emmanuel, God with us. In one person, a covenantally representative person, God dwelt with us, as us."

There are multiple Biblical statements and declarations here mixed in with the Trinity language that came centuries later. The Bible never says the Son is a separate eternal person that "shared" deity with the Father and Holy Spirit. You can remove the Trinity language and lose nothing of Biblical value in this description.

---

[34] Original from article: *Christ as Mediator: The Offices of Christ*, Thomas J. Nettles, https://www.thegospelcoalition.org/essay/christ-mediator-offices/

"The Person of Christ in his incarnation logically and ontologically [fulfills] his work as prophet, priest, and king. The eternal person of God, uncreated, infinite, by means of an inexplicable miracle embraced the nature of humanity [when God made the Son].

Thus, the eternal existed simultaneously as the temporal, the uncreated as the created, the infinite as the finite, the immutable as one who would increase in 'wisdom, stature, and favor with God and man' (Luke 2:52). In short, Jesus was Emmanuel, God with us. In one person, a covenantally representative [human] person, God dwelt with us, as us."

I removed the non-Biblical language of multiple persons in God, and my insertions are [bracketed] in the revision above. I find the revised description Biblically consistent and beautiful. I see no advantage to adding eternal persons to the scripture, and no Biblical meaning is lost by their removal. Scripture already explains the incarnation majestically and consistently without the additions of Catholic Church theology.

We can just stick with the language of the Bible, provided by God, to explain God, and we don't need extra words like "Eternal Persons" to get the job done.

For the record, we don't need extra words like "Adjacency" either. I am only using it to build a bridge. I want to establish that the Bible verses about separation between the Father and Son are beautiful and scriptural.

You don't need the Trinity to understand them, and we find no declaration of eternal, separate persons of God in scripture. So why add it? We can use and celebrate scriptural language to understand and pursue God.

We don't need Catholic definitions to get us there. The Bible does NOT say:

> *"All Scripture, plus the first six Catholic Ecumenical Councils, are given by inspiration of God, and are profitable for doctrine..."*

If your spiritual authority was originally Bob from Chicago, I understand that you think your group can add to the Bible. I don't want to force you to change your mind. I do want to encourage you to examine your model and ask why the Catholic Church is somehow superior to following scripture alone.

I don't see it. I am not angry with you. I just don't see the moral authority of the Catholic Church. I see Greek philosophical influences as early as the mid-100s. I see human ego, corruption, greed, and murder in Catholic leadership all the way back to the 300s. Then it got a whole lot worse over the centuries. I'm not remotely convinced of their spiritual or moral authority.

I am thankful the Catholic Church has stood strong for the sanctity of life and has worked tirelessly to preserve the Word of God. Thank you, Catholics. Sincerely. But I am not Catholic. My beliefs come directly from the Bible.

If you are not Catholic, stop pursuing Catholic doctrine in your belief system. Stop Protesting the Catholic church as well. You can stop being Catholic and cease being Protestant and just follow the Scriptures. The Bible doesn't need the Trinity; it adds confusion about God, violates the plain meaning of multiple verses, takes away from the majesty of Jesus, takes away from the supremacy of the name of Jesus, and leads to people being baptized differently than how the Apostles did it.

The Trinity offers no advantages, just confusion and division. Why would non-Catholics demand that you acknowledge a model for God not declared or taught in the Bible? It makes sense for Catholics, since they believe (incorrectly) that they are allowed to add and change doctrines in the Bible. For non-Catholics, claiming to follow Scripture alone, it makes absolutely zero sense to adopt the Catholic Church's model for God.

The main reason for the confusion is this idea of Adjacency. Once you acknowledge that Adjacency is not the same thing as the Trinity, you can embrace all the Adjacency verses and drop the Catholic language. Drop the magic "T-word" and stop saying persons and just embrace and use the language of the Bible.

Can we examine the Adjacency verses without the Trinity Model? Will they still make sense? You can even examine them without the Apostolic model. Just take the basic and agreed-upon common ground and look at Scripture.

All Bible-believing Christians agree on the following:

- ✓ There is one, and only one, God.
- ✓ God was manifested in the flesh in Jesus Christ, called the Son of God.
- ✓ Jesus was fully God and fully man.
- ✓ Jesus sometimes acted and spoke in His divinity.
- ✓ Jesus sometimes acted and spoke in His humanity.

You might be shocked at how far you will get when you consider scripture, remembering just the Deity and Dual-Nature of Jesus Christ.

John 3:16-17 NKJV
For God so loved the world that He gave His only begotten Son, that whoever believes in Him should not perish but have everlasting life. [17] For God did not send His Son into the world to condemn the world, but that the world through Him might be saved.

2nd Corinthians 5:19 NKJV
...God was in Christ reconciling the world to Himself...

God begat a Son, that means He made a Son, and He sent that Son into the world. That son was God in Christ. This is God manifested in the flesh – divine and human. Praise be to God! No problems so far.

God spoke His approval of the Son at the baptism of Jesus, demonstrating Supernatural authority in Jesus

Christ and showing the connection of God's Spirit with this Son to John. Amazing.

The Son was a genuine human, and our high priest, our Kinsman Redeemer and mediator. He prayed and spoke about God to others. Why did He pray? He prayed as a genuine human should pray. He had to pray to fulfill the will of God in His life. His struggle of wills was not two divine wills, but the will of the man, Christ Jesus, to submit to the will of God.

Luke 22:41-44 NKJV
And He was withdrawn from them about a stone's throw, and He knelt down and prayed, [42] saying, "Father, if it is Your will, take this cup away from Me; nevertheless not My will, but Yours, be done."

[43] Then an angel appeared to Him from heaven, strengthening Him. [44] And being in agony, He prayed more earnestly. Then His sweat became like great drops of blood falling down to the ground.

This is not a word picture of God wrestling with God, nor would deity need strength from an angel. This is humanity struggling with the very difficult and pending reality of Calvary looming on the horizon.

Hebrews 4:15 NKJV
For we do not have a High Priest who cannot sympathize with our weaknesses, but was in all points tempted as we are, yet without sin.

Jesus also struggled and was tempted and truly experienced the human condition. Because of His genuine humanity, it was a true human test.

John 8:58 NKJV
Jesus said to them, "Most assuredly, I say to you, before Abraham was, I AM."

In other places in scripture, we see Jesus speak and exercise His full authority as divine. He is fully God and fully man, and Jesus declared His self-existent and eternal identity in the most profound way possible. We can embrace all of this without Eternal Triune persons.

Then we can consider a passage with one of the clearest examples of Adjacency in the Gospels.

John 8:16-18 NKJV
"And yet if I do judge, My judgment is true; for I am not alone, but I am with the Father who sent Me. [17] It is also written in your law that the testimony of two men is true. [18] I am One who bears witness of Myself, and the Father who sent Me bears witness of Me."

The Son, as a man, is a real and separate person from the Father. There is nothing here that demands or even teaches Eternal Persons. We have one witness in God, and another witness in the man Christ Jesus. That is enough to settle a  matter in a Jewish court, and I think enough to settle the matter in my heart. Between the testimony of the God of the Bible, and the demonstrated love of God, shown in the man, Christ Jesus, I have found enough evidence to believe the plan of God for my life.

This adjacency passage is 100% compatible with the Apostolic model. For the record, it also fits the Trinitarian model, but it does not specifically teach a Trinity of persons or require us to believe in multiple Eternal Persons. John 8:18 is just another demonstration of the Adjacency pattern found throughout the New Testament. Many don't understand that the Apostolic model doesn't dismiss but embraces New Testament Adjacency. **Jesus Christ was absolutely a genuine human man, and in that way, He was separate from the Father, while having the divinity of the Father in Him.**

This next verse, John 14:23, feels a little different than the general Adjacency pattern and is likely the best example in the Bible of a verse that reads well into the Trinitarian model or at least feels very Trinitarian to many Christians.

> **John 14:23 NKJV**
> *Jesus answered and said to him, "If anyone loves Me, he will keep My word; and My Father will love him, and We will come to him and make Our home with him."*

We should study this verse (and all verses) in the context of the larger passage to better understand what this means. In this case, we are in the midst of John 14, on the night of the Passover dinner, the Last Supper. As the disciples struggle to know where Jesus is going, He answers by declaring the overlapping identities of the Father and Son. Jesus declares that He reveals the Father to the disciples and to us. If you know the Son, you know the Father, and if you've seen the Son, you have seen the Father[35]. He explains that the Father dwells in the Son[36].

Then Jesus introduces a new way in which we will experience God. There have been previous hints and even direct statements of God's Spirit coming and changing both our relationship and our worship[37], but this passage introduces a lot more details for the first time in the Gospels.

Jesus announces "another helper", another way in which we will experience God, "the Spirit of Truth".

---

[35] John 14:7-9

[36] John 14:10

[37] John 3:5, John 4:24, John 7:37-39

> **John 14:16-18 NKJV**
> *"And I will pray the Father, and <u>He will give you another</u>*
> *<u>Helper</u>, that He may abide with you forever— [17] the*
> *Spirit of truth, whom the world cannot receive, because*
> *it neither sees Him nor knows Him; <u>but you know Him,</u>*
> *<u>for He dwells with you and will be in you.</u> [18] <u>I will not</u>*
> *<u>leave you orphans; I will come to you.</u>*

He clearly continues in the language of Adjacency here, describing the Holy Spirit as external, but at the same time, Jesus makes it abundantly clear that this Spirit is His Spirit. "You know Him, for He dwells with you and will be in you." Jesus introduces the Holy Spirit using 3rd person language, but then makes it very personal and direct, "I will come to you."

His explanation that He is that Spirit is intentional and clearly established at its very introduction. Do not ignore this and focus on the 3rd person language. Jesus twice refers to Himself in the 3rd person in this chapter, so this type of language here, what I call the language of Adjacency, is not indicative of a true and external 3rd person.

> **14:7** *"...from now on you know Him and <u>have seen Him</u>"*
> **14:17** *"...but you know Him, <u>for He dwells with you</u>*
> *and will be in you."*

In the broader context of this chapter, Jesus introduces a new way we will be comforted and experience God –

through the Spirit of Truth, the Holy Spirit. This passage and others make it clear that we receive one Spirit, God dwelling in us, leading us, guiding us, and perfecting us[38].

John 14:19-21 NKJV

"A little while longer and the world will see Me no more, but you will see Me. Because I live, you will live also. [20] At that day you will know that I am in My Father, and you in Me, and I in you. [21] He who has My commandments and keeps them, it is he who loves Me. And he who loves Me will be loved by My Father, and I will love him and manifest Myself to him."

I would guess everyone understands and agrees on the figurative context of verses 19-21. How will we see Jesus after He is gone? We see Him working and moving in our lives and other believers. How will He manifest Himself? Through His Spirit – as our Comforter – He will not leave us as orphans, He will come to us.

John 14:22-23 NKJV

Judas (not Iscariot) said to Him, "Lord, how is it that You will manifest Yourself to us, and not to the world?"

[23] Jesus answered and said to him, "If anyone loves Me, he will keep My word; and My Father will love him, and We will come to him and make Our home with him.

---

[38] Eph 4:4-6, 1st Cor 12:13, Gal 5:16, Rom 8:9, Heb 10:14

At least one Judas still doesn't understand, so Jesus explains further. Is the "we" in Jesus' answer either literal or metaphoric?

I believe we all understand that when we receive the Holy Spirit, we receive the Spirit of God, which is the Spirit of the Son, the Spirit of Christ, the comforter, and the Spirit of Truth. Your model for God might not allow for all these overlaps, but it is clearly scriptural to understand that these are all valid Biblical descriptions for the one Spirit of God. The Bible never describes people receiving more than one Spirit – at least for those on the good team. Some men and unfortunate pigs get extra spirits... Christian believers only receive one Spirit.

The best explanation, no matter your model for God, is that the "we" in verse 23 is a figurative expression that gives a beautiful promise. If you love God, and keep His Word, you will receive everything found in the ministry and identity of the Son, as well as the power and presence of the Father. All of this will be manifest in your life if you do it God's way. The "we" of verse 23 is metaphorical, you only receive One Spirit, but the promise is literal. We get filled with ALL of God's Spirit. Nothing will be withheld to those who love Him.

I would agree that reading John 14:23 in isolation sounds very Trinitarian, but then, should we read any verse in isolation, including the ones that sound extra Apostolic? Reading this verse in context, we see a beautiful promise from God that I want in my life and yours. John 14:23 is compatible with both the Apostolic and Trinitarian models. When understood in context, it doesn't specifically teach one model or the other. It does give us reason to rejoice at the promises of God.

There is one last Adjacency passage I want to mention. It may surprise you. In the middle of the Last Supper instructions, Jesus makes a surprising declaration.

John 16:25 NKJV

These things I have spoken to you in figurative language; but the time is coming when I will no longer speak to you in figurative language, but I will tell you plainly about the Father.

What can John 16:25 mean? This passage is enigmatic, but it does directly give us instruction both on the mediation and role of the Son at some future point. This role of the Son includes the plain declaration that the Son will not be active or answer our prayers in some way. I would hazard a guess that you may have never noticed the details in this passage before.

John 16:23, 26 NKJV

And in that day you will ask Me nothing. Most assuredly, I say to you, whatever you ask the Father in My name He will give you... [26] *In that day you will ask in My name, and I do not say to you that I shall pray the Father for you.*

Jesus, in the midst of the Last Supper discourse, makes this amazing declaration about not asking the Son for needs, and that Jesus will NOT ask the Father for them. This is connected, and these verses sandwich the declaration that Jesus spoke in figurative language. A day is coming when it will be plain. On that day, you will go directly to the Father, and there is no reason to go through the Son to get your needs met.

The connected instructions around John 16:25 de-emphasize the role and mediation of the Son at a future point. You won't need to ask the Son, just ask the Father in the name of the Son. And there is no need or cause to go to the Son with your needs.

John 16:26 AMPIFIED
*In that day you will ask in My name, and I am not saying to you that I will ask the Father on your behalf [**because it will be unnecessary**].*

We learn from multiple other scriptures that the Father was in Jesus, that the name of Jesus is the name of the Father, and that the deity of Jesus is the deity of the Father. Therefore, it makes tremendous sense to know we can address the Father directly in this name.

So the Bible actually declares, Jesus declares, that at some point, we don't need to ask the Son to get to the Father. We can just go to the Father by the name. This passage astounds me, and I can objectively say that it doesn't match the Trinity model for God at all. In the Trinitarian model, you pray to the Son so that He can ask the Father. According to Scripture, you should go to the Father directly.

Please remember this clear figurative declaration in John 16:23-26 and keep this in mind as we look earlier in the same chapter. We should be very careful about looking for declarative and ontological truth in the midst of clearly figurative instructions. There are two interesting verses in the first half of this chapter worth looking at a bit more.

John 16:7 NKJV
Nevertheless I tell you the truth. It is to your advantage that I go away; for if I do not go away, the Helper will not come to you; but if I depart, I will send Him to you.

This verse raises questions. Even with figurative language, there is a basic truth here. We cannot receive God's Spirit (the Helper) while Jesus remains bodily on Earth. Why? What does this mean?

Trinitarians have brought up this verse as proof of multiple persons, but I don't think it works well in that context. If this verse reveals something about God's specific nature, then it would seem to violate the Trinity model.

Why would we only experience one person of the Trinity at a time? If God is "three Who's and one What" as often declared by Trinitarians, then why couldn't we experience the 2nd person and the 3rd person of a Triune God simultaneously and separately? We never see that idea expressed in scripture. Instead, we experience God as a single Who, although we encounter Him through multiple means: as our Creator, through His Word, through His Spirit, and through the life of Christ lived on Earth. The Bible declares God largely as "one Who" revealed through "multiple What's".

John 16:7, if read out of context, would support a Modalistic model[39] for God. This wouldn't match the Apostolic or Trinitarian models. Taking any verse in isolation is not a great practice, but I hope you could see where a model that believes God "switches modes" would fit well here.

But we don't (or shouldn't) take verses out of context, and I do not believe this verse helps or hinders the Trinity model. It also doesn't help or hinder the Apostolic model. Based upon other verses, I do not believe John 16:7 is about limits on God's ability to reveal or show Himself in different ways. Something else "blocks" God's Spirit from coming. Something else is going on here.

---

[39] Turn to the section on Strict Monotheism, specifically page 107, to learn more about the difference between Modalism and Apostolic views.

> **John 7:37-38 NKJV**
> *On the last day, that great day of the feast, Jesus stood and cried out, saying, "If anyone thirsts, let him come to Me and drink.* ³⁸ *He who believes in Me, as the Scripture has said, out of his heart will flow rivers of living water."*

In John 7, Jesus sneaks into Jerusalem and interrupts the Feast of Tabernacles and makes this bold declaration about living water. John adds explanation in verse 39.

> **John 7:39 NKJV**
> *But this He spoke concerning the Spirit, whom those believing in Him would receive; for the Holy Spirit was not yet given, because Jesus was not yet glorified.*

At a minimum, this is a much better explanation of John 16:7, in that the Apostle, inspired by God, adds this note in John 7 to let us know that the Spirit could not come until the glorification of Jesus happened.

Recall that John 16 happens on the same evening as John 14, and Jesus already identified this Spirit of truth when He first formally introduced and described the Holy Spirit just minutes earlier on the same night.

> **John 14:17-18 NKJV**
> *... The Father... will give you another Helper, the Spirit of truth... but you know Him, for <u>He dwells with you and will be in you.</u>* ¹⁸ *I will not leave you orphans; <u>I will come to you.</u>*

This Spirit, the Helper, is another way to receive and experience Jesus, and He makes that explicitly clear.

John 7:39 states that the Spirit cannot come until Jesus is glorified. Does the Bible declare the fulfillment of this glorification? When does this happen?

1st Peter 1:20-21 NKJV
He indeed was foreordained before the foundation of the world, but was manifest in these last times for you 21 who through Him believe in God, who raised Him from the dead and gave Him glory, so that your faith and hope are in God.

When we consider John 16:7 and whatever "blocks" the Helper from coming, there is no evidence in scripture that this is the interaction of multiple persons in God or that one of these "persons" causes a block for the other. This figurative language is better understood through the larger plan of God and the glorification of the Son at the resurrection. God will then send His Spirit to us.

John 16:7 NKJV
"Nevertheless I tell you the truth. It is to your advantage that I go away; for if I do not go away, the Helper will not come to you; but if I depart, I will send Him to you."

This beautifully fulfills one of the most powerful prophecies in scripture. The Old Testament prophet, Zechariah, declares that God will pour out His Spirit on

Jerusalem, and the timing occurs after the Lord Himself will be pierced. A careful reading shows that God Almighty, Yahweh Himself, was pierced, yet the figurative word picture in Zechariah 12:10 describes this as a Son dying. This prophetic and figurative picture matches the Oneness model quite beautifully with God described as one Who revealed in different ways.

Zechariah 12:10 NKJV
"And I will pour on the house of David and on the inhabitants of Jerusalem the Spirit of grace and supplication; then they will look on Me whom they pierced. Yes, they will mourn for Him as one mourns for his only son, and grieve for Him as one grieves for a firstborn."

This prophetic picture finds its fulfillment on the day of Pentecost, and we see the heartache and desperation of the crowd when they respond to Peter.

Acts 2:37 NKJV
Now when they heard this, they were cut to the heart, and said to Peter and the rest of the apostles, "Men and brethren, what shall we do?"

John 16:7 does not provide any support for a Trinity model for God and would even disagree with the Trinity regarding co-equal persons. This is not about specifics in God's divine nature. This verse doesn't specifically support or disprove the Oneness model either.

John 16:7 really speaks more to the conditions required before God will pour out His Spirit.

Just a few verses further down, we find a more interesting Adjacency verse:

> **John 16:13 NKJV**
> "However, when He, the Spirit of truth, has come, He will guide you into all truth; for He will not speak on His own authority, but whatever He hears He will speak; and He will tell you things to come."

If you don't think about it much and read this verse in isolation, it sounds Trinitarian, but there are issues here. This verse does nothing to support a teaching of co-equal persons in a divine triad. If this is supposed to reveal a declared truth about God's nature, then the Spirit is subordinate and not co-equal. It just does what it is told.

The Apostolic perspective understands this verse as a figurative expression of God revealing truth through His Spirit. This could refer to the operation of the gifts in the church, but ultimately, God's Spirit leads the church into truth through the inspiration of the Apostles, by the Holy Spirit, to write the New Testament.

I am generally uncomfortable with the idea of interpreting verses as "figurative" to fit a model. In normal practice, if you have to "dismiss" a passage as figurative or limited in its context, that might be evidence that your model is controlling your thinking and that your model is the root issue. I have no desire to dismiss any passage of scripture. In this case, the verse occurs in the same discourse where Jesus declares this is figurative language, and so the proximity to John 16:25 demands we listen to Jesus. He said He was speaking "in proverbs" (KJV) or "figuratively" (NKJV, NIV), and so any interpretation that ignores this would be irresponsible.

John 16:13, if it were ontological and declarative, would be an example of Adjacency that doesn't fit the Apostolic model well. It might better fit the Trinity, except that it would reveal subordination and not co-equal persons. But reading this verse in context makes it clear that this is better understood as a figurative picture of how God's Spirit will guide the Church and specifically the Apostles after the resurrection. I believe this verse is a great example of a careful fit for the Apostolic model that works well in the context of the passage.

All the Adjacency passages fit the Apostolic model with no trouble. Maybe one or two are a careful fit, but most fit easily. Therefore, this Adjacency pattern in the Bible is compatible and supports the Oneness view of God.

My only criticism would be that some Apostolic believers do not fully understand this pattern of Adjacency and its full compatibility with the Oneness position. But in terms of the Apostolic model, we have no difficulties here and rejoice in all these verses. They fit beautifully.

Some Adjacency verses work well in the Trinity model, but others cause problems. The Trinity goes beyond Biblical Adjacency to teach that the Persons of the Triune God are co-equal and the Son is "Eternally Begotten". These are Catholic definitions that are not taught or supported by scripture – in fact, scripture disagrees with both points.

We see in the Adjacency verses that the Father is greater than the Son, and the Son has some declared limits and depends on the Father. This contradicts the Trinity teaching of co-equal persons. We talk about this more in the Subordination chapter, but here is a clear case where the Adjacency verses disagree with the Trinity model.

John 14:28 NKJV
"...because I said, 'I am going to the Father,'
for My Father is greater than I."

We see another problem for the Trinity when we ponder the idea of an Eternally Begotten Son. The Bible says that Jesus is the "only begotten Son", and the concept of being eternally begotten is self-contradictory and not taught in the Bible.

John 3:16 NKJV
For God so loved the world that He gave His only
begotten Son, that whoever believes in Him should not
perish but have everlasting life.

We will discuss this more in the chapter on Firstborn, Begotten, and Logos.

So the Trinity model attempts to explain the Adjacency verses but actually doesn't fit all the passages very well. I find myself surprised in my own analysis here. I started this book contemplating the Oneness and Trinity models, and I organized the major New Testament themes into twelve patterns to see where it led me.

As an Apostolic, I suspected that the Oneness model would do better than the Trinity on most of the patterns, but I guessed that the Trinity would at least be a better fit for the Adjacency verses. After spending a lot of time working through the details, I see that the Oneness model fits all these verses, and the Trinity model has gaps and issues here. Whether a Trinitarian can see the issues is a harder question.

I'm hoping Trinitarian readers can see the differences between Adjacency in scripture and the Catholic doctrine of the Trinity. They are not the same thing and actually disagree on several key points.

Let's look at a short list of differences...

Adjacency in the Bible	The Trinity Model
Always connected to the Incarnation and Creation	Eternal Persons in a Triune God in Heaven
The Father is Greater than the Son The Spirit does whatever it is told	Persons are Declared Co-Equal
The Bible says the Son is made and begotten	The Catholic Church says the Son is Eternally Begotten
Adjacency verses can be understood through the Dual-Nature of Christ	The Trinity is Difficult to understand, so we say it's a mystery
Verses that show Adjacency: Dozens	Verses declaring God is Triune or Three: 0

I'm hoping you can see the difference between the two. It really is that simple.

Jesus is not part of God or one of three persons of God in Heaven. He is the genuine and true image of the invisible God.

Colossians 1:15 NKJV
He is the image of the invisible God,
the firstborn over all creation.

When you understand this, you can see how astounding the declarations of the incarnation really become.
Jesus truly is the fullness of deity bodily (Colossians 2:9). Receiving the Holy Spirit is receiving the Spirit of Jesus (Romans 8:9), also described as the Spirit of the Son (Galatians 4:6). There is one Spirit, one God, one Lord who is Father of all.

Ephesians 4:4-6 NKJV
There is one body and one Spirit, just as you were called in one hope of your calling; [5] one Lord, one faith, one baptism; [6] one God and Father of all, who is above all, and through all, and in you all.

Jesus is that one Lord, Father of all, above all, and through all, and in you all. Once you understand who Jesus really is, it changes everything!

#5 – SUBORDINATION IN SCRIPTURE

Of all the patterns in scripture, this one is the simplest to establish and describe, but still difficult for some to explain. Jesus plainly declares that the Father is greater than the Son, and the Father knows things that the Son does not know. As  Christians, we believe that Jesus, as the Son, is also God, even if wrapped in flesh, and so these statements can cause confusion, for both Apostolic and Trinitarian Christians.

John 14:28 NKJV
"You have heard Me say to you, 'I am going away and coming back to you.' If you loved Me, you would rejoice because I said, 'I am going to the Father,' for My Father is greater than I."

Mark 13:32 NKJV
"But of that day and hour no one knows, not even the angels in heaven, nor the Son, but only the Father."

John 5:30 NKJV
I can of Myself do nothing. As I hear, I judge; and My judgment is righteous, because I do not seek My own will but the will of the Father who sent Me.

The Apostolic answer is fairly simple, in that these differences are best understood through the limitations of His humanity. We are not fully told why, but we conclude that these limitations are necessary or preferred in the manifestation of God in Christ, reconciling the world to Himself.

Maybe these human limitations make Jesus a better or more valid high priest and mediator, but again, the specific reason is not given in the Bible. Only that the Father is greater than the Son.

There are a couple other places in scripture implying subordination. Jesus prayed to God, demonstrating a clear act of submission. Prayer is automatically a relational act from an inferior being towards a superior being. Then He specifically prayed, "not My will, but Your's be done". This implies the superiority of the Father's will over the Son's will.

John 16 includes two further examples of subordination that are difficult to reconcile with the idea of co-equal persons in the Trinity model. John 16:13 describes the Spirit with limited authority, only speaking that which comes from the Son. John 16:23-26 talks about a day when the role of the Son will be diminished[40] and we can and should directly address the Father in the name, and "in that day, you will ask me nothing" (NKJV 16:23).

---

[40] Discussed in detail in the section on Adjacency, starting on page 156.

The Apostolic answer remains the same. These acts are done out of His humanity, as the actions and prayers of a 100% authentic human being. Yes, Jesus is also deity, and His divinity is not just equal with the Father. The deity of Jesus is the deity of the Father. Yet when he acted in His humanity, as explained by His Dual-Nature, these actions are done as a genuine man. Therefore, they can be subordinate without contradiction from the Apostolic perspective.

Examining our list of options for model fitting, these are a valid example of a careful fit for the Apostolic Oneness model.

From the Trinitarian perspective, there are basically two options to address this scriptural pattern. Recall that the Trinity claims three co-equal persons in one God. One cannot be both co-equal and inferior at the same time.

If you reject the Apostolic view that the limitations come from the humanity of Jesus, then you have a simple contradiction between scriptural statements and the definition of the Trinity. Either the Trinity is true, or John 14:28 is true. Both cannot be true at the same time.

John 14:28 NKJV
"You have heard Me say to you, 'I am going away and coming back to you.' If you loved Me, you would rejoice because I said, 'I am going to the Father,' for <u>My Father is greater than I</u>."

But Trinitarians also believe in the Dual-Nature of Jesus Christ, so it is acceptable for them to appeal to the humanity of Jesus exactly as the Apostolics do. This does come with a price for the Trinitarian position, in that appealing to the humanity of Jesus waters down the whole reason for deciding God is a Trinity.

The logic ends up going something like this:

- Why did Jesus pray?
- He must be separate in some way from the Father.
- How is He separate?
- Maybe He is a separate divine being?
- But if God, then He must be equal with the Father.
- Okay, then why did Jesus pray if He is equal?
- Oh… then He actually prayed in His humanity.

Once you realize that the widely accepted doctrine of the Dual-Nature of Jesus actually answers most or all of the reasons for creating a Trinity, you realize that the Trinity doesn't actually explain anything anymore.

When we consider the Subordination verses in the New Testament, knowing that Jesus has two natures, fully God and fully man, we can best understand these verses as reflecting the limitations in the humanity of Christ. These verses easily fit the Apostolic model with no trouble.

#6 – ETERNITY REFERENCES TO THE SON

This is likely the most mysterious of the Biblical patterns, because we have a number of declarations in scripture about the Son, where a statement is made, but not fully explained. In cases where scope and explanation are lacking, we see the clearest examples of the models taking over where scripture doesn't provide the rest of the details.

Maybe a neutral example would help here. Let's start with a word picture in scripture that intrigues us but lacks details to fully explain it – the Book of Life.

> **Revelation 3:5 NKJV**
> *He who overcomes shall be clothed in white garments, and I will not blot out his name from the Book of Life; but I will confess his name before My Father and before His angels.*
>
> **Luke 10:20 NKJV**
> *Nevertheless do not rejoice in this, that the spirits are subject to you, but rather rejoice because your names are written in heaven.*

This Book of Life remains mysterious. We know it exists, and the language in multiple references is declarative and not easily dismissed as metaphoric. Names are written in the Book of Life, and some are blotted out. It's mentioned specifically in Exodus, Psalms, Daniel, and maybe in Malachi[41], as well as Luke, Philippians and multiple times in Revelation[42].

We know little about this book, but that hasn't stopped preachers from delivering numerous sermons with a lot more details than the scriptures might provide. I am not saying it is wrong to preach this, and I don't think it's wrong to paint vivid word pictures while preaching (in most cases). Please follow me carefully here, I'm not trying to make a new doctrine or attack the Book of Life. I'm only trying (again) to get you to think about your models. I believe in an actual and physical Book of Life.

Here's what we know for sure:

✓ There's a book.
✓ Your name better be in it.
✓ A name can be blotted out because of sin.

These texts, as far as I can tell, do not declare or explain exactly when your name is written in the book. Maybe a verse exists that I have missed, and I would love to know about it, but this is the part where your model for this book can dominate your thinking more than the verses. Let's look at three models for how this Book might work.

---

[41] Exodus 32:33, Psalms 69:28, Daniel 12:1, Malachi 3:16

[42] Luke 10:20, Philippians 4:3, Revelation 3:5, 13:8, 17:8, 20:12-15, 21:27

The Born-Again Book of Life Model - Some believe that a Christian's name is added when they are born again, but if you walk away from God or die without an active faith in God, it is blotted out.

The Life-Means-Life Model - Others believe everyone's name is written in the book when you were born (it is, after all, called the Book of Life) and that your name is blotted out when you stop living, which for the Christian, happens if you die without an active faith in Jesus.

The Calvinist-Elect Model - Calvinists believe this book was written before Creation and has a list of all the names of the Elect in it. But when was it written?

Revelation 13:8 NKJV
...whose names have not been written in the Book of Life of the Lamb slain from the foundation of the world.

Maybe you can see where the model controls their thinking here. Was the "Lamb slain from the foundation of the world" as the declared plan of God, determined before Creation and fulfilled later in time? Or is this the Book of Life, and names were written in the book "from the foundation of the world"? Calvinists, because of their model, believe the second version, but that isn't what this verse says. The verse points to an event described before the foundation of the world as part of the plan of God but fulfilled later in time.

The Book of Life belongs to the owner from the event.

Calvinism teaches that the Elect, before Genesis 1, were declared by God to be saved, and everyone else was literally made to go to hell. They would contend that this Book of Life has our names from before creation, and then this model must ignore the verses about blotting out names, because that completely destroys their pre-destination assumptions. Apparently, God looks in His book, quite surprised, "Oh, how did that name get in here? That one wasn't supposed to make it to heaven... Where is my white-out?"

I tend to believe the Born-Again model over the second one, and the third model makes me chuckle. I can't prove from scripture that the first model is right because the Bible doesn't provide enough declared details on this point. The second model for the Book of Life might also be correct. I have enough scripture to dismiss the Calvinist model as broken and useless.

The Book of Life serves as a beautiful example of something declared in scripture but not fully explained. The reference in Revelation 13:8 only makes it more interesting by referencing the foundation of the world. We should learn from this to be careful about connections to eternity past. Was the lamb slain from the foundation of the world? Or was the lamb slain at Calvary roughly 2,000 years ago? I believe the answer is yes, both are somehow true. I would argue that in the mind of God and plan of God, whatever He declares as true and coming to pass is already reality and valid, even if time needs to catch up to fulfill it.

There are multiple amazing statements in scripture referencing the Son of God that point to or hint at an Eternal connection. Many of these are not fully explained. Some are hardly explained at all. These paint vivid word pictures of sublime beauty and majesty, but also raise questions in our understanding of God and how this might work.

There are also multiple references to the Son being sent, as well as the beautiful descriptions of Jesus as the firstborn of creation or the only begotten Son of God. They deserve extra attention and will be discussed in the next chapter, so for now, let's focus on the scriptural word pictures that specifically connect the Son of God to the foundation of the world and eternity past.

Can we start with my favorite of the Messianic prophecies about the birthplace of Jesus?

Micah 5:2 NKJV
But you, Bethlehem Ephrathah, though you are little among the thousands of Judah, yet out of you shall come forth to Me the One to be Ruler in Israel, whose goings forth are from of old, from everlasting.

The One who is coming, even called the LORD Himself in Isaiah 40:3, is given an address in history, both in time and space, in which to arrive.

Bethlehem, a small town about 25 miles south of Jerusalem, bears the great honor as the birthplace of the Messiah. But Micah's prophecy, along with other verses, indicates that this Messiah would be more than just an anointed man or another prophet. This One is different, and something about Him goes back to eternity, "from everlasting".

This is beautifully explained and easily understood when we look at who made Jesus. His mother, Mary, was human, and so He is called the Son of Man, indicating He came from humanity. The Bible also tells us Jesus uniquely comes from God, and scripture even tells us why He is called the Son of God.

Luke 1:35 NKJV
And the angel answered and said to her, "The Holy Spirit will come upon you, and the power of the Highest will overshadow you; therefore, also, that Holy One who is to be born will be called the Son of God."

At this point, there is no need to even consider the Apostolic or Trinitarian models. The Word of God provides all the details we need to understand Micah's prophecy. He is called Son of Man because of Mary, and the Bible tells us why Jesus is to be called the Son of God, because He also came directly from the Spirit of God acting as His Father in this supernatural conception.

Note the Bible never declares that Jesus is the Son of God because He is the 2nd person of a Triune being.

Luke 1:35 would naturally have been a great place to introduce or explain this concept if it were Biblical. The verse even contains a "therefore" establishing that the reason explains the result:

Work of the Holy Spirit → Therefore → Son of God

We never see the Trinity model declared in scripture, which would be something more like:

2nd Person of Trinity → Therefore → Son of God

This language and model came from the Catholic Church a couple of centuries later.

If we focus on scripture to drive our model for the incarnation, the language of scripture gives us a simple and beautiful framework for the passage in Micah 5:2 and elsewhere. How is Jesus from everlasting? Because He is deity and has the same divine nature and being as God. As a Son, He had a beginning, but as God, He is also eternal.

The Apostolic model is content to understand that the deity of Jesus is obviously eternal, and His humanity had a beginning. Any attempt to force an eternal Son into the text feels like reading your model into scripture instead of letting the scripture determine your model.

One of the most famous examples of this is the discussion in Philippians 2 and what Jesus did to "empty Himself" – often called the Kenosis of Christ.

Philippians 2:5-9 NKJV

Let this mind be in you which was also in Christ Jesus,

⁶ who, being in the form of God, did not consider it robbery to be equal with God, ⁷ but made Himself of no reputation, taking the form of a bondservant, and coming in the likeness of men.

⁸ And being found in appearance as a man, He humbled Himself and became obedient to the point of death, even the death of the cross. ⁹ Therefore God also has highly exalted Him and given Him the name which is above every name...

The Greek word, Kenosis, in verse 7, for emptying or "making Himself of no reputation", forms the basis of lots of publications on how this might have worked. For the Trinitarian model, they see this passage as proof of the pre-existent Son, and that the Son had to "empty" Himself of some of His divine attributes for the incarnation. Discussions follow on whether it was an "ontological kenosis" or a "functional kenosis". Did the Son really give up his omnipotence and omniscience? Or just limit their use in the incarnation[43]? This gets too technical too quickly for most, but the shared goal is to

---

[43] *Christ Emptied Himself – The Kenosis of Christ*, Nick Campbell, May 16, 2022, https://christisthecure.org/2022/05/16/christ-emptied-himself-the-kenosis-of-christ/

show how the second person of the Trinity existed in the past and gave up certain powers in the incarnation.

The idea that Jesus emptied Himself of divine attributes is already problematic. If this refers to His deity, then did He become less divine in the incarnation?

Malachi 3:6 NKJV
For I am the Lord, I do not change...

If this references His deity, then how can the Second Person of God become less God? It doesn't work. And the objection gets worse when we consider:

Hebrews 13:8 NKJV
Jesus Christ is the same yesterday, today, and forever.

If Philippians 2 is about the deity of the Second Person of the Trinity, then one of these verses cannot be true. Hebrews 13:8 says that Jesus did not change, so Apostolics understand Philippians 2 in light of the humanity of Jesus. As a genuine man, He emptied Himself of self-will to instead be a servant and fulfill the plan of God. But in His deity, Jesus is the same yesterday, today, and forever. These verses fit together beautifully in the Apostolic Model because of the doctrine of the Dual-Nature.

On a more basic level, does Philippians 2:5-9 even require or prove that the Son existed separately from the Father before the incarnation? You can force that reading into the text, but there is an easier way to understand this entire passage. It not only explains the Kenosis, but once you see it, it invalidates any claim that Philippians 2 is about a pre-existent Son of God.

I love the rule, "any text without a context is a pretext for a prooftext". This means that failing to look at the surrounding verses and what they say about a passage can set one up for using a text incorrectly as a poor support for a doctrine.

We are told in verse 5 to "let this mind be in you which was also in Christ Jesus". That's the context. Whatever follows is to help us adopt or pursue a given mental attitude and perspective. Think about it this way...

Does Philippians 2:5 ask the impossible of us?

> *"Let this mind be in you which was also in the second divine person of the Triune God?"*

How would anyone even remotely attempt such a thing? Even taking the Trinity out of the picture, this verse still would be impossible if the context is divinity:

> *"Let this mind be in you which was the mind of God?"*

We cannot take on such a mindset, and it would be illogical and unreasonable to be instructed to do so. God asks us to do the part that we can do and trust Him for the rest. God does not ask us to think like Him.

"For My thoughts are not your thoughts, nor are your ways My ways," says the Lord. ⁹ "For as the heavens are higher than the earth, so are My ways higher than your ways, and My thoughts than your thoughts."

Philippians 2:5-9 is NOT about the divinity of Christ or somehow being asked to think like God thinks. It's clearly and entirely about the humanity of Jesus. Although He is, in fact, God, and being in the form of God, it would be valid and reasonable to declare His divinity as full and equivalent. Yet this passage is about His choice as a man to submit and be a servant. You can actually and reasonably follow this kind of example.

"Let this mind be in you which was also in the man, Christ Jesus, who submitted and humbled Himself and served humanity even sacrificially. You can be a servant to humanity as well."

Jesus emptied Himself of self-will and pride, and of any claim to a higher station that He legitimately deserved to serve humanity and the greater plan of God.

This passage doesn't specifically support the Apostolic model or the Trinity model. It just beautifully establishes the mindset of Jesus as a legitimate human servant, an attitude and commitment that we should copy. The classic interpretation of the pre-existent Son, if it were Biblical, gets no support here because of the clear context of Philippians 2:5. This passage must be about the humanity of Jesus, or it makes no sense and has no application for us.

There are a few other passages often discussed as support for the pre-existent Son. Other than John 1, which we will talk about in the next chapter, the most famous passage used to teach the pre-existent Son is John 17, where Jesus prays to be glorified.

John 17:4-5 NKJV
I have glorified You on the earth. I have finished the work which You have given Me to do. ⁵ And now, O Father, glorify Me together with Yourself, with the glory which I had with You before the world was.

Similar to Philippians 2, we must answer a question to establish the context for how we interpret this prayer. Is Jesus speaking and acting in His divinity or His humanity? Both are valid parts of the Apostolic and the Trinitarian models for God – both models believe in the dual-nature of Christ, but your answer affects how you attempt to read John 17.

If this is divinity praying to divinity, it creates a couple of issues. It raises the subordination question again, because prayer is fundamentally a relational act from an inferior being towards a superior being. The case for deity talking to deity gets worse in John 17:5, because this would be one person of God asking to be restored in their attributes from another person of God. How could

Jesus lose His divine glory and then get it back? How does that remain consistent with Malachi 3:6 and the unchanging deity of Hebrews 13:8?

Hebrews 13:8 NKJV
Jesus Christ is the same yesterday, today, and forever.

Both the act of prayer and the content of the prayer in John 17 are difficult to reconcile with other verses if done in Jesus' divinity. They do, however, work beautifully and consistently if understood in the context of Jesus praying as a man. It's a better understanding of the prayers of Jesus, and it fits these specific verses well.

What is the glory that Jesus mentions in John 17:5? It is the glory of the plan of God, established in the Logos, or the mind of God, at the beginning of Creation, and shortly to be revealed for all to see. The Bible declares this as the glory of God's foreordained plan.

1st Peter 1:18-21 NKJV
Knowing that you were not redeemed with corruptible things, like silver or gold, from your aimless conduct received by tradition from your fathers, 19 but with the precious blood of Christ, as of a lamb without blemish and without spot. 20 He indeed was foreordained before the foundation of the world, but was manifest in these last times for you 21 who through Him believe in God, who raised Him from the dead and gave Him glory, so that your faith and hope are in God.

Not only does 1st Peter 1 explain this as the plan of God, but it also specifically connects the glory to Christ, as a lamb, as our sacrifice, receiving glory from God through the resurrection and victory over death and the grave. Nothing in this passage demands or declares the glory of a pre-existent Son, but the glory of the plan of God in the man Christ Jesus.

If this is the humanity of Christ praying in John 17, we should expect to find further evidence to support this understanding.

> **John 17:22-23 NKJV**
> *"And the glory which You gave Me I have given them, that they may be one just as We are one:* [23] *I in them, and You in Me; that they may be made perfect in one, and that the world may know that You have sent Me, and have loved them as You have loved Me."*

The context of this passage demands a human focus and understanding. Jesus includes His followers in the request, "that they may be one just as We are one". This is completely possible in the context of a human praying to God, but not possible if this is communication between the Second person of a Triune being to the First person. How could we be one with each other or one with the Trinity in the same way as the persons of the Trinity are with each other?

The language and context are clear, as this prayer comes from the man Christ Jesus, and I pray it becomes true in my life and yours as well.

John 17:24 NKJV
"Father, I desire that they also whom You gave Me may be with Me where I am, that they may behold My glory which You have given Me; for You loved Me before the foundation of the world."

Verse 24 is probably the most mysterious and intriguing in this passage. Taken out of context, I would agree that verse 24 is compatible with the Trinitarian model. I have some issues, as stated above, believing that Jesus could pray in His divinity, but I am trying to see the world through someone else's viewpoint.

It can also be understood in the Apostolic model, in that God loved humanity from the beginning of the world, and I would think that God loved the man Christ Jesus as well. Verse 24 could also be a prophetic declaration similar to Revelation 13:8, where the Lamb is slain from the foundation of the world.

I don't see a compelling proof-text for the Trinity model here. I see some verses in John 17 that fit parts of the model and other verses in John 17 that should be a challenge to the Trinitarian understanding. All of these verses can fit the Apostolic model just fine.

Genesis 1:26 and Genesis 11:7 are sometimes cited as evidence of plurality within God and a pre-existent Son.

Genesis 1:26-27 NKJV
Then God said, "Let Us make man in Our image, according to Our likeness; let them have dominion over the fish of the sea, over the birds of the air, and over the cattle, over all the earth and over every creeping thing that creeps on the earth." ^{27} *So God created man in His own image; in the image of God He created him; male and female He created them.*

Genesis 11:7-8 NKJV
"Come, let Us go down and there confuse their language, that they may not understand one another's speech." ^{8} *So the Lord scattered them abroad...*

For the Jew or the Apostolic Christian, this feels an awful lot like reading your theology into the text instead of building your doctrine from the text. God speaks in the plural but acts in the singular with nothing signifying a three-ness in God's nature. Nothing here demands that God be understood to have a plural identity that opposes the numerous declarations of Strict Monotheism.

God could be speaking to the angels, deliberating with Himself, or using the plural of majesty, a valid construct in Hebrew grammar. Jewish scholars have referenced all three interpretations as the likely explanations for these verses.

"Mankind is described as in a special sense created by God Himself. To enhance the dignity of this last work and to mark the fact that man differs in kind from the animals, Scripture represents God as deliberating over the making of the human species (Abarbanel). It is not 'let man be created', or 'let man be made', but 'let us make man'.

The use of the plural, 'let us make man', is the Hebrew idiomatic way of expressing deliberation, as in 11:7 or is the plural of Majesty, royal commands being conveyed in the first person plural, as in Ezra 4:18."

Explains Rabbi Hertz in his classic commentary on the Pentateuch[44]. Or as David Bernard explains in his book, *The Oneness View of Jesus Christ*[45]:

The simplest explanation is that God was communing within Himself. Ephesians 1:11 informs us that God "worketh all things after the counsel of His own will." If a finite human being can make plans with himself by saying "Let's see" ("Let us see"), and if the rich fool could address his own soul (Luke 12:19), then is it not unreasonable to suppose that the infinite, omniscient God could counsel with Himself?

---

[44] *Pentateuch and Haftorahs*, Dr. J. H. Hertz, 1960, Soncino Press, p. 4-5.

[45] *The Oneness View of Jesus Christ*, David Bernard, 1996, Word Aflame Press, p. 53.

There are multiple, valid explanations for Genesis 1:26 as well as claims about the plural case for the word God, in Hebrew, "Elohim". For a devout Jew, to attempt to redefine the God of Israel as anything other than "one", disagrees with numerous Bible verses. Consider Rabbi Tovia Singer's analysis of attempts to find the Trinity in the Hebrew scriptures[46]:

> *"The doctrine of the Trinity has no greater foe than the Hebrew Scriptures. It is on the strength of this sacred oracle that the Jew has preserved the concept of One, single, unique Creator God Who alone is worthy of worship. Missionaries undertake a daunting and unholy task as they scour the Jewish Scriptures in search of any text that can be construed as consistent with the doctrine of the Trinity.*
>
> *No prophet remained silent on the uncompromising radical monotheism demanded by the God of Israel. The Jewish people, therefore, to whom these sublime declarations about the nature of the Almighty were given, knew nothing about a trinity of persons in the godhead."*

If you are hunting for it and fixed on your beliefs, you can likely find a verse compatible with any idea. For the serious, Bible-believing Christian, we shouldn't read our

---

[46] Article on *Finding the Trinity in the First Chapter of the Bible*, Rabbi Tovia Singer, April 28, 2014, https://outreachjudaism.org/trinity-genesis/

doctrine into the Bible but let declarative scripture and Biblical patterns drive our beliefs and models.

Nothing in Genesis 1:26 or Genesis 11:7 compels us to consider that God might be different in nature than the Strict Monotheism found throughout scripture. This aligns in full agreement with the Apostolic model.

Considering John 17, Philippians 2, Micah 5:2, and others, in light of the Apostolic Model, all of these passages fit easily or carefully within an Apostolic understanding with no issues or violence to the text.

Thinking about eternity, past or future, has certain challenges, but knowing that we serve a God who loved us so much that He planned to take care of sin before He even created the world... astounds me when I ponder it.

I enjoy the puzzling challenge of these verses, but see a clear and beautiful picture where God set His plan in motion in Jesus Christ to make a way for us. Before Calvary, Jesus did pre-exist. In His divinity, He existed as God Almighty. And in the plan of God, the Bible also tells us that the Son of God was foreordained but then manifest in these last times for us.

(We will focus more on this foreordained plan in the next chapter, discussing the Logos and other references to the Son's role in creation.)

1st Peter 1:18-21 NKJV

Knowing that you were not redeemed with corruptible things, like silver or gold, from your aimless conduct received by tradition from your fathers, ¹⁹ but with the precious blood of <u>Christ</u>, as of a lamb without blemish and without spot. ²⁰ <u>He indeed was foreordained before the foundation of the world, but was manifest in these last times for you</u> ²¹ who through Him believe in God, who raised Him from the dead and gave Him glory, so that your faith and hope are in God.

Galatians 4:4-5 KJV

But <u>when the fullness of the time was come, God sent forth his Son, made of a woman, made under the law</u>. To redeem them that were under the law, that we might receive the adoption of sons.

None of the verses so far declare or necessitate a Trinity or multiple divine persons in God to be true. Instead, multiple friction points in these verses do not match or fit the Trinity model without stretching the words beyond their plain meaning.

All of these verses discussed do fit the Apostolic model through the Dual-Nature of Christ. Jesus in His divinity is Eternal, and in His humanity He prayed. In His deity, He did pre-exist as God Almighty. In the mind of God, the plan for the Son and Calvary was foreordained, but the Son of God was also firstborn, begotten, and made, which we will discuss in the next chapter.

#7 – FIRSTBORN, BEGOTTEN, AND LOGOS

Let's start with the most famous Bible passage in Christianity – the most profound declaration of the love of God and plan of God for each of us.

As a reminder of context, John 3:16 occurs in the nighttime conversation between Jesus and a pharisee with a sincere heart, Nicodemus.

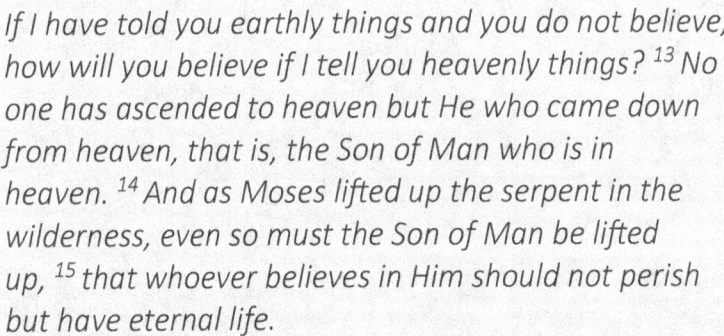

John 3:12-17 NKJV

If I have told you earthly things and you do not believe, how will you believe if I tell you heavenly things? [13] No one has ascended to heaven but He who came down from heaven, that is, the Son of Man who is in heaven. [14] And as Moses lifted up the serpent in the wilderness, even so must the Son of Man be lifted up, [15] that whoever believes in Him should not perish but have eternal life.

[16] For God so loved the world that He gave His only begotten Son, that whoever believes in Him should not perish but have everlasting life. [17] For God did not send His Son into the world to condemn the world, but that the world through Him might be saved.

I heard once that it's harder to learn from a beloved passage than a new one, since our brains categorize familiar phrases and words and more easily overlook the details. Is there another passage more familiar, more loved, than this amazing promise?

Let's deliberately pause and consider the word choices and phraseology in this sublime account:

- ✓ The Son of Man "who is in heaven"
- ✓ The Son of Man "came down from heaven"
- ✓ His only begotten Son
- ✓ God sent His Son into the world

Most of our conversation will focus on begotten and sent, but the first verses are worth a pause. Am I just as earthly or worse than Nicodemus? I struggled with the "Son of Man" reference in John 3:13. I love the surprises I have found or seen anew while writing this book. Although I'm happy with the explanatory power of the Dual-Nature of Christ, I'm adjusting my model to realize that wholeness and identity of the Son is more integrated than I had believed.

"Son does not refer to the humanity alone but to the one person of Christ, who was simultaneously human and divine. For example, the Son has power to forgive sin (Matthew 9:6), the Son was both in Heaven and on Earth at the same time (John 3:13), the Son ascended up into heaven (John 6:62), and the Son is coming again in glory to rule and judge (Matthew 25:31)."

In his book, *The Oneness of God*, David Bernard's summary of Biblical Terminology for the Son has been very useful in my understanding of this passage[47]. The one person of Christ, fully God and fully man, according to scripture, in some manner still resides in Heaven while also on Earth. We have another reference to the Deity of the Son coming down from heaven in John 6:33. Since the Son is fully and truly God as well, this is compatible with both the Apostolic and Trinity models.

SENT FROM GOD

The language of sent or sending does not confirm or deny either the Apostolic or Trinitarian model. Both models affirm the full deity of Jesus. The concept of sending the Son does not require, for instance, an Eternal Son as taught in the Trinity. The only challenges would come from the surrounding language and word choices in a given Bible verse.

God can send the Son in the Apostolic model with no trouble and full support. There remains a question in the Trinitarian model that Apostolics sometimes wonder about. With John 3:16, did all three persons of God love the world to send the Son, or was it just the Father who loved the world? I presume all three, but the language of scripture on many of these Adjacency verses leaves no room for the actual Trinity. Scripture interchangeably says God so loved or God sent the Son, and the Adjacency described in scripture is often the Adjacency

---

[47] *The Oneness of God*, David Bernard, 2012, Word Aflame Press, p. 100.

of God and the Son, not the later language developed by the Catholic Church. In those cases, they have to redefine God to mean different persons or substance in different passages. We will see more definition challenges for the Trinity when we explore the Logos in this chapter.

John 17:3 NKJV
"And this is eternal life, that they may know You, the only true God, and Jesus Christ whom You have sent."

John 17:3 presents us with another language challenge for the Trinity, in that we have clear Adjacency here. If this is a picture of plurality in the Trinity, this would also show that only one of the persons in God is deity. God, presumably the Father, is "the only true God", and then there is Jesus Christ. The Trinity model assumes that Adjacency verses like John 17:3 prove the Trinity, but if this is the Trinity, then the second person is not deity.

Oneness believers recognize that Jesus is praying – a uniquely human act. Prayer demonstrates a relational interaction between an inferior being and superior one, and so Jesus, praying in His humanity, as a man, can sincerely say these words with no violation of the Apostolic model. It is completely valid to recognize the only true God, and the man Christ Jesus, as God in the flesh, whom God sent. A Trinitarian might not like or agree that this works in the Apostolic model, but it works just fine in John 17:3 and elsewhere.

THE LOGOS

Many believe that John 1:1 comes before Genesis 1:1. Before God made a tree or a goldfish or the first star, this begins with the Logos, a declaration of the Word of God or mind of God from Eternity past. In time, this Word became flesh and dwelt among us.

John 1:1, 14 NKJV
In the beginning was the Word, and the Word was with God, and the Word was God...

14 And the Word became flesh and dwelt among us, and we beheld His glory, the glory as of the only begotten of the Father, full of grace and truth.

The translators picked Word as the best equivalent for this uniquely Greek idea. This adds another flavor to how we know Jesus. He is the Way, the Truth, and the Life, the Good Shepherd, and our Passover Lamb. John adds "Word" to the amazing titles for our Lord.

As much as we celebrate Jesus as the Word, this choice is also limited compared to the full meaning in Greek. The Greek for "word" is "Logos", and any study of Logos shows it means so much more. I like the explanation[48] on GotQuestions.org, a Trinitarian website.

---

[48] *What is the Logos?*, Article on GotQuestions.org, https://www.gotquestions.org/what-is-the-Logos.html

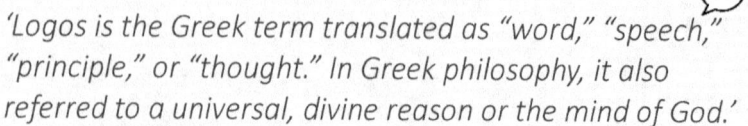

'Logos is the Greek term translated as "word," "speech," "principle," or "thought." In Greek philosophy, it also referred to a universal, divine reason or the mind of God.'

The Jews had one understanding of the Word of God, and the Greeks brought another loaded perspective to this word, "Logos". John selected this word under the inspiration of God to grab the attention of both Jews and Greeks. This Word points both to Jesus Christ and His true divine nature in a powerful way.

So "word" means "word", but it goes much deeper: the mind of God, the thoughts of God, the plan of God, the blueprint of God... This is recognized as true for both Apostolics and Trinitarians. The differences come in how we understand this definition and its application. The Apostolics look to the specific Greek word choices in John 1 (and Colossians 1 and elsewhere) as the driving forces in understanding this text.

In the beginning was the plan and mind of God, which was with God, and God is ultimately operating in His plan and through His thoughts. These are divine thoughts; they are with God and from God. How much can you separate anyone from their thoughts? It should be valid to say that "your thoughts are with you" and "you are your thoughts", at least the ones that genuinely reflect your heart and character. With no one capable of influencing God's thoughts, this certainly holds for God.

This question, "Who or What is the logos?", really is the focus of this chapter. Who was firstborn, begotten, and sent? What do these words mean? Was this the eternal second person as described by the Catholic Church or not? The meaning and interpretation of Logos becomes central, and we will circle back shortly. Let's look at the next verses in John 1 and their connection in Colossians.

John 1:1-3 NKJV
In the beginning was the Word, and the Word was with God, and the Word was God. ² He was in the beginning with God. ³ All things were made through Him, and without Him nothing was made that was made.

Colossians 1:15-17 NKJV
He [the Son] is the image of the invisible God, the firstborn over all creation. ¹⁶ For by Him all things were created that are in heaven and that are on earth, visible and invisible, whether thrones or dominions or principalities or powers. All things were created through Him and for Him. ¹⁷ And He is before all things, and in Him all things consist.

These passages clearly describe the same event revealed supernaturally to two authors, John and Paul. The Logos, as the mind and plan of God, is now active in fulfillment through the Son, the firstborn over all creation. This is the agency and source of everything else created.

So we can learn more about the Logos when we contemplate the meaning of the firstborn.

THE FIRSTBORN

With just a handful of verses, this unique word only shows up 9 times in the Textus Receptus Greek text.

Most of the uses of prōtotokos (πρωτότοκος G4416) connect to Jesus, but only one of these verses directly connects Jesus as firstborn to creation, which is then confirmed by the declarations in John 1:1-3.

Usage	Reference
Mary's firstborn	Matthew 1:25 Luke 2:7
Jesus, firstborn among many brethren	Romans 8:29
Jesus, firstborn from the dead	Colossians 1:18 Revelation 1:5
Firstborn of Egypt who were judged	Hebrews 11:28
The church of the firstborn	Hebrews 12:23
Firstborn begotten into the world	Hebrews 1:6
Firstborn of creation	Colossians 1:15

At its root meaning, firstborn comes from two Greek words, prōto, meaning first, and tokos, meaning birth or offspring. Unfortunately, passed this point, our models take over and take two completely different directions on the meaning of this word.

Does firstborn actually mean first and born? The Catholic Church and the Trinity model says no. The Son is eternal, and this word is effectively mangled and ignored for Trinitarians. For the Apostolic, we believe that Jesus is the firstborn through the Logos, declared in the mind and plan of God and fulfilled in time.

1st Peter 1:19-20 NKJV
...precious blood of Christ, as of a lamb without blemish and without spot. [20] He indeed was foreordained before the foundation of the world, but was manifest in these last times for you.

Revelation 13:8 NKJV
...have not been written in the Book of Life of the Lamb slain from the foundation of the world.

Apostolics recognize that God can speak His plan into existence, and the Bible declares that the Lamb was slain from the foundation of the world. This plan was foreordained from the very beginning.

Romans 4:17 NKJV
...God, who gives life to the dead and calls those things which do not exist as though they did.

We see this pattern declared and well supported in scripture. With the specific declaration of the Logos as well as Colossians 1:15-17, we understand that this is the most scriptural and reasonable explanation for how Jesus is the firstborn. This declaration places Calvary and the Incarnation at the center of God's plan for creation and should thrill every believer.

Everything that was made, was done through and for the Son, Jesus Christ, which prioritizes and demonstrates how much more God really loves us and proves that love. This puts John 3:16 in an even more profound light.

ONLY BEGOTTEN

Returning to John 3:16, we understand that the Son was firstborn and sent as the fulfillment and manifestation of the Logos, the Word, from John 1. Everything that was made was done through, for, and by the Son.

John 3:16 NKJV
For God so loved the world that He gave His only begotten Son, that whoever believes in Him should not perish but have everlasting life.

This treasured promise brings us to the next attribute for the Son. He is declared the "only begotten" of the Father.

In Greek, this is monogenēs (μονογενής G3439), and like firstborn, it also doesn't show up very often in the New Testament.

Usage	Reference
The only son or only daughter of an unnamed human parent	Luke 7:12, Luke 8:42, Luke 9:38
Isaac, the only begotten of Abraham	Hebrews 11:17
The only begotten Son of God	John 1:14, 1:18, 3:16, 3:18, 1st John 4:9

The root idea of "genēs" is to make, bring to pass, be made, be done, etc... It's where we get the book name for Genesis. It might seem silly to some readers to dig into the details here, but the meaning of "begotten" is controversial when discussing the Incarnation because the Catholic Church decided that the Son is actually NOT begotten in any normal understanding of this word.

The bishops of the church declared the Son is "eternally begotten", and this was first affirmed officially at the Ecumenical Council in Nicaea in 325[A.D.]. Here is the second clause of the creedal statement from Nicaea:

> *"And in one Lord Jesus Christ, the Son of God, begotten of the Father [the only-begotten; that is, of the essence of the Father, God of God,] Light of Light, very God of very God, **begotten, not made**, consubstantial with the Father"*

Some might be wondering how "begotten not made" is any different than "made not made". I understand your confusion. The declaration of an eternally begotten Son sounds like a basic contradiction of terms. It sounds like "jumbo shrimp", "Dodge Ram", or "congressional ethics". It just doesn't go together or make sense. If you ask, you might be told it's a mystery, but if you want to stick with scriptural language to define and understand God, this is a mystery you can skip.

The Bible uses multiple expressions and verses to indicate that the Son had a beginning. It gets even clearer in the case of the begetting of the Son.

Hebrews 1:5-6 NKJV

For to which of the angels did He ever say: "You are My Son, <u>today I have begotten You</u>"? And again: "I will be to Him a Father, and He shall be to Me a Son"?

⁶ But when He again brings the firstborn into the world, He says: "Let all the angels of God worship Him."

This is a hypothetical question never asked of the angels, but the clear meaning is that it does apply to the Son. Hebrews 1:5 clearly explains that the Son came into being on a given day.

Galatians 4:4 KJV

But when the fullness of the time was come, God sent forth his Son, made of a woman, made under the law.

I am quite aware that modern translations prefer the word "born" over made, but the Greek word underlying this verse appears hundreds of times in the New Testament, and consistently carries the meaning of becoming, coming to pass, being made, done, or fulfilled.

The case for an eternally begotten Son, from scripture alone, is ridiculously weak, and when you ask Trinitarians about it, many are aware of how Catholic this sounds.

ONE MORE WORD ABOUT THE WORD

This chapter and these specific words, Begotten, Firstborn, and Logos, get very technical and deep quickly. This book attempts to explore the Incarnation in a way that most Christians, Trinitarian and Apostolic, would find understandable and approachable. I hope I have not lost you in this chapter with technical details and Greek word usage. If you want to dig deeper, I highly recommend David Bernard's book, *The Oneness View of Jesus Christ*, especially chapter 2, *The Word Became Flesh*.

I want to mention one last aspect of the Logos that needs to match either of our models. The Logos, as a basic concept, represents the words, thoughts, mind, and reasoning of God.

If the Trinity model is true, and the Logos is the second person of a Triune God, then the declaration of John 1:1 brings up a great difficulty. If all three persons in God have their own mind, will, and center of consciousness, then wouldn't each have their own Logos as well?

Why and how does the second person of the Trinity have a monopoly on Logos? Shouldn't there be three individual Logos, one for each person? I would be very hesitant to stand before the first person of God and explain that I thought it was only the second person who gets the mind, reason, and thoughts of God.

If there is only one Logos, as described in scripture, that much better matches the Apostolic model, in that God has one consciousness, one mind, and one voice. God speaks and identifies Himself in the singular in both the Old and New Testament. God is one! Then God put His single Logos into action and fulfillment in the created Son, in the man Christ Jesus. Because of this great plan, we can see the glory of the Father in the Son.

John 1:14, 18 NKJV
And the Word became flesh and dwelt among us, and we beheld His glory, the glory as of the only begotten of the Father, full of grace and truth...

18 No one has seen God at any time. The only begotten Son, who is in the bosom of the Father, He has declared Him.

In the Trinity model, they approach the scriptures by modifying the definitions of words throughout the verses for firstborn, begotten, and logos. It feels like the Trinity model is far more loyal to the unique definitions established by the Catholic Church than the specific word choices found in the Bible. Firstborn does not mean born, but eternal. Begotten does not mean made, but eternally begotten – whatever that means.

Even logos does not mean "mind of God" but is a name for the second person of the Trinity, and the first and third person don't apparently get their own Logos.

Apostolic Definition	Trinity Definition
Logos = mind or plan of God, the thoughts of God	Logos = 2nd person of the Trinity
Firstborn = the Logos, the plan of God	Firstborn = not born, not first, but eternal person
Begotten = begotten	Begotten = an eternal mysterious process where the Son is Co-Equal with the Father, but somehow also directly and continually dependent on the Father in an ongoing begetting process the Bible never describes

Even the word God changes in meaning in the Trinity model depending on where it falls in any given verse.

John 1:1 NKJV

In the beginning was the Word, and the Word was with God, and the Word was God.

In John 1:1, the definition of God has to switch mid-verse to match the Trinity model. Trinitarians often describe God as "one What and three Who's". When they read John 1:1, they have to change the meaning of God as first a "Who" and then immediately afterwards as a "What".

John 1:1 NKJV

In the beginning was the Word, and the Word was with GOD AS A WHO, IN THIS CASE, THE FATHER,

and the Word was GOD AS A WHAT, MADE OF THE SAME SUBSTANCE AS THE OTHER TWO PERSONS OF THE TRINITY.

Is this a great way to exegete and understand scripture? Is there another place in the Bible where we redefine a word in a single passage to mean two things? This is likely evidence of forcing a model and external definitions into the Bible instead of letting scripture define our understanding.

In the Apostolic model, we look to the word definitions and usage in the text, and not the declared model of the Catholic church. We see the Logos as the mind and plan of God, with God from everlasting, and truly as God. Then God's plan activates with the Incarnation, where Calvary was planned from the beginning of the world. God declared there would be a Son, and everything was made by, for, and through this plan and declaration. This is how Apostolics see the firstborn – as truly first and truly born in the plan of God.

John 1:1-3 NKJV
In the beginning was the Word, and the Word was with God, and the Word was God. ² He was in the beginning with God. ³ All things were made through Him, and without Him nothing was made that was made.

Colossians 1:15-16 NKJV
He [the Son] is the image of the invisible God, the firstborn over all creation. ¹⁶ For by Him all things were created that are in heaven and that are on earth, visible and invisible, whether thrones or dominions or principalities or powers. All things were created through Him and for Him.

1ˢᵗ Peter 1:19-20 NKJV
...precious blood of Christ, as of a lamb without blemish and without spot. ²⁰ He indeed was foreordained before the foundation of the world, but was manifest in these last times for you.

Then, when the time was right, the Eternal took on temporal flesh, the Creator stepped into creation – the Word became flesh. And through the created Son, we see the glory of the Father revealed.

John 1:14, 18 KJV

And the Word became flesh and dwelt among us, and we beheld His glory, the glory as of the only begotten of the Father, full of grace and truth... [18] *No one has seen God at any time. The only begotten Son, who is in the bosom of the Father, He has declared Him.*

Galatians 4:4 KJV

But when the fullness of the time was come, God sent forth his Son, made of a woman, made under the law.

The idea of a created Son requires that you abandon the Catholic definitions for these words and embrace the word choices in the Bible instead. Firstborn must somehow mean first and born. Begotten should mean begotten. God inspired the authors of scripture to use these words, and changing the meaning of begotten to eternally begotten should strike any sincere truth seeker as a massive perversion of language and word meaning. You are not allowed to declare that a word means effectively the opposite of its natural meaning.

Trinitarians will struggle with this, claiming that it is not scriptural or possible for Jesus to be both Creator and created. In their article on Jesus being the Firstborn, the Trinitarian website GotQuestions.org raises this very point in their discussion[49] of Colossians 1.

---

[49] *How Is Jesus the FirstBorn?*, Article on GotQuestions.org, https://www.gotquestions.org/Jesus-first-born.html

"In a letter to the church at Colossae, the Apostle Paul gave an intriguing description of Jesus. In it, he explained Christ's relationship to God the Father and to creation. Some have claimed that Paul's description of Christ as the firstborn of creation means that Jesus was created—not eternal, not God. Such a doctrine, however, conflicts with the rest of the Bible. Christ could not be both Creator and created; John 1 clearly names Him Creator. Let's take a careful look at the passage where Jesus is called the firstborn."

This seems compelling, but this is exactly the claim made by the Bible. Creator stepped into creation.

John 1:14 NKJV
And the Word became flesh and dwelt among us

Revelation 22:16 NKJV
"I, Jesus, have sent My angel to testify to you these things in the churches. I am the Root and the Offspring of David, the Bright and Morning Star."

In the last chapter of Revelation, Jesus declares that He is both Creator and created. He made David and calls Himself the root of David, but He also came from David. So, according to scripture, when the Word became flesh, Christ was absolutely Creator and created simultaneously.

When we consider the meaning of these words, and their use in the Bible, we see that the Apostolic model easily accommodates the Biblical declarations for the firstborn, begotten, and the Logos. I could objectively see some resistance to the idea that God's plan was declared at the beginning and fulfilled at the right time. Some might not like how Jesus is the firstborn of all creation, but that's also what the Bible plainly says about itself in the verses listed earlier in the chapter.

For the Trinity model, these words and verses only fit if you change their meaning to basically mean the opposite of the natural definitions. Firstborn isn't actually born but has to become eternal. Begotten must mean eternally begotten.

These alterations go beyond a careful fit or even a stretch fit, and the Trinity just doesn't match the plain word choices found in the New Testament for the firstborn and begotten Son of God.

#8 – SUPREMACY OF THE NAME

On the simplest level, the name of God shines as an important theme throughout the Bible, and in the New Testament, the name of Jesus is featured as the revealed name of God and the name of Salvation for believers. God's name represents His character, His authority, His power, and His presence. His name acts as a placeholder for God Himself and for the manifestation of His activity.

> **Proverbs 18:10 NKJV**
> *The name of the Lord is a strong tower;*
> *The righteous run to it and are safe.*

Jesus comes directly from God and is more than an anointed prophet or messenger. Scripture declares Him as the Word made flesh, the image of the invisible God, and the fullness of deity bodily[50].

So His name celebrates both His identity and His mission. Jesus literally means "Yahweh is our salvation" or "Yahweh has become our salvation". He was not the first to have this specific name as pronounced in Hebrew, but was the first to fully embody this name.

---

[50] John 1:14, Colossians 1:15, Colossians 2:9

A name is a placeholder for the person. Complimenting their name complements them, and complimenting the person gives them a "good name". We see this beautifully fulfilled in Isaiah 9:6, where the name of the Son is called an astounding list of attributes, some of which can only be true of Almighty God.

Isaiah 9:6 NKJV
For unto us a Child is born, unto us a Son is given;
And the government will be upon His shoulder. And His name will be called Wonderful, Counselor, Mighty God, Everlasting Father, Prince of Peace.

Jesus, fulfilling the mission as our High Priest, submits to the will of the Father. Philippians 2:5-11 explores the humility of Jesus Christ as a man and servant obeying the plan of God. Although also divine, He acted in full submission in His humanity.

Philippians 2:9-10 NKJV
Therefore God also has highly exalted Him and given Him the name which is above every name, [10] that at the name of Jesus every knee should bow...

We see the importance and emphasis on His name even more in baptism, in that the instructions for baptism and their fulfillment in scripture beautifully honor the Biblical emphasis on the supremacy of the name of Jesus.
The baptism discussion includes enough verses and questions to warrant a separate chapter of its own, so

we'll limit comments here to the other verses in scripture emphasizing the superiority of the name of Jesus.

Acts 4:12 NKJV
Nor is there salvation in any other, for there is no other name under heaven given among men by which we must be saved.

Colossians 3:17 NKJV
And whatever you do in word or deed, do all in the name of the Lord Jesus, giving thanks to God the Father through Him.

Before we consider our models, a note on pronunciation seems warranted. I've run into people obsessed with the Hebrew pronunciation of Jesus, in both Apostolic and Protestant circles. It goes beyond the scope of this book to deal with all their arguments, but as part of our models, two thoughts put this in perspective:

✓ The New Testament was largely written in Koine Greek, including Acts, written by the Greek historian Luke, who travelled with Paul. He translated the name of Jesus into Greek, setting a translation precedent for the name.

✓ The power is not found in the specific pronunciation, but in faith in the name, and this power has been effectively and empirically demonstrated with miracles and deliverance in numerous languages throughout the world. The name works in Greek, English, Spanish, and dozens of other languages.

Trinitarians strive to honor this name in general and in their worship. Many beautiful songs have been written and sung celebrating the name of God and specifically the name Jesus. Trinitarian songwriters often use phraseology found throughout the Bible.

"What a Beautiful Name it is" by Hillsong Worship
"I Know a Name" by Elevation Worship
"Blessed Be the Name of the Lord" by Clinton Utterbach
"Blessed Be Your Name" by Matt Redman
"His Name is Jesus" by Phil Wickham
"There's Something About that Name" by the Gaithers

Trinitarians generally agree that Jesus is a valid name for God or at least divinity, and to this extent, their model is compatible with the Bible. The trouble begins when you ask if Jesus is the name above every name. They want to say yes, but also struggle because they don't truly view Jesus as the fullness of God, but as one person of three, and they don't want to leave the other two out.

You really see this if you ask, "Is Jesus also the name of the Everlasting Father?" They want to answer yes, but often try to explain away the language in Isaiah 9:6. Some struggle to embrace the word picture that Isaiah clearly declares. Other Trinitarians just roll with it, because of the majesty and simplicity of this prophetic utterance.

They recognize that this is a reference to Jesus' deity, and their desire to honor scripture is admirable[51].

"Isaiah is highlighting the divine nature of the Messiah."

This answer, from a Trinitarian, aligns beautifully with scripture and what Apostolics believe about Isaiah 9:6 and the name of Jesus. In my experience, most Trinitarians struggle with this and often put this verse in Isaiah on the list of things they don't want to think about very much. They love the verse, but not its details, since it contradicts their internal model for God.

Apostolics embrace the name of Jesus plainly and wholeheartedly in all its glory. We take the statements of scripture on the majesty and supremacy of the name, and we go nuts over it, as well we should.

We sing, dance, and jump up and down about the name of Jesus. We baptize in this beautiful and precious name. We pray for healing in this name. We've seen lives delivered through this name. We know that praying to Jesus is praying to God. We know we are praying to the one true God, and we know Jesus truly as "Yahweh is our salvation!"

---

[51] From the Gospel Coalition article: https://www.thegospelcoalition.org/article/how-can-jesus-be-our-everlasting-father/

#9 – THE RIGHT HAND OF GOD

Of all the Biblical patterns, this one remains the most misquoted by Christians. Many commonly believe that the Bible describes Jesus in Heaven as sitting at the right hand of the Father. Scripture remains consistent in describing this amazing picture, but in the Bible, it is ALWAYS with the Son at the right hand of God. The specific verb of sitting or standing varies, with sitting being the most common.

Sitting	Psalm 110, Matt 22, 26, Mark 16, Luke 22, Eph 1, Col 3, Hebrews 1, 8, 10, 12
Standing	Acts 7
Exalted	Acts 2
Unspecified	Rom 8, Acts 5, 1st Peter 3

If you haven't been exposed to Apostolic thinking, you should know that our general approach in studying scripture is to look at all possible relevant passages and attempt to let the context and word choices drive the study and results.

In this case, there is a declarative truth in these verses, but in examining the scriptures, this picture also feels figurative in nature, so we should be careful in our conclusions.

> **John 4:24 NKJV**
> *"God is Spirit, and those who worship Him must worship in spirit and truth."*
>
> **Colossians 1:15 NKJV**
> *He is the image of the invisible God, the firstborn over all creation.*
>
> **1ˢᵗ John 4:12 NKJV**
> *No one has seen God at any time. If we love one another, God abides in us, and His love has been perfected in us.*
>
> **1ˢᵗ Timothy 6:15-16 NKJV**
> *He who is the blessed and only Potentate, the King of kings and Lord of lords, ¹⁶ who alone has immortality, dwelling in unapproachable light, whom no man has seen or can see, to whom be honor and everlasting power. Amen.*

The Bible is clear and consistent that God is Spirit and invisible, so the language of the right hand, indicating power and authority, should not be taken as a literal and physical arrangement.

It also does indicate Adjacency, in that the one at the right hand is "next to" and in some way "not the same as" the one with the right hand. This is why Trinitarians often want to read this verse as Jesus next to the Father, because they want this picture in scripture to be two persons of the Trinity in Heaven.

> **Colossians 3:1 NKJV**
> *If then you were raised with Christ, seek those things which are above, where Christ is, sitting at the right hand of God.*

But that is not the picture in scripture. We have God and an entity next to God. So if this is a reference to the deity of Jesus, this is clearly two deities side-by-side and would violate the pattern of Strict Monotheism.

Jesus Christ   **God**

For the Trinitarian, I understand their deep desire to see their model expressed in scripture. If this were specifically the Father next to the Son in Heaven, it would support their model, but that is not the language that God provides in the Bible. This is a figurative picture of God and another entity next to God, Jesus Christ.

The Apostolic model often makes the claim that any difficulties in understanding why Jesus prayed, or any language of separation between Jesus and the Father, can best be explained through His Dual-Nature. Could this be a better way to understand the right-hand passages?

There are quite a few passages mentioning God's right hand, so let's examine the relationship and word choices to see if this confirms or challenges the Apostolic model.

The one on the throne is the Father	0 Passages
The one on the throne is God	16 Passages

We don't find two divine persons of a Trinity next to each other in Heaven, at least not in the Bible. We do see this in Catholic art in their cathedrals. The Biblical picture is Jesus next to God. What does that mean? Let's look at how Jesus is identified:

Lord	Psalm 110, Matt 22, Mark 16
Jesus, Christ, or Jesus Christ	Acts 2, Acts 5, Romans 8, Eph 1, Col 3, Hebrews 12, 1st Peter 3
God's Son	Hebrews 1
Our High Priest	Hebrews 8
Son of Man	Matt 26, Luke 22, Acts 7
This man	Hebrews 10

I don't think the title Lord or God's Son or the references to Jesus or Christ by name do enough to objectively explain, confirm, or deny the Apostolic model. You could make the case that "Christ" as a title pertains to the incarnation, and I would agree.

We do have 5 of the 16 references that specifically and strongly draw our attention to the humanity of Jesus, which beautifully fits the Apostolic model and makes this word picture in scripture both clear and majestic.

Hebrews 8:1 NKJV
Now this is the main point of the things we are saying: We have such a High Priest, who is seated at the right hand of the throne of the Majesty in the heavens.

Hebrews 10:11-14 NKJV
And every priest stands ministering daily and offering repeatedly the same sacrifices, which can never take away sins. [12] But this Man, after He had offered one sacrifice for sins forever, sat down at the right hand of God, [13] from that time waiting till His enemies are made His footstool. [14] For by one offering He has perfected forever those who are being sanctified.

Both of these passages clearly describe Jesus, as our human high priest, seated at the right hand of God. This is exactly how the Apostolic model explains the Son, operating as a perfect man, in human agency. Now that the mission of mediation at Calvary is accomplished, this is a beautiful and figurative word picture of the humanity sitting because "it is finished".

The remaining three humanity references come from an answer Jesus gave at His trial, as well as a vision shown to Stephen immediately before his stoning.

Matthew 26:64 NKJV

Jesus said to him, "It is as you said. Nevertheless, I say to you, hereafter you will see <u>the Son of Man sitting at the right hand of the Power,</u> and coming on the clouds of heaven."

Luke 22:69-70 NKJV

Hereafter <u>the Son of Man will sit on the right hand of the power of God.</u>" ⁷⁰ Then they all said, "Are You then the Son of God?" So He said to them, "You rightly say that I am."

Acts 7:55-56 NKJV

But he, being full of the Holy Spirit, gazed into heaven and saw the glory of God, and Jesus standing at the right hand of God, ⁵⁶ and said, "Look! <u>I see the heavens opened and the Son of Man standing at the right hand of God!</u>"

All three of these vivid word pictures identify Jesus by the title, Son of Man, specifically calling out His genuine human identity.

An objective look at the Right Hand of God passages provides no support for the Trinity. It actually raises polytheistic questions if this is deity next to deity in Heaven. These passages fit the Apostolic model beautifully and provide a picture of God accomplishing His mission through the Son, in the man Christ Jesus. Once the mission was finished, the humanity, the Son of Man, sits in a place of honor and authority in this beautiful and figurative word picture.

I should end the chapter right here. This is a tight analysis of 16 passages very consistent with Apostolic teaching, giving fantastic support for the Oneness model and raising challenges for the Trinity model.

As a sincere student of scripture, I'm compelled to deal with one last word picture in the Bible. It's not the right hand of God, but it's close enough. This next passage mentions two thrones in an interesting way.

Apostolics do not, or should not, pick and choose which verses we like and ignore the rest. Ignoring difficult verses and focusing on our favorites causes the disease of Selectaversitis to run rampant among Christians. Almost every theology book out there pushes a model, and will ignore some evidence that challenges their position, or at least doesn't fit easily. I have zero interest in what is really a deceptive presentation.

So let's look at an interesting and related text found in Revelation 3. To set the scene, let's remember that Revelation is full of symbolism and figurative language, so we need some caution in pulling declarative, ontological truth out of these verses.

In Revelation 1:1-18, we start with Jesus, clearly identified as Jesus, but also described in His full divine glory as God Almighty. In Revelation 5:6, we see a lamb that initially appears "in the midst of the throne". Some of this is declarative, and some is clearly figurative. If someone started a religion claiming lambs are divine because of Revelation 5, we would rightly conclude they need a mental evaluation. It's also worth noting that Jesus shows up in multiple ways and in multiple roles in Revelation. (See Revelation 22:16 for one of the most profound examples of this.) I bring this up only to say that there is a lot of figurative language happening here.

Let's look at the mini epistle to the church of Laodicea:

Revelation 3:14-18 NKJV

And to the angel of the church of the Laodiceans write,

'These things says the Amen, the Faithful and True Witness, the Beginning of the creation of God:

* 15 I know your works, that you are neither cold nor hot. I could wish you were cold or hot. 16 So then, because you are lukewarm, and neither cold nor hot, I will vomit you out of My mouth.*

17 Because you say, "I am rich, have become wealthy, and have need of nothing"—and do not know that you are wretched, miserable, poor, blind, and naked— 18 I counsel you to buy from Me gold refined in the fire, that you may be rich; and white garments, that you may be clothed, that the shame of your nakedness may not be revealed; and anoint your eyes with eye salve, that you may see.'

The correction to this church is real, but the instructions and rebuke are clearly full of figurative language. Their hot and cold works are real works, but not based on physical temperature. And God is not going to place the congregation here in His physical, giant mouth and then upchuck them back out.

Laodicea had some wealth because of its location at a useful intersection of two Roman roads in Southwest Asia Minor. History tells us they were famous for their wool and some kind of medicine produced locally. So the instruction to get real wealth, better garments, and eye salve remains one of the harshest corrections in the Bible. Even the hot and cold references pointed to the water supply of the neighboring towns. The less wealthy town of Colossae was their primary source of water. It started cold and fresh but ran downhill through about six miles of aqueducts before reaching Laodicea. The sun-baked aqueduct would heat the water to a less pleasant lukewarm experience.

Although the language was figurative, the rebuke to the Laodicea church was quite literal, and I doubt they struggled to catch the meaning behind the words.

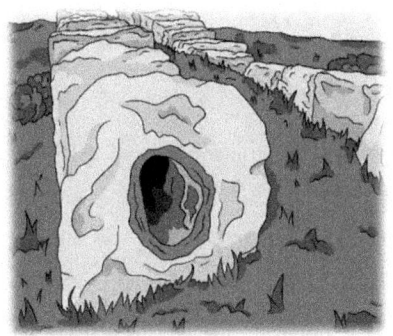

Aquaduct Remains from Colossae to Laodicea

The rebuke ends on a positive note with an interesting reference to thrones.

Revelation 3:19-21 NKJV

*'As many as I love, I rebuke and chasten. Therefore be zealous and repent. *20* Behold, I stand at the door and knock. If anyone hears My voice and opens the door, I will come in to him and dine with him, and he with Me.*

21 To him who overcomes I will grant to sit with Me on My throne, as I also overcame and sat down with My Father on His throne.'*

This entire epistle overflows with figurative language. Even the invitation in verse 20 is figurative. Jesus is interested in more than stopping by for a friendly bite to eat. It is quite reasonable to understand verse 21 as figurative as well. The word picture here points to sharing authority and honor. It would be awkward and ridiculous if this were an invitation for two adults to sit on a throne together, side-by-side.

This picture is quite compatible with the idea of humanity adjacent to deity, similar to the right-hand-of-God language discussed earlier in this chapter.

Even a Trinitarian would have to agree that verse 21 has to include humanity sitting next to deity.

We who Overcome → Sit next to Jesus
Jesus Overcame → Sits next to the Father

No matter your model for God, at least one of these seating arrangements is humanity sitting next to deity.

Jesus overcame sin as a man. He conquered sin, "in the flesh", as our High-Priest and Mediator. Scripture declares and explains this consistently. So the best explanation for the Right-Hand of God verses is that the humanity of Christ sits and rests in completion of the mission.

This picture in Revelation 3:21 is best understood as a figurative picture where we as humans, can overcome by the power of God, and share in the honor of Jesus Christ. Just as Jesus overcame, in His humanity, and sits next to the Father, we can find victory because of Calvary over sin and death!

Although figurative, this passage does fit the Apostolic model. It also fits the Trinity model. I would suggest it fits the Trinity much better than Genesis 1:26, for example. Reading the Trinity into the Old Testament is a terrible way to interpret scripture. But a verse, like the one above, does have a natural reading that would fit the Trinity.

This is the part where Apostolics might attempt to see the world through someone else's eyes. Revelation 3:21 would be a valid verse in the Trinitarian model. It doesn't prove the Trinity, because it works in the Apostolic model as well, but it would help if Apostolics could step outside our own viewpoint long enough to understand a different perspective.

In the overall picture, the passages referencing Jesus at the Right Hand of God are often listed as support for the Trinity. This is mainly because Trinitarians want to pretend that the Bible says Jesus is at the right hand of the Father. The Bible never says this. The actual word picture in scripture NEVER clearly declares two divine persons next to each other in Heaven, which would basically support polytheism. In this regard, the way Trinitarians consistently mis-quote the Right Hand passages shows that their model doesn't match scripture well in this pattern.

We are given multiple reasons (5 passages for example) to believe that the picture of the right hand points to Jesus, as the Son of Man, our high priest, in His humanity, next to God.

Hebrews 8:1 NKJV
Now this is the main point of the things we are saying: We have such <u>a High Priest</u>, <u>who is seated at the right hand of the throne</u> of the Majesty in the heavens.

One last thought on the sitting part. I like the explanation that humanity sits, because "It is finished". I need the divinity of Jesus to be active. I'm a pastor, working with people who desperately need Jesus, and I am thrilled that once the mediation was finished, Jesus didn't stop working, but continues quite actively in our lives.

Jesus explained it another way at the Last Supper, that God would give us another helper. This would be a new way to experience God, and Jesus made it clear that the Holy Spirit was the same Spirit of Jesus, that He would come to us and be with us.

John 14:16-18 NKJV
And I will pray the Father, and He will give you another Helper, that He may abide with you forever— [17] the Spirit of truth, whom the world cannot receive, because it neither sees Him nor knows Him; but you know Him, for He dwells with you and will be in you. [18] I will not leave you orphans; I will come to you.

He is not resting, but Jesus is active in our lives today!

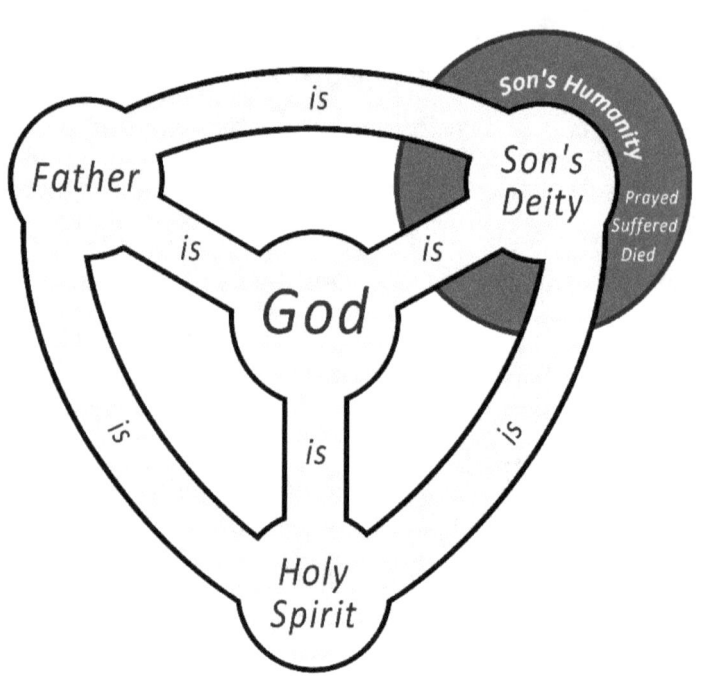

#10 – OVERLAPPING ACTIVITY

Of all the patterns in scripture, this one remains the most ignored by modern Christian theology. In the general sense, this pattern recognizes numerous places where God as Father, in His Spirit, or in the Son, occupies overlapping roles, effectively making it impossible to identify many parts of God's activity that might be done through only one manifestation or expression of God's presence.

For example, born-again Christians are filled with the Holy Spirit, which is the Spirit of the Son, called the Spirit of Christ, which is the Father in us, also God in us[52]. If you know the Son, you know the Father. If you see the Son, you've seen the Father[53]. If Scripture is your final authority in doctrine, it remains impossible to say that some things are done only by the Holy Spirit and not the Son or the Father.

This isn't found in just one or two examples. This pattern is numerous and abundant in scripture, and our models for the incarnation should account for it, both Apostolic and Trinitarian. We'll look at multiple examples of overlapping roles and identity in this chapter. Others can be found, but the ones selected are declarative and clear.

---

[52] John 3:5, Gal 4:6, Rom 8:9, Eph 4:4-6, Phil 2:13

[53] John 14:7-9

> **Isaiah 9:6 NKJV**
> *For unto us a Child is born, unto us a Son is given; And the government will be upon His shoulder. And His name will be called Wonderful, Counselor, Mighty God, Everlasting Father, Prince of Peace.*

The name of the Son is called the name of the Everlasting Father and Mighty God. Quite simply, this beautiful prophetic declaration should fit your model for God, and it clearly describes that the child coming is not just a man, but divine, and more than deity, this child's name is also the name of the Everlasting Father.

> **John 4:24 NKJV**
> *"God is Spirit, and those who worship Him must worship in spirit and truth."*
>
> **Ephesians 4:4-6 NKJV**
> *There is one body and one Spirit, just as you were called in one hope of your calling; ⁵ one Lord, one faith, one baptism; ⁶ one God and Father of all, who is above all, and through all, and in you all.*

In this second example, God is Spirit, and there is one Spirit, and so the Spirit of the Father is the Holy Spirit above all, through all, and in us all. In other words, **the Holy Spirit is the Spirit of the Father in us**.

> **John 14:7 NKJV**
> *"If you had known Me, you would have known My Father also; and from now on you know Him and have seen Him."*

In the next examples, we have a list of interchangeable observations declared by Jesus. John 14:7 plainly tells us that **if you know the Son, you also know the Father.**

> **John 14:8-9 NKJV**
> *Philip said to Him, "Lord, show us the Father, and it is sufficient for us."* **9** *Jesus said to him, "Have I been with you so long, and yet you have not known Me, Philip? He who has seen Me has seen the Father; so how can you say, 'Show us the Father'?"*

Starting in verse 7 and continuing, Jesus expands the declaration further. They **not only know the Father but have now seen the Father. Seeing Jesus is seeing the Father.** This makes sense if we understand that Colossians 1:15 declares the Son is the image of the Invisible God. These observations directly oppose the Orthodox Trinitarian belief that each person of the Trinity is clearly differentiated with no overlap between them.

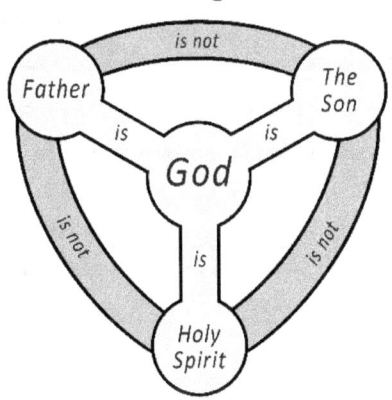

This is commonly shown in a triangle diagram where each person of the Trinity is God, but each person IS NOT another person. The Father IS NOT the Son, and the Son is NOT the Holy Spirit. If we revisit James White's explanation of the Trinity, he said it this way:

[The doctrines that flow into the Trinity] are as follows:

1) There is one and only one God, eternal, immutable.

*2) There are three eternal Persons described in Scripture – the Father, the Son, and the Spirit. **These Persons are never identified with one another – that is, they are carefully differentiated as Persons.***

3) The Father, the Son, and the Spirit are identified as being fully deity—that is, the Bible teaches the Deity of Christ and the Deity of the Holy Spirit.

Apostolics agree with points #1 and #3, but we find his second point to not only be wrong, but profoundly wrong when compared to the Bible. We've looked at examples of the Father revealed in Jesus. Now let's consider how the scriptures describe God's Spirit.

John 14:17 NKJV
"The Spirit of truth, whom the world cannot receive, because it neither sees Him nor knows Him; but you know Him, <u>for He dwells with you and will be in you</u>."

Jesus describes the Spirit of Truth, which dwells with them (as Jesus) but will be in them. He continues...

> **John 14:18 NKJV**
> *"I will not leave you orphans; I will come to you."*

These persons "are never identified with one another", except, of course, repeatedly in scripture. Dr. James White is not stupid, but I'm scratching my head here.

> **Romans 8:9 NKJV**
> *But you are not in the flesh but in the Spirit, if indeed the Spirit of God dwells in you. Now if anyone does not have the Spirit of Christ, he is not His.*

The epistles continue this pattern of significant overlap, and in Romans, we see the Holy Spirit called the Spirit of God and also the Spirit of Christ. This is definitely not distinctive persons, and instead clearly interchangeable.

> **Galatians 4:6 NKJV**
> *And because you are sons, God has sent forth the Spirit of His Son into your hearts, crying out, "Abba, Father!"*
>
> **2nd Corinthians 3:16-17 NKJV**
> *Nevertheless when one turns to the Lord, the veil is taken away. [17] Now the Lord is the Spirit; and where the Spirit of the Lord is, there is liberty.*

The Bible continues, with **God's Spirit also called the Spirit of the Son as well as the Spirit of the Lord**.

One more example shows **the Holy Spirit as the Spirit of the Lord and also the Spirit of God**, all in one passage in

1st Corinthians. The passage concludes by pointing out that the same singular God is the one who works all in all, for His purposes.

1st Corinthians 12:4-6 NKJV
There are diversities of gifts, but the <u>same Spirit</u>.
5 There are differences of ministries, but the <u>same Lord</u>.
6 And there are diversities of activities, but it is
the <u>same God</u> who works all in all.

The baptism command and fulfillment make up the last example of overlap in this chapter. This is covered in chapter 12 in detail, so we just observe here that the baptismal instruction in Matthew 28:19 and its fulfillment in every single baptism described in the Bible asks a simple question. It's a question Trinitarians struggle to answer.

Matthew 28:19 NKJV
Go therefore and make disciples of all the nations,
baptizing them in the name of the Father and of the Son
and of the Holy Spirit.

Acts 2:38 NKJV
Then Peter said to them, "Repent, and let every one of
you be baptized in the name of Jesus Christ for the
remission of sins; and you shall receive the gift of the
Holy Spirit."

See also Acts 8:14-17, Acts 10:46-48, Acts 19:1-7, Acts 22:16

Do these passages describe a legitimate fulfillment of Jesus' instruction or a violation of His command? Did the Apostles disobey the Lord or honor His words through their actions? Apostolics believe that the Baptisms in Acts beautifully fulfill Matthew 28:19.

If you don't agree, then you are left playing word games with these verses, claiming they didn't actually baptize specifically in the name of Jesus, or you have to dismiss the clear descriptions of Jesus' name baptism just because they don't match your model for God.

The Bible makes it very clear. The name of Jesus is the name of the Father and of the Son and of the Holy Spirit. This is just another clear example of overlapping roles, and it beautifully confirms the Apostolic model.

From the Trinitarian model:

*"There are three eternal Persons described in Scripture – the Father, the Son, and the Spirit. **These Persons are never identified with one another – that is, they are carefully differentiated as Persons.**"*

Note the common Trinitarian diagram indicating zero overlap between the different persons in the Trinity. Do we see this when we examine the Bible?

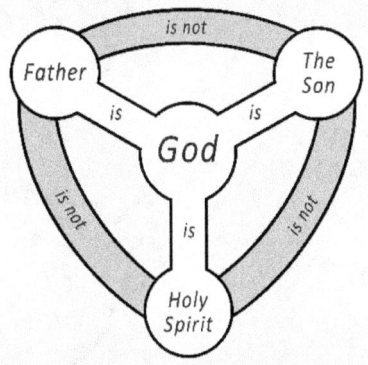

The Biblical pattern:

Jesus Christ is identified as the Father and shows us the Father, and the Father is found in us through the Spirit. The Holy Spirit is clearly declared to be the Spirit of the Son, the Spirit of Christ, and Jesus coming to us. And the baptism descriptions demonstrate that the name of Jesus is the legitimate name of the Father and the Spirit. Saying they are never identified with one another is either dishonest or ignorant of Biblical declarations.

I want to share a corrected version of the Trinity diagram. The following was created by Pastor James Roberts. He is a Presbyter, Bible Teacher, and also my favorite Father-in-Law. He has permitted me to include his "corrected" diagram in this chapter.

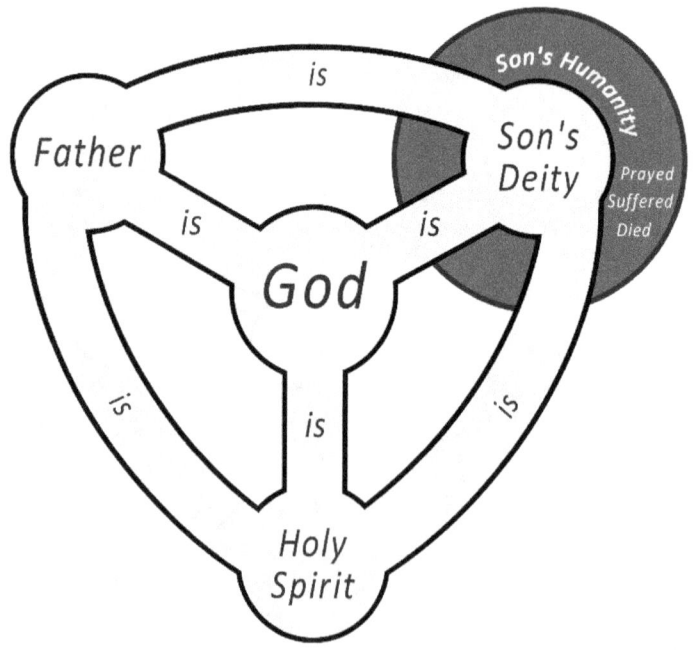

This attempts to explain how God's roles and activity are described in the Bible with multiple examples of overlap, and his diagram differentiates between the deity and humanity of the Son through the Dual-Nature of Christ. A diagram might not perfectly describe the incarnation, but this much better matches the clear pattern of Overlapping Activity we see in scripture.

These ten examples of overlapping roles go beyond challenging the Trinity model. They don't fit that model at all. The Biblical pattern of overlapping roles and the Trinity's claim of no overlap are incompatible. A stretch fit is not enough to accommodate these verses.

Overlapping Roles	Bible References
The name of the Son is also the name of the Everlasting Father.	Isaiah 9:6
God is Spirit, and there is one Spirit, so the Spirit of the Father is the Spirit of the Son, which is the Holy Spirit – the Father in us.	John 4:24 Ephesians 4:4-6
If you know the Son, you know the Father.	John 14:7
If you have seen the Son, you have seen the Father.	John 14:9
The Spirit of truth is with you in Jesus and will be in you when you receive the Holy Spirit.	John 14:17

Overlapping Roles	Bible References
Jesus will come to us in the Holy Spirit and not leave us as orphans.	John 14:18
The Holy Spirit is the Spirit of Christ.	Romans 8:9
The Holy Spirit is the Spirit of the Son.	Galatians 4:6
The baptisms in Acts in the name of Jesus fulfill the Great Commission and demonstrate that this is the name of the Father, and of the Son, and of the Holy Spirit.	Matthew 28:19 Acts 2:38, 8:16, 10:48, 19:5, 22:16
Bonus overlap example: The Holy Spirit is called the Spirit of Truth and the Spirit of Wisdom. Jesus is the Truth and Wisdom of God.	Eph 1:17, John 14:6, 14:17, 15:26, 1st Cor 1:30

All of these verses fit the Apostolic model beautifully. We believe that God has revealed Himself in multiple ways, but that God's greatest self-revelation is in the Son, who is the express image of God and the image of God's single person (Hebrews 1:3).

These examples of overlapping roles confirm and support the Apostolic model and plainly contradict the Trinity.

#11 – THE BIBLICAL EMPHASIS IN MEDIATION

Of the Biblical patterns, this observation might be the most overlooked in this list. But with multiple scriptures being consistent on this, we find the Bible describing the act of mediation as being a specifically human and bodily act.

This should not take away from the deity of Christ, only that He must be a genuine human to be our Kinsman Redeemer. So we shouldn't be surprised that the mediation verses so consistently point to the body, the flesh, and the humanity of Christ.

Romans 8:3 NKJV
For what the law could not do in that it was weak through the flesh, God did by sending His own Son in the likeness of sinful flesh, on account of sin: He condemned sin in the flesh.

Colossians 1:21-22 NKJV
And you, who once were alienated and enemies in your mind by wicked works, yet now He has reconciled [22] in the body of His flesh through death, to present you holy, and blameless, and above reproach in His sight.

See also Ephesians 2:14-16 NKJV

Besides teaching us a clear truth about the incarnation, these verses also serve to thoroughly reject the Gnostic Greek model that God Himself could not come to corrupt Earth or be near human flesh. Gnostics have caused all kinds of trouble in Christianity, and their influence remains in odd doctrines still around. They opposed anything involving pleasure or the flesh, and obsessed over special calendar observances, angels, and which foods you were allowed to eat. Gnosticism also led to celibacy in the Catholic priesthood.

Paul comes in guns blazing in Colossians 2 to let us know how Christians should respond to these teachings:

Colossians 2:16-18 NKJV
So let no one judge you in food or in drink, or regarding a festival or a new moon or sabbaths, ¹⁷ which are a shadow of things to come, but the substance is of Christ.

¹⁸ Let no one cheat you of your reward, taking delight in false humility and worship of angels, intruding into those things which he has not seen, vainly puffed up by his fleshly mind.

Paul tells us to not chase the shadows, since we have Christ, and are alive in Christ, and he asks why would we go back to ordinances and shadows?

It is hard for us to realize how shocking Paul's words might be to a Gnostic. Because of their model for God and the world, they didn't believe that Jesus could be both fully God and fully human. One of the two must be limited or an illusion. Maybe He just appeared as a human, or maybe He was not fully God but some other kind of created and supernatural being. If you know about the Greek Apologist, Justin Martyr, that was the path he took when he claimed to be a Christian and published odd writings about 120 years after Calvary. He called Jesus, "another God... numerically distinct from the Father". Should we be amazed that the Catholic Church granted him sainthood? They did... to a heretic.

Read Colossians 1 & 2 and look for evidence that Jesus was deity in the flesh. Look for references to angels and food and calendar observances, and be amazed at how much the Bible opposes these Gnostic teachings.

Then consider the incarnation. Could the Bible be clearer about the full deity and full humanity of Christ?

Colossians 2:8-9 NKJV
Beware lest anyone cheat you through philosophy and empty deceit, according to the tradition of men, according to the basic principles of the world, and not according to Christ. [9] For in Him dwells all the fullness of the Godhead bodily.

The closest we come to a mediation verse that doesn't directly mention flesh is 1st John 2:1-2. Jesus is called our advocate with the Father in a word picture of a legal setting. The text beautifully points again to Calvary, but it remains unclear if this is a literal or figurative account.

1ˢᵗ John 2:1-2 NKJV

My little children, these things I write to you, so that you may not sin. And if anyone sins, we have an Advocate with the Father, Jesus Christ the righteous. ² And He Himself is the propitiation for our sins, and not for ours only but also for the whole world.

Some Christians treat this as a literal courtroom arrangement where Jesus is our defense attorney and God the Father is the judge. If Jesus mediates in His humanity, this still does not necessitate an eternal Trinity of persons. It also doesn't match all the other accounts instructing us to pray directly to God.

And if God's holiness demands a mediator, and the second person of the Trinity is also divine, no one ever adequately explains why the Holiness of Jesus doesn't also require a mediator. This is solved when you look at the pattern in scriptures that teach this mediation was done through perfect humanity, in the flesh.

This idea of ongoing mediation inspires the Catholics to provide numerous ways to indirectly reach the Father. You could pray to Jesus and He would forward your request. You might add some saints into the mix to fast-track your prayers through the bureaucracy. Saint Anthony knows how to cut through red tape if you need a miracle. Saint Matthias handles alcoholic prayers and apparently various carpentry issues. Saint Denis helps with headaches. I can't imagine how excited Saint

Timothy was when he was assigned irritable bowel syndrome. With hundreds of Saints covering all manner of needs, they even have a representative for ice skating requests, Saint Lidwina.

When it really matters, some go right to the Catholic top floor and ask Jesus' mom to intercede. They think she has special access to Jesus, which fast-tracks some needs to the Father. If you have any Bible knowledge, this all looks ridiculous and stinks of man-made religion. The Bible tells us that we can and should pray directly to God, and we don't need intermediaries.

Philippians 4:6 NKJV
Be anxious for nothing, but in everything by prayer and supplication, with thanksgiving, let your requests be made known to God.

We pray by the authority of the name of Jesus, but John 16:23-26 (and other passages) instructs us to pray directly to the Father in this name. Numerous other verses let us know that praying to the Father is praying to Jesus, and the advocacy of Jesus was completed at Calvary, and for this reason, Jesus declared, "It is finished".

John 19:30 NKJV
...He said, "It is finished!" And bowing His head, He gave up His spirit.

It's no accident that the Scriptures use exact wording to clearly teach us doctrine. When it comes to the topic of mediation, specific and consistent words are used to emphasize the flesh and human agency at Calvary.

Deity cannot die, nor can divinity be our Kinsman Redeemer. The man, Christ Jesus, lived a perfect life and died a perfect death to fulfill the plan and law of God. Our mediator, although divine, mediates as a man.

1st Timothy 2:5 NKJV
For there is one God and one Mediator between God and men, the Man Christ Jesus.

The emphasis and language point to flesh and humanity, not to take away from His deity, but to focus our attention on Jesus' role as the perfect human high priest.

Hebrews 10:11-12 NKJV
And every priest stands ministering daily and offering repeatedly the same sacrifices, which can never take away sins. 12 But this Man, after He had offered one sacrifice for sins forever, sat down at the right hand of God.

Serious students of the Bible might know that "man" is not literally found in the Greek text here but is implied. The passage focuses our attention on Jesus as our perfect and human high priest, and there are multiple other verses referencing humanity in the "right hand of God" references.

So the KJV and NKJV rendering is valid and a fantastic word picture of Jesus' mediation and the fulfillment of the mission of the Son of Man.

We want to consider one last verse on mediation.

Galatians 3:20 NKJV
Now a mediator does not mediate for one only, but God is one.

This verse speaks strongly to the Oneness Apostolic model and might be clearer in modern translations. Galatians 3:20, as translated by multiple Trinitarian scholars, reads like this:

Galatians 3:20 NIV
A mediator, however, implies more than one party; but God is one.

We know that mediation implies multiple parties, which is affirmed here. It can better be explained as a reflection of the humanity of Christ. This matches the pattern we see in the other verses discussed in this section. Galatians 3:20 clearly declares that this mediation SHOULD IN NO WAY cause us to consider a plurality in God's divine nature. This beautifully supports the Apostolic Model, and it contradicts the Trinitarian Model for God.

All these verses easily and perfectly fit the Apostolic model. Jesus is declared and revealed as God manifested in the flesh in the Son. He is a genuine man and acts as our high priest. He mediated our sins on the cross, in the flesh, and then declared, "It is finished".

The Trinity model struggles with these verses. Some Trinitarians embrace scriptural language and recognize that the mediation is clearly done in the humanity of Christ, but this (again) reduces and removes the need for the Trinity. So you can embrace scripture and dilute the value and role of the Trinity, or you can embrace the Trinity and contradict scripture.

In orthodox Trinitarian thinking, all three persons of God, or perhaps just the first person of God, sent the second person of God to be our sacrifice and mediator. They typically minimize the humanity of Christ and emphasize the second person of God in this role. When you point out the clear pattern in scripture that our sins were mediated on the cross, in His body, in the flesh, as a man, they just ignore these verses and their specific meaning.

It feels like Trinitarians just fundamentally do not believe that 1st Timothy 2:5 and Galatians 3:20 are true. They believe that the mediation is done by an eternal, second person of the Trinity that the Bible never describes or declares.

#12 – BAPTISM INSTRUCTION AND FULFILLMENT

Knowing God truly matters, and there is no pursuit more worthy for the serious believer. I'm very committed, and even if you disagree with the Apostolic model for God, I hope you can see my sincerity in putting  scripture first and attempting to let the language of the Bible determine my beliefs and not church traditions.

You might think some of this debate gets bogged down in semantics and theology. Maybe you're wondering how much our theological models really matter? If so, then this chapter is for you. In the analysis of two models, Oneness and Trinity, the baptism discussion affects what we actually do more than the 11 previous chapters. This chapter is the most applicable and pragmatic of the list.

After the resurrection, Jesus commissioned the church on three different occasions. Most don't realize why the commands in Matthew 28, Mark 16, and Luke 24, as well as Acts 1, don't appear to match. If you look a bit closer, you will realize that He commissioned the church three times, recorded in four places in the Bible. Jesus used different words on each occasion. If this surprises you, then pay attention to almost anyone involved in leading and public speaking.

Preachers and leaders will say the same things in different ways, using different words, on almost every occasion to hold your attention. They often return to a core list of themes that matter to them, but they use different phrases and illustrations to get us there.

We have a running joke in my house. I think it's a joke. I am not sure that my wife agrees. I will be working on typically 1 to 3 sermons at any one time, depending on my mood and the hecticness of life. Towards the end of many weeks, my wife will ask, "What are you preaching this Sunday?" I almost always reply, "Probably something about Jesus." I am only kidding a little bit. Some weeks, I know exactly what I am preaching, and other times, I pray and study longer before I settle on a direction, but it's almost always about Jesus. As a pastor, I often speak on a core list of themes, but use different word pictures, approaches, and illustrations to get there.

In a similar fashion, Jesus used different words in the commissioning passages to emphasize different aspects of the Gospel. The most famous of these commissions is likely labeled in your Bible "The Great Commission". It's found in Matthew 28:16-20. These beautiful words have inspired millions over the centuries.

Matthew 28:19 NKJV
"Go therefore and make disciples of all the nations, baptizing them in the name of the Father and of the Son and of the Holy Spirit."

Just days later, on the day of Pentecost, Peter, standing with the eleven, gave a baptism command and promise to the crowd in his famous closing in Acts 2.

Acts 2:38 NKJV
Then Peter said to them, "Repent, and let every one of you <u>be baptized in the name of Jesus Christ for the remission of sins</u>; and you shall receive the gift of the Holy Spirit."

These two passages capture the initial divide in the Apostolic and Trinitarian models for baptism. Oneness Apostolics consistently and strongly hold that baptism should be done by immersion in water in the name of Jesus, and that baptism is clearly connected in scripture to Salvation. This is the New Birth as described in the John 3 meeting with Nicodemus.

The Trinitarians believe strongly that you should be baptized in the titles or names of the Trinity, "of the Father, and of the Son and of the Holy Spirit", and that the words of Jesus should probably outrank Peter. I've had Trinitarians even say to me, "I would rather listen to Jesus than to Peter."

This raises a troubling question. Did the Apostles ignore the command of Jesus? The eleven stood with Peter on the day of Pentecost and allowed Him to command baptism in the name of Jesus. Philip, likely taught by the Apostles, also baptized in Jesus' name in Samaria. Paul used the same name and followed the same pattern in Ephesus. Every baptism record with details, since the commissioning of the church, was done in the name of Jesus or calling on the name of the Lord.

Acts 8:14-17 NKJV

Now when the apostles who were at Jerusalem heard that Samaria had received the word of God, they sent Peter and John to them, [15] who, when they had come down, prayed for them that they might receive the Holy Spirit. [16] For as yet He had fallen upon none of them. They had only been baptized in the name of the Lord Jesus. [17] Then they laid hands on them, and they received the Holy Spirit.

Acts 10:46-48 NKJV

...Then Peter answered, [47] "Can anyone forbid water, that these should not be baptized who have received the Holy Spirit just as we have?" [48] And he commanded them to be baptized in the name of the Lord. Then they asked him to stay a few days.

Acts 19:5 NKJV

When they heard this, they were baptized in the name of the Lord Jesus.

Acts 22:16 NKJV

"...Arise and be baptized, and wash away your sins, calling on the name of the Lord."

It isn't just Acts that connects Baptism specifically with the name of Jesus. Compare the commissioning of the church in Luke 24 with Peter's instructions in Acts 2. We can see that even our Lord connected baptism, the remission of sins, and His name.

> **Luke 24:46-47 NKJV**
> *Then He said to them, "Thus it is written, and thus it was necessary for the Christ to suffer and to rise from the dead the third day, ⁴⁷ and <u>that repentance and remission of sins should be preached in His name</u> to all nations, beginning at Jerusalem.*
>
> **Acts 2:38 NKJV**
> *Then Peter said to them, "Repent, and let every one of you <u>be baptized in the name of Jesus Christ for the remission of sins;</u> and you shall receive the gift of the Holy Spirit."*

Luke, who wrote both the gospel of Luke and the book of Acts, records Jesus' instructions in His first appearance to the disciples after Calvary (see Luke 24 and Mark 16). Jesus explains that remission of sins should be preached in His name. Then Luke records the command in Acts 2:38, that baptism in the name of Jesus is for the remission of sins.

Jesus described baptism in two ways in the Gospels. He first instructed that remission of sins (at Baptism) should be preached in His name, then Jesus gave us more details and explanation in Matthew 28:19 with the titles.

So Jesus connected baptism to His own name. Then Jesus said to baptize in the name of the Father, and of the Son, and of the Holy Spirit. This isn't a disagreement between Jesus and Peter. Do we have Jesus, Jesus and Peter all saying different things? I hope not...

The connection between baptism and the name and identity of Jesus continues in the epistles.

Romans 6:3-4 NKJV

Or do you not know that as many of us as <u>were baptized into Christ Jesus</u> were baptized into His death? [4] Therefore <u>we were buried with Him</u> through baptism into death, that just as Christ was raised from the dead by the glory of the Father, even so we also should walk in newness of life.

Galatians 3:26-27 NKJV

For you are all sons of God through faith in Christ Jesus. [27] For as many of you as <u>were baptized into Christ have put on Christ</u>.

The epistle to the Romans specifically connects baptism to the death and burial of Jesus. Galatians tells us that those who were baptized have "put on Christ".

What do we make of all this? For the Apostolic, this is one tremendously beautiful and consistent pattern of instruction and fulfillment. All of these verses agree with one another and reinforce each other, and they all point to baptism in the name of Jesus.

Jesus instructed us to baptize in His name for the remission of sins. He also explained that we should do this in the name of the Father, and the Son, and the Holy Spirit. This was the same command described in two beautiful ways. The disciples clearly understood His words. When we get to Acts, we see them repeatedly baptizing in the name of the Father, and the Son, and Holy Spirit. **They fulfilled Jesus' command every single time, because the name of Jesus IS the name of the Father, and Son, and Holy Spirit.** It all matches, and there is no contradiction or disconnect in the baptismal instructions and fulfillment. Praise God! It's amazing how God's Word makes so much sense.

Unless you are a Trinitarian...

Then this whole thing turns into a series of awkward questions. In the Trinity model, you have to say that they didn't REALLY baptize in Jesus' name, or maybe it was for Jesus, or by the authority of Jesus? Why did they never use the titles of the Trinity in actual baptisms? Or maybe you shouldn't be bothered that it wasn't recorded, not once, in any of the accounts in scripture. Then the Trinitarians largely ignore the link between remission, baptism, and Jesus' name in Luke 24:47. I have never seen this directly addressed in Trinitarian writings.

If you bring up Isaiah 9:6 as further evidence that the name of the Son is the name of the Everlasting Father, I have seen Trinitarians even attempt to discredit the witness of this beautiful prophecy.

It used to be more common to recognize the disconnect between the baptisms in Acts and the Trinitarian understanding of Matthew 28:19. You can find more common examples of this in older commentaries and Bible dictionaries. For example, from 1898, here is

James Hastings' classic, *A Dictionary of the Bible,*
in the entry on the History of Baptism:

*The Institution of Christian baptism is to be dated from
Christ's farewell command... (Matt 28:19),* **This
command the Twelve do not attempt to carry out until
they are free from the earlier charge** *(Luke 24:49)...
Peter begins to exhort the people to "repent, and be
baptized in the name of Jesus Christ unto the remission
of their sins" (Acts 2:38), and with very great success.*

**But here we are at once struck by the fact that, in spite
of Christ's command to baptize into the name of the
Trinity, no mention is made of the Trinity, but only of
"the name of Jesus Christ."**

*And this first and important record of Christian
baptisms does not stand alone. The Samaritans who
were converted by Philip were "baptized into the name
of the Lord Jesus" (Acts 8:16). Peter at Caesarea
commanded that Cornelius and those with him should
be "baptized into the name of Jesus Christ" (Acts 10:48).
And the Ephesian disciples of John's baptism, were
"baptized into the name of the Lord Jesus" (Acts 19:5).*

**Moreover, there is no mention in the NT of anyone
being baptized into the name of the Trinity;** *and the
expression 'baptized into Christ' (Rom 6:3, Gal 3:27;
compare 1st Cor 1:13, 6:11) is more in harmony with
the passages in the Acts than with the divine command
as recorded [in] Matt 28:19.*

Dr Hastings description[54] is more candid than I often see in modern Trinitarian literature, but you can see where the Trinity model affects his theology and reading of scripture. He clearly sees the Trinity in Matthew 28:19, but to his credit, he also sees the disconnect with all the places the Apostles actually baptized in Jesus' name.

He then provides a list of reasons for how and why the Apostles disobeyed Christ, none of which would be acceptable to modern Christians. (1) They just plainly disobeyed. (2) Baptism in Jesus' name is actually baptism into the Trinity. (3) They actually were baptized in the titles of the Trinity, it just wasn't recorded correctly a single time. (4) Matthew 28:19 was added decades later and not part of the original instructions.

With the Trinity model firmly in His head, it is just inconceivable to Dr. Hastings and many others that Jesus might be the name of the Father, Son, and Holy Spirit.

I understand their struggle and motivation. Baptism in the titles of the Trinity is essential to defending the Trinity model. The baptism instruction in Matthew 28:19 is one of their favorite examples demonstrating any kind of Trinity declaration in the New Testament. But every single baptism fulfillment with details was actually done in Jesus' name.

---

[54] *Baptism – The History of Christian Baptism*, A Dictionary of the Bible, James Hastings, T & T Clark, Edinburgh, 1898, p. 241.

If you think about it for a couple of minutes, baptism in Jesus' name utterly destroys the basic idea of the Trinity. It gives you a simple Biblical proof that the name of Jesus is the name of the Father, Son, and Spirit. It draws your attention back to the one and not three.

Next time you hear a Trinitarian mention Matthew 28:19 as proof of the Trinity, I want you to note how they leave out important but pesky issues. They rarely mention that every baptism with details was done in Jesus' name. Then you realize that the Trinitarian making the claim is either grossly ignorant of their Bible or dishonest.

Even if the Acts accounts didn't exist, Matthew 28:19 still wouldn't teach or prove the Trinity. It would just be another example of Adjacency in the Bible. But with the actual Baptism details in Acts as well as the epistles linking Baptism specifically with the name and identity of Jesus, we have an incredibly strong case for Matthew 28:19 supporting the Oneness Apostolic model.

Trinitarians still quote this one verse while ignoring all the accounts connected to it, and they pretend this is a profound demonstration of the Trinity in scripture.

This is the worst example of a raging case of Selectaversitis. They are picking a verse to prove their side, then ignoring how that verse is actually applied in every single baptism account with details.

They have to ignore the connected verses, especially in Acts, because each example gives profound Biblical evidence against the Trinity.

When it comes to the baptism pattern and fulfillment, this is one of the easiest and clearest examples where the Apostolic model fits easily and beautifully. Baptism in Jesus' name strongly supports the Oneness Apostolic position.

For the Trinitarian, their best response is to ignore Jesus' words in Luke 24 and the connection to remission of sins. Then they should pretend Acts isn't part of the Bible or useful for doctrine, which is what lots of Christians in the modern world actually do. Most Trinitarians know they cannot Biblically object to people getting baptized in Jesus' name, but they also know they need to stay away from Jesus' name baptism to stay loyal to the Trinity. The baptism instructions and their fulfillment, throughout the New Testament, is a train wreck for the Trinity model.

I want every Christian to know they don't have to pick their favorite baptism verses and ignore the others. They can embrace all the baptism verses as beautiful, wonderful, and consistent, if they just drop the Catholic Church model of God as a Trinity. Then, you can be baptized in the same way and under the same amazing name that the Apostles used in the 1st-century church.

ANALYSIS

We've covered a lot of ground. In the first part, we introduced models and how they affect not only Christian debates but most disagreements between humans. We then explored Biblical models and Christian models about the Bible before diving into the most important model, the model that you and I might use to understand God and the incarnation.

In part 2, we dug deeper by looking at two models for the Incarnation in light of 12 different patterns and observations found in the Bible. I tried to be as objective as possible in presenting and discussing all the relevant scriptures, and not just my favorites for each chapter. I hope anyone reading would agree that I didn't pick the favorite verses for Apostolics and shy away from any "difficult" passages. The Apostolic method of study is to look at all relevant passages for a given topic and attempt to put God's Word in charge of the conclusion.

We're drawing near to attempting to grade the two models. The tribe mentality wants us to give our own side all A's and the other side a variety of lower grades, but I want both of us to resist this and attempt to be objective. Scan each chapter and consider the verses listed or any verses that I might have missed. Think about how well each model explains or fits the verses. Since these are declarative models, they should fit all the relevant verses, but we should leave some wiggle room for metaphoric verses that might not require a tight and complete fit. All Bible verses with ontological statements need to fit a model for that model to be valid.

Remember, we are not grading God's Word but our models and how well they explain and fit God's Word. There is nothing wrong with assigning a lower grade or changing the model to fit scripture better.

As you consider the observations and Bible verses, maybe the best way to review is to consider individual Bible verses. Which verses specifically support one model while giving difficulty to the other model? I am tempted to list Bible verses that specifically declare the Apostolic model, but we just went through 150+ pages covering a lot of passages – I don't see a reason to do it twice...

As a summary, let's consider Bible verses that make clear and declarative ontological statements that violate a model for God. We should minimize metaphoric examples and look for cases where a plain statement of scripture gives trouble to a model.

Some Trinitarians may likely disagree, but I don't see a single Bible verse that troubles or violates the Apostolic model. The Trinitarian may struggle with this, mainly because they don't understand that the Apostolic model also believes in and affirms the Adjacency verses throughout the New Testament. We also believe that Jesus Christ is separate from the Father as a man, and that His true human identity explains the Adjacency language in scripture while not violating His deity. You might not like or agree with this, but this is our model, derived from scripture, and it fits the verses just fine.

Some passages may sound more Trinitarian, such as John 8:18 or John 14:23, but understood in context, they fit the Apostolic model as well. Although I have been studying the Bible for 30 years, I actually began this project expecting a couple of passages to be more challenging from my perspective.

Although I knew multiple verses challenge the Trinity model, I was far more surprised at how many Bible passages make declarations incompatible with the Trinity. These are often simple, declarative Bible verses that should fit if the model is true.

Let's look at a summary of at least 25 Bible passages that most disagree with the Trinity model for God:

- ✗ **Deuteronomy 6:4**
  The Bible emphasizes that God is one.
  The Bible never says God is three.

- ✗ **Colossians 2:8-9**
  All of God, the fullness of deity is in Christ,
  It is not the 2nd person of the Trinity in Christ.

- ✗ **John 14:28**
  Jesus declares the Father is greater than I, which disagrees with the Trinity teaching of Co-Equality.

- ✗ **John 3:16, Hebrews 1:5, Galatians 4:4**
  The Bible declares the Son is begotten and made. Hebrews 1:5 reinforces that this happened at a point in time. This disagrees with the Catholic doctrine of the Eternally Begotten Son.

- ✗ **Colossians 1:15**
  Something about the Son is firstborn. Yes, His deity is eternal, but to say the Son is eternal is incompatible with the description of firstborn.

- ✗ **Isaiah 9:6**
  The name of the Son is the name of the mighty God and Everlasting Father. Trinitarians do not believe that Jesus is a valid name for the Everlasting Father.

- ✗ **1st Timothy 2:5, Hebrews 10:11-14**
  The Trinity teaches that the 2nd Person of the Trinity mediates our sins, but the Bible says the Son mediated as a man, as our human high priest.

- ✗ **1st Peter 1:18-21**
  The Bible says the Son was foreordained before the foundation of the world as part of the plan of God and then manifest at the right time. Foreordained is not the same as an eternal Son.

- ✗ **Luke 1:35**
  The Son is not called the Son because He existed in Eternity Past as the Trinity teaches, but the Son is called the Son because He came from God.

× John 14:8-10

The Trinity teaches that the persons are clearly differentiated and do not overlap, but the Bible overlaps the Father and the Son. If you know the Son, you know the Father. If you've seen the Son, you've seen the Father.

× John 14:16-18

The overlap continues between the Son and Holy Spirit. The Spirit is already with them as Jesus but will be in them. Jesus will come to us in the Spirit.

× Ephesians 4:4-6, Romans 8:9, Galatians 4:6

The overlap continues in the epistles. There is one Spirit, and the Father is the Spirit in us, which is the Spirit of Christ, which is the Spirit of the Son.

× Matthew 28:19, Luke 24:47, Acts 2:38, Acts 8:14-17, Acts 10:46-48, Acts 19:1-7, Acts 22:16, Romans 6:3, Galatians 3:27

The baptism instructions and their fulfillment and description in the epistles strongly teach that the name of Jesus is the name of the Father, and the Son, as well as the Holy Spirit, which directly contradicts the Trinitarian model.

× Colossians 1:15, Hebrews 1:1-3

The Bible declares that the Son is the image of God and the express image of God's single person.

These are simple, declarative examples where the Trinity model and the Bible plainly disagree.

Think about it, review and pray about it, and grade both models against the 12 observations and patterns.

Biblical Observation	Oneness Model	Trinity Model
Strong Commitment to Monotheism		
The Deity of Jesus Christ		
Dual-Nature of Christ		
The Adjacency Language		
Subordination in Scripture		
Eternity References to the Son		
Firstborn, Begotten and the Logos		
The Supremacy of the Name of Jesus		
The Right Hand of God		
Overlapping Activity		
Biblical Emphasis on Mediation		
Baptism Instruction and Fulfillment		

Grade on a scale from A to F. I promise I am not going to give the Apostolic side all A's. I ask you to sincerely consider each category as compared to the Bible.

PUTTING GOD'S WORD IN CHARGE

You made it this far, so I
believe with confidence that
you are someone who wants
the truth and likely loves the
Bible, even if you disagree
with some of my views. I
struggle to see how you could
make it this far if you didn't want God's Word in charge.

After a lot of study and prayer, I want to share my grades
for the 2 models. Realizing that I am biased towards one
team here, I intentionally am looking to judge my side
(Team Apostolic) more harshly than the Trinity model.
I will explain this more shortly when we look at grades.

So I am judging the 2 models across the 12 categories of
Biblical observation. For the Trinitarian side, I have
considered the classic, orthodox Trinitarian model as
presented in published works and by prominent leaders
in Trinitarian organizations. I am not judging the Trinity
based on what various church members and random
Christians have said to me.

For Team Apostolic, I am largely looking at published
authors, but I am also looking at how a lot of ministers
and seasoned Apostolic saints describe God and the
Incarnation. This is a lop-sided view and probably grossly
unfair, but I am interested in identifying any area where

Team Apostolic could do better in our pursuit of Biblical truth and its presentation.

MY GRADES FOR THE MODELS

Biblical Observation	Oneness Model	Trinity Model
Strong Commitment to Monotheism	A	D
The Deity of Jesus Christ	A	B
Dual-Nature of Christ	A	B
The Adjacency Language	B	B
Subordination in Scripture	A	D
Eternity References to the Son	B	C
Firstborn, Begotten and the Logos	B	D
The Supremacy of the Name of Jesus	A	D
The Right Hand of God	A	D
Overlapping Activity	A	F
Biblical Emphasis on Mediation	A	C
Baptism Instruction and Fulfillment	A	F

APOSTOLIC GRADES EXPLAINED

I'm not interested in rehashing the whole book, but the Apostolic model mainly uses scripture to directly declare the identity, full deity, and humanity of Jesus, so obviously, it will receive high grades.

When Colossians 2:9 says that Jesus is "the fullness of deity bodily", and then Apostolics say that Jesus is "the fullness of deity bodily", of course, it matches up. We just keep repeating Bible verses to explain what we believe.

In three of the categories, I believe it is more accurate to give the Apostolic model lower marks and room for improvement.

- ✓ The Adjacency Language
- ✓ Eternity References to the Son
- ✓ Firstborn, Begotten and the Logos

In each area, I believe our Apostolic leaders and published sources do a fantastic job explaining these verses, and absolutely deserve an A. To be clear, I don't think my explanations are as good as many given by others, and I am praying that this book doesn't give a know-it-all vibe. I am humbled by great teachers and amazing Apostolic resources that explore scripture and doctrine beyond my understanding.

It has been the modeling question that drove me to attempt this book. I've seen how models control conversations and blind us to the root causes of our disagreements, and I hope and pray this book plays a role in getting others to examine their models better. I think this can help Apostolics and others be better Christians and witnesses.

So I humbly suggest that Team Apostolic could do better in three areas, mainly because of our models, and I'll explain in reverse order.

In the area of Firstborn and Begotten, I have found that a lot of Apostolics really struggle to understand how the Son can be Firstborn. It's a really deep question, and the answer is profound and sublime, so it shouldn't surprise us that some struggle here. The explanations by David Bernard and other Apostolic authors are fantastic and rooted in scripture, but this remains a hard question for many. The Apostolic grade should likely be higher, and I am judging very harshly here, maybe it would be more accurate as a B+ or A-. If you ask the average Trinitarian, they have no idea how Jesus is the firstborn, and I would guess most Trinitarian ministers struggle here as well.

The **B for Eternity References** might also be harsh for Team Apostolic, for the same reasons as above. Again, our authors and leaders do great here, but I believe some Apostolic ministers struggle to explain or understand passages such as Philippians 2 and John 17. I believe our answers are excellent and put the Word of God first, but in my experience, I have seen Apostolics generally avoid texts such as John 17 and others.

My strongest criticism of Apostolics would be in the area of Adjacency Language in the Bible. To be clear, no one needs to agree with my word choice of Adjacency to describe this. I picked the word, and you are free to dismiss it. But the word is a container for a whole list of scriptures that reveal a very present pattern in the Bible.

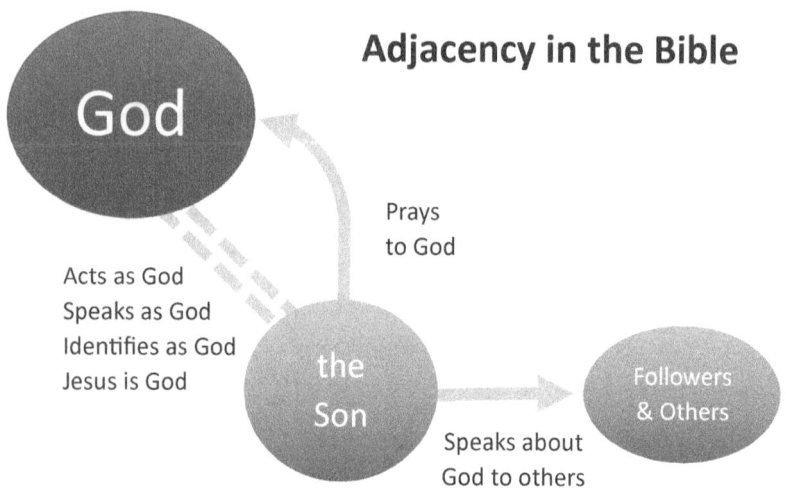

Adjacency in the Bible

God

Prays
to God

Acts as God
Speaks as God
Identifies as God
Jesus is God

the Son

Followers
& Others

Speaks about
God to others

This pattern is found in the Scriptures, repeatedly, and I am only giving it a name for the sake of this discussion.

In numerous conversations with Apostolics, including ministers, I have found that some of our ministers and many of our saints act like this is NOT something real and in the Bible. When you ask if there is any difference between the Father and the Son, they sometimes squirm and act like you are talking nonsense. I would love to know that my experience is unique, but I doubt it.

I believe Apostolics may be sensitive to "sounding Trinitarian" and that explains part of this, but it creates a wall and makes us less effective when talking to Christians from other groups.

In fairness, most Apostolic ministers have no issue with the Adjacency verses. When you ask how Jesus sits at the right hand of God, or about the two witnesses in John 8:18, or "we will come to him" in John 14:23, Apostolics have great and consistent answers, and most ministers do not squirm or struggle with these verses. The general tone is clear and Biblical. I have heard variations of, "Yes... God had a Son. Jesus is a real person, a real man, God incarnate in flesh... What's the problem?"

I hope and believe that Apostolics could connect better with Trinitarians if we could effectively communicate that we also believe in all the Adjacency verses in scripture. These verses are wonderful and true, and there is a profound difference between Adjacency and the Trinity.

Adjacency is a pattern observed in the Bible repeatedly. The Trinity is an attempt to explain the Adjacency that is compatible with the worldview and background of Church leaders in the centuries after the book of Acts. You can abandon the Catholic definitions and their model for God and still embrace all the Adjacency verses. You will find it only makes scripture more powerful and clear.

You will enjoy not being left with "well... it's a mystery" when asked why some aspect of the Trinity doesn't make sense. Instead, you can answer, "The only mystery in scripture[55] is the Incarnation, and this mystery has been revealed to us through the mighty God in Christ!"

TRINITY MODEL GRADES EXPLAINED

I hope I've been objective in evaluating the Trinity through these Biblical patterns. I believe I understand the Trinity well, and I am confident that I would receive an A on a multiple-choice test on the doctrine of the Trinity. I have talked to many Trinitarians, including a number of Pastors, and I doubt many would even pass a multiple-choice test on the Oneness Apostolic model.

I think most of us don't realize how much our models control our thinking. This is especially true for Trinitarian beliefs. Maybe an example would help here. Leighton Flowers and Mike Winger, two serious Bible teachers whom I really enjoy and respect, were discussing Calvinism and the book of Romans. Mike Winger made this comment[56] about finding Calvinism in Romans 9.

"If I ignore Calvinism for a minute, and then I read and teach through Romans, I don't get Calvinism... But if I start with Calvinism, and I read Romans 9, I get what I started with."

---

[55] 1st Timothy 3:16

[56] *Beware of Establishing Your Theology on This...*, Soteriology 101, https://www.youtube.com/watch?v=lWD1Jiz0-gg

This is exactly how models control our thinking. The Calvinist starts with the ideas and precepts of Determinism and TULIP, and they find what they expect when they look in scripture. Their model determines and controls what they see when they look at Bible verses.

I believe the same is true for the Trinity. If you could set aside the T-word and the idea of eternal, co-equal persons and read scripture, you would find that God is described and emphasized as one, not three, and you won't get to the Trinity from the Bible alone.

Now Mike Winger and Leighton Flowers are Trinitarian, and would likely not agree with the following statement, but I believe the same thought they apply to Calvinism also applies to the Trinitarian model.

> *"If I ignore the Trinity for a minute, and then I read and teach through the Bible, I don't get a Trinity… But if I start with the Trinity, and I read the New Testament, I get what I started with."*

When the Bible says the Father is greater than the Son, would you conclude, "Nope, that's wrong, they are co-equal." When the Apostles fulfilled Matthew 28:19 by baptizing in the name of Jesus, would you conclude, "Well, they disobeyed Christ, but the Catholic popes are the ones who got it right when they told us to baptize into the Trinity." When the Bible says that the Son is the image of the Invisible God, would you conclude, "Nope, that's not what God looks like, I think God is more like a triangle of three persons, not the one person shown to us in Christ Jesus." When the Bible says the Son is begotten and even "Today, I have begotten you", would you reply, "Nope, I think the Father eternally begat a Son through a mysterious and ongoing process." What about firstborn? "Nope, that means eternal and not born."

I don't think you get to the Trinity from the Bible alone. It requires some outside help and mixing in some philosophical ideas that are contrary to scripture to get there. You can check out the third appendix for a brief and documented history of how this happened.

When it comes to the Trinity and the Biblical patterns and observations, most readers do not realize they are reading their model into the text. When a scripture mentions God, most Trinitarians automatically read which part and definition of God fits that verse. They swap their definition into the text subconsciously while reading the verse.

John 1:1 uses the word God twice, and Trinitarians change the definition mid-verse to make sense of this.

John 1:1 NKJV

In the beginning was the Word, and the Word was with God [OH… GOD AS A WHO, THAT MUST BE FATHER],

and the Word was God [OH… THIS MUST BE GOD AS A WHAT, MADE OF THE SAME SUBSTANCE AS THE OTHER TWO PERSONS OF THE TRINITY].

I believe it is easier to just understand that the Logos is the mind of God and thoughts of God. This belongs to God and is, in fact, God. This mind and plan were in the beginning. Every thinking person has a logos, and it is hard even to separate your logos from you. You can put your thoughts into action in something that you do or make. When you do that, you put a part of you out there into the world.

We are not identical to God, although made in His image, but otherwise, this revelation in John 1 makes sense to me. God has a logos, and through that logos, the mind or plan of God, everything that was made, was made in accordance with the plan. That plan, including the Incarnation and Calvary, was established before the foundation of the world, then when the time was right, God made a Son, made of a woman, made under the law, and His only begotten Son, fully human and fully divine, in the fulfillment of the logos, became flesh and dwelt among us, and we beheld His glory, the glory of the only begotten of the Father.

We don't need the Trinity or eternal persons to understand any of this. But if you start with the Trinity, you can attempt to read it into the Bible. A number of Biblical patterns and observations will overlap and be compatible with parts of the Trinity. Many of the Adjacency verses will work fine in the Trinity model, especially since the Trinity attempts to explain a lot of the Adjacency language.

But **the Trinity only gets a B on the Adjacency verses** because other verses with Adjacency, such as the overlapping roles in John 14 and the fulfillment of Matthew 28:19, actually contradict the Trinity model.

In other areas, the Trinity deserves a lower grade when compared to scripture. The **Strict Monotheism** of scripture emphasizes that God is one, and clearly the Trinity emphasizes the number three, and it does so without a single verse in scripture to credibly[57] support that declaration.

In several of our categories, the Trinity model just runs roughshod over scriptural language and declarations. The Bible says the Father is greater than the Son. The Trinity disagrees. The Bible declares the Son is firstborn and begotten. The Trinity redefines these words to mean almost the opposite. The Bible celebrates and emphasizes the name of Jesus as the supreme name of God in the New Testament. The Trinity dilutes that emphasis and teaches people to be baptized in a way different than every single baptism account with details. These are contradictions and real problems for Trinitarians, and I believe I am being generous in giving the Trinity model a grade of D for these.

In the category of **Overlapping Activity**, the Trinity just completely disagrees with scripture. It gets an F.

---

[57] Check out the 4th Appendix if you are thinking about 1st John 5:7.

In the area of **Baptism Instruction and Fulfillment**, I would give the Trinity a grade lower than F if I could. Not only is the Trinitarian position on Baptism incoherent and flawed, but the Trinity model leads to a conclusion that most reasonable believers find unacceptable.

How do you compare and resolve the differences between Matthew 28:19, Acts 2:38, and the other verses on baptism? Pick an option.

A) The Apostles disobeyed Jesus, and every recorded baptism in the Bible was done incorrectly, but the Catholic Church bishops were the ones who got it right. We cannot trust the example of the Apostles in understanding Baptism. We should follow the Catholic Church on this and not the Biblical precedent set by Peter, Paul, and others.

B) The Apostles understood and fulfilled the instruction of Jesus by baptizing in Jesus' name in every recorded instance in the Bible. Acts and the Epistles, along with Luke 24, all beautifully align with Matthew 28:19 in teaching that Jesus is the name of the Father, the Son, and the Holy Spirit.

I understand why Catholics would pick Option A. I still think it's the wrong choice, but if you are not a Catholic, why are you picking this option? As a Bible-believing Christian, option B is the only choice that honors scriptural authority. If you pick Option A, then stop pretending you are a Bible-believing Christian.

THANK YOU

We've covered a lot of ground in this book. I am honored, humbled, and thrilled that you made this journey with me.

I hope I have challenged your thinking and especially how you view models and how they control so many of our interactions. My goal is that we would both have better models and be more aware of how models impact our conversations and disagreements.

This is more than a church issue. Models control so many human interactions. They are not only responsible for a lot of progress in higher learning but also cause many of the conflicts in politics and world affairs.

We need models to help us understand the world and even the Bible, but we need good and great models, not flawed and incomplete models.

Our model for God, because it has such a huge impact on our lives, needs to be the best model it can be. We've spent a lot of time in this book exploring two major models for understanding God and the Incarnation. We've covered a lot of details, but I want to end by zooming out and asking a simple question.

According to the Bible... what does God look like?

WHAT DOES GOD LOOK LIKE?

Model disagreements can get technical quickly, and I can understand if you are frustrated with the details and wrinkles that come up in a discussion like this.

They can get even worse if you watch a debate between experts. I enjoy the details, but I have noticed that even in Oneness and Trinity debates, it sometimes gets bogged down with specific Greek words, such as a conjunction or pronoun in a given Bible verse. Truth matters, but a debate can be won by the better presenter who is faster on their feet and has witty replies. I love Oneness and Trinity debate videos, and I believe Team Apostolic does quite well, but I was also on a debate team in high school, and learned early on that winning a debate was not the same thing as discovering or defending the truth.

In a model fight, each side builds their position and looks for weaknesses in the statements of their opposition. This kind of disagreement can get bogged down in exchanges where both sides are just fighting for their model. They rarely look at the underlying facts or common grounds between their positions.

The details matter, but in the bigger picture of the identity of Jesus, there really is a simpler way to understand and answer the question, "Who is Jesus?"

Yes, let's dive into the details, and we can learn a lot there, but let's start with a very simple question:

What does God look like?

Fundamentally, the disagreement that makes up the second part of this book is a disagreement about two different models, two different ways to understand and see God. Some might balk at visualizations, but I doubt anyone would disagree that the Catholic Church provides a distinct picture of what God looks like. It shows up in stained glass windows in church buildings all over the world.

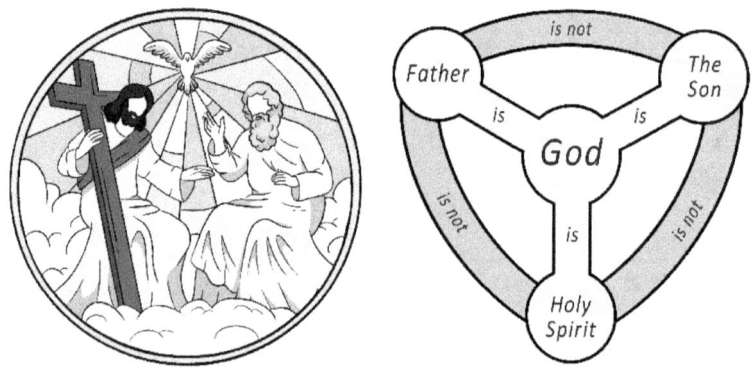

Even if you don't agree with the stained-glass version, you likely know that diagrams of triangles and word pictures of an egg or an apple are commonly used as visuals to understand this picture of God.

I just find it incredibly odd that people attempt to give a picture of God, when God already provided a clear image of Himself. If this sounds like an idol, then you have not thought this through. If a person makes an image, it is by definition a man-made (or woman-made) image, and it could be an idol. If God makes an image, then by definition, it is not a man-made idol.

God has given us an image of what He looks like to better understand His nature, character, and intentions towards us. Whatever you believe about God and His eternal nature, it definitely should NOT disagree with God's provided image.

Colossians 1:15 NKJV
[the Son] is the image of the invisible God...

We know that God is Spirit, and we cannot see Him, but God has given us a representation we can see. This word, image, likely makes you think of a reflection, a painting, or a photograph. This is not the root understanding in the 1st century church. Reflections in water were understood, and even polished bronze mirrors existed in wealthier homes, but the idea of an image was most often understood as a carving, a statue, or stamped impression on a coin. In Colossians, the word "image" comes from *"eikon"*, a likeness, a statue, or profile. An image is a representation. Another verse declares the same idea using a different specific word.

Hebrews 1:3 NKJV
[the Son is] ...the brightness of [God's] glory and the express image of [God's] person.

In this case, the word for image is *"charactēr"*, a mark or figure, burned in or stamped on, an impression, or precise reproduction in every way.

God provided His own image for us to better understand Him. What is that image? Which one of these better represents how God wants us to understand and know Him according to the Bible?

Very simply, God's image and self-revelation is Jesus Christ. We can see and understand God better through the single person of Christ. He is the fullness of Deity bodily. He is the image of the Invisible God.

Hebrews 1 goes further than just declaring the image.

Hebrews 1:1-2 NKJV
God, who at various times and in various ways spoke in time past to the fathers by the prophets, ² has in these last days spoken to us by His Son, whom He has appointed heir of all things, through whom also He made the worlds.

Hebrews 1 uses language that sounds a lot like Colossians 1 and John 1, in that the creation of the world was done through this Son. This is beautiful and astounding, but let's not lose "sight" of the image provided here:

Hebrews 1:3-4 NKJV
Who [the Son] being the brightness of His glory and the express image of His person, and upholding all things by the word of His power, when He had by Himself purged our sins, sat down at the right hand of the Majesty on high, [4] having become so much better than the angels, as He has by inheritance obtained a more excellent name than they.

There's a lot to unpack here. The Son, this express image, completes the mission of Calvary and sits at the right hand of majesty – other scriptures would say the right hand of God. I would guess that Trinitarians and Apostolics would agree that verse 4 cannot be a reference to divinity since God cannot go from a state lower than the angels to higher than the angels – God cannot change nor can God receive an inheritance He already possessed – verse 4 would point to the human agency of Christ in accomplishing the mission and receiving the inheritance.

This is all quite powerful and beautiful, but I want to draw your attention to the simple, declarative, and ontological truth in the middle of these verses.

Colossians 1:15 NKJV
[the Son] is the image of the invisible God...

Hebrews 1:3 NKJV
[the Son is] ...the brightness of [God's] glory and the express image of [God's] person.

Hebrews 1:3 NIV
[the Son is] ...the radiance of God's glory and the exact representation of His being.

Hebrews 1:3 goes further to specifically declare that the Son is the express image of God's person, nature, or being. The word for person, in Greek, is *"hypostasis"*. You can focus and dive as deep as you wish on the hypostasis side of this verse. This verse directly opposes the Trinity.

I understand why modern translations moved away from the KJV and NKJV rendering. This is the only verse in the entire Bible using the word "person" connected to God's nature. This verse, in the King James, declares that God is one person, and we see that person expressed in Jesus Christ. That is a slam-dunk rejection of the Trinity.

It doesn't get better in the Greek. Look at the usage of the Greek word, hypostasis, which is the specific word used to define plural persons in the Trinity. One substance and three persons, or one "homoousios" and three "hypostasis". Hebrews 1:3 says God is one hypostasis, and we see that hypostasis in Jesus Christ. Directly from the Greek, we have a slam-dunk rejection of the Trinity.

These verses provide another solid, declarative, and ontological rejection of the Trinity model, but I would rather focus on the power and significance of God manifested in the flesh in Jesus Christ.

We can have all kinds of profound conversations about the Son and what it means for Him to be God in the flesh, fully God and fully man. We can discuss how He is firstborn, and His dual-nature, and explore the wonder of so many Bible declarations and descriptions.

What we cannot do is lose sight of this simple and powerful declaration in Colossians 1 and Hebrews 1.

Do you want to know what God looks like? He looks like the man, Christ Jesus. God looks like one perfect person in Jesus Christ.

This is the inspiration for the title of this book. **Jesus is the Express Image of God**. God reveals Himself to us through this model and expression so that we can better know Him.

I represented this as an impression in the dirt of a human handprint with a barely hidden hint of God's love drawn in.

God tells us what He looks like, and it isn't a triangle relationship of three persons or an apple or an egg. God gave us an image of Himself, and it looks nothing like the Trinity. Whatever else you decide about God, it had better match the image God has provided for Himself.

Otherwise, you are creating a different image – a man-made image, and most of us know that is not a great idea according to the Bible. If you visualize God as a triangle, or an old man, young man, and a dove, you have moved away from the Biblically inspired image God gave you.

How could it possibly be better to replace God's provided image, Jesus Christ, with a man-made version?

The Bible warns us specifically about this kind of broken thinking. The mystery of God is revealed in Christ, yet we risk being deceived by fine-sounding arguments. The solution is to keep your faith firmly in Christ, to focus on Jesus Christ.

Colossians 2:2-4 NKJV
My goal is that they may be encouraged in heart and united in love, so that they may have the full riches of complete understanding, <u>in order that they may know the mystery of God, namely, Christ</u>, [3] in whom are hidden all the treasures of wisdom and knowledge.

[4] <u>I tell you this so that no one may deceive you by fine-sounding arguments</u>.

We are never told to chase after a Trinity, but that we should pursue Christ and apprehend Christ.

The warning and instruction in Colossians continue...

Colossians 2:6-10 NKJV
As you therefore have received Christ Jesus the Lord, so walk in Him, [7] rooted and built up in Him and established in the faith, as you have been taught, abounding in it with thanksgiving.

[8] Beware lest anyone cheat you through philosophy and empty deceit, according to the tradition of men, according to the basic principles of the world, and not according to Christ. [9] For in Him dwells all the fullness of the Godhead bodily. [10] and you are complete in Him, who is the head of all principality and power.

Receive Christ, walk in Him, and don't let anyone cheat you through philosophy and man-made traditions. If someone comes along and says that Jesus is one person in a three-person divine arrangement, the Bible answers emphatically no. He is the fullness of divinity bodily!

When you have Jesus, you also have the Father, and when you have Jesus, you already have the Spirit too! His presence and His name represent all of God, the fullness of God. Jesus is the image of the invisible God and the express image of God's person. You are complete in Him.

APPENDIX 1 – DEFINITIONS, SCRIPTURES & SOURCES

Key Definitions

I'm not attempting a full dictionary, but I do want to give you a cheat sheet to make this book more approachable and enjoyable. Warning: these are biased definitions, written with a mild smirk but real joy in my heart. I believe these are accurate but do contain some humor.

After all, there are only two kinds of people who read definitions. Some are stumped and desperate, and maybe I can make you smile. The other group includes grumpy, fact-checking types. They don't like fun definitions (and I do).

Adjacency – label created by the author in this book to describe Bible verses where Jesus spoke about the Father, prayed to the Father, and also spoke and acted with authority as the Father at other times. In the General sense, Adjacent means "next to".

Apostolic – Refers to beliefs and practices demonstrated and directly taught by the Apostles, specifically in the New Testament. Apostolic would be contrasted to Catholic Church or Protestant beliefs and practices that come from confessional statements, church councils, or the decrees of Popes.

In the Apostolic tradition, you might hear someone say that we "speak where the Bible speaks and try to remain silent where the Bible is silent".

Begotten – From the Greek word, "monogenēs", in the Bible, this means to beget or give birth to a child. "Genēs" is similar to the Greek word, "genesis", and indicates a clear beginning – except for Trinitarians, who believe the Son was eternally begotten by the Father in a mysterious process that defies logic and isn't taught in the Bible.

Calvinism – The generic term for the belief that God already determined who would be saved and who would be lost. Calvinism teaches that humans play zero role in deciding to live for God or accept God's gift of grace and salvation. Although taught by John Calvin, who executed people for disagreeing with his theology, there are variations today in how different Calvinists understand predestination.

Christology – The fancy and academic term for the study of the Deity of Christ and the Incarnation.

Co-Equal – When two or more are equal with each other in rank. In the case of the Trinity, this was first proposed by Origen around 230 [A.D.] but not adopted until the Council of Constantinople in 381 [A.D.].

Co-Eternal – Indicating two or more have co-existed from eternity past. First proposed by Origen around 230 [A.D.] and officially adopted in the 325 [A.D.] creedal statement from Nicaea, with the clause, "begotten not made".

Declarative – This is a statement that asserts facts and makes a truth claim that should be objectively true, especially in theology. "Bacon comes from pigs" is declarative. "Bob ate some bacon" does declare something, but is not a fundamentally declarative statement about the nature and essence of bacon or, for that matter, Bob.

Dual-Nature (Hypostatic Union) – The widely held belief that Jesus was one person with two natures and two wills fully integrated within His person. He was fully God and fully man.

Eternally Begotten – This is the Catholic way of ignoring the Bible verses that indicate the Son had a clear beginning at some point and instead believe that there is an ongoing and mysterious process where the Father continually begets the Son from eternity past into eternity future.

Figurative – Language or words that depart from literal and declarative truth and instead use forms and representations to convey an idea or picture. If you are "happy as a clam", this is not a literal declaration comparing your mental state to a mollusk or even a declaration of the heightened mental happiness of bivalves in general.

Firstborn – From the Greek word, "prōtotokos", from the root words for first and offspring. Used consistently in scripture to indicate the first child with a beginning, but in the Trinitarian model, firstborn is defined as the Eternal Son, which is not by definition born.

Homoousios – The Greek word for substance or essence. It is used in the definition of the Trinity to explain how the persons of the Trinity can be plural but still one God because they share the divine nature. "One Homoousios and Three Hypostasis."

Hypostasis – The Greek word for person or being or confidence and also substance, depending on context. Used in the definition of the Trinity to explain how the persons of the Trinity can be one God, yet each has their own personhood. "One Homoousios and Three Hypostasis."

Hebrews 1:3 declares that God is one hypostasis.

Jesus-Only – A typically derogatory term for the Oneness Pentecostal view of the Deity of Jesus, mistakenly believing that Apostolics don't believe in the Father or the Holy Spirit – they only believe in Jesus. Some Apostolics, including this author, enjoy the label Jesus-Only, since we know that Jesus is the Father, and the Spirit of Jesus is the Holy Spirit.

If all I have is Jesus, I have everything I need!

Logos – The Greek word for "word" and likely so much more than "word" because this includes the thoughts, plans, and mind of God as well. This is a keyword in the opening of John 1:1 and plays a contentious role in the discussion of the Deity of Jesus Christ.

Metaphoric – A word picture, model, or story that uses figurative language and word pictures to convey a hidden or deeper meaning. "Take up your cross and follow Him" is not about finding two pieces of perpendicular attached wood and carrying them around behind Jesus.

Modalism – An often-misunderstood view about the Deity of Jesus. We don't actually know what ancient Modalists taught, since most of our information comes from their opponents. At a minimum, Modalists teach that God has revealed Himself in different modes and forms, but Modalism sometimes goes further than that basic claim to believe that God has to somehow switch modes.

Apostolics are often compared to Modalists, but some odd statements by modern Modalists show incompatibilities between the Apostolic perspective and Modalist teachings.

Model – In the context of this book, this is a word for an idea box with a label, and that box can contain one or more ideas that explain a subject or the world we live in. Geometry can be a model. Capitalism is a model, as well as Monotheism, the Dual-Nature of Christ, and the idea that you can be a Born-Again Christian. Models are building blocks that allow us to think deeper thoughts about Life, the Universe, and Eternity.

Oneness – This is the Apostolic Model for the Deity of Jesus Christ and the Incarnation, namely that God is presented consistently as one being, one person in scripture, and that God made a Son, where He put His divine nature in a genuine human life and God stepped into His own creation in the man, Christ Jesus, our Lord. Through Jesus, this world saw both the perfect life lived and also the perfect death, paying the price for sin and making it possible for those who choose Jesus to be filled with His Spirit and live forever with God.

Ontological – Pertains to the study of the nature of being or what exists. Ontology explores fundamental categories and the structure of reality. "A triangle has three sides" is ontologically true, but if you describe someone as a "married bachelor", it is false and impossible, because each word invalidates the meaning of the other.

Pentecostal – Recognizes the Day of Pentecost as the birthday of the New Testament church, and also the distinctive "Day of Pentecost experience" should be normal and expected in the conversion of a believer. A sinner should turn to God, repent of their past, be baptized (immersed) in water in Jesus' Name, for the remission of Sin, and they will be filled with God's Spirit in a distinct, supernatural experience.

Selectaversitis – A disease named by Scott Lynn in the early 2000s and rampant in modern Christianity, where a believer carefully picks certain verses to explain their beliefs while avoiding other verses that would awkwardly challenge their position. It is highly contagious and difficult to treat.

Subordination – The general idea that two are not equal and one is greater and superior to the other. The earliest version of the Trinity, as described by Tertullian around 213 [A.D.], included Subordination. Origen later introduced the idea of co-equal persons, but not with that exact title.

Trinity, Trinitarian – The popular belief among Christians that there is one eternal being of God that is shared by three co-equal, co-eternal persons, the Father, the Son, and the Spirit.

Charts and Scripture Lists

Scripture Index

The Gospel

Book of Acts Referenced on Pages

Pauline Epistles	Referenced on Pages
Romans 4:17	201
Romans 5:1-2	58
Romans 6:3-4	256, 258, 266
Romans 8:3	84, 93, 243
Romans 8:9	59, 85, 93, 154, 168, 233, 237, 242, 266
Romans 8:29	200
Romans 8:34	93, 219, 222
Romans 9	274-275
Romans 10:9	57-59
Romans 12:1-2	59
1st Corinthians 1:13	258
1st Corinthians 1:30	242
1st Corinthians 6:11	258
1st Corinthians 8:4	66, 82, 92, 104
1st Corinthians 12:4-6	238
1st Corinthians 12:13	154
1st Corinthians 13:5	53, 317
2nd Corinthians 3:16-17	237
2nd Corinthians 5:19	82, 113, 148
2nd Corinthians 13:14	5, 92
Galatians 3:20	249-250
Galatians 3:26-27	256, 258, 266
Galatians 4:4-7	85, 92, 168, 192, 204, 210, 233, 237, 242, 265, 266
Galatians 5:16-18	59, 154
Ephesians 1:11	189
Ephesians 1:17	242
Ephesians 1:20	219, 222
Ephesians 2:8-9	58

Primary Sources Used

(✶ Highly Recommended Resource)

✶ *New King James Bible*, 1982, Thomas Nelson.

A Brief Definition of the Trinity, Dr. James White,
April 29, 1998, Alpha and Omega Ministries,
https://www.aomin.org/aoblog/theology-matters/a-brief-definition-of-the-trinity

Baptism – The History of Christian Baptism,
A Dictionary of the Bible, James Hastings,
1898, T & T Clark, Edinburgh.

Greek and English Interlinear New Testament (KJV, NIV),
William Mounce and Robert Mounce, 2008, Zondervan.

✶ *I Am, A Oneness Pentecostal Theology*, Dr. David
Norris, 2009, Word Aflame Press Academic.

✶ *John: The Gospel that had to be Written*, Fred Kinzie,
1995, Word Aflame Press. (Difficult to find but worth it!)

A Textual Commentary on the Greek New Testament,
Dr. Bruce Metzger, Fortress Press, 2008.

The Trinity, Encyclopedia of Religion and Ethics,
James Hastings, 1921, Volume 12.

The Trinity, Holy, New Catholic Encyclopedia,
1967 Edition, Volume 14.

The Trinity, **The New Encyclopedia Britannica**,
1993 Edition, Volume 11 Micropedia.

The Doctrine of the Trinity, **The New Schaff-Herzog Encyclopedia of Religious Knowledge**, 1969, Volume 12.

✳ *The Oneness of God*, Dr. David Bernard, 2012, Word Aflame Press,

✳ *The Oneness View of Jesus Christ*, Dr. David Bernard, 1996, Word Aflame Press.

Pentateuch and Haftorahs, Dr. J. H. Hertz, 1960, Soncino Press.

Most of my research was from actual books, which for our younger readers, are like tablet computers, except with no batteries or electricity, and the ink is on actual paper. Think of a Kindle, except you can smell the history and happiness of written words and paper.

There were several online resources I found very helpful. I have thoroughly enjoyed **Dr. Bernard's videos in the Apostolic Life in the 21st Century series**. I have enjoyed his perspective and thoughts on a lot of Bible passages. His love for the Bible, and logical and careful responses, have influenced how I study God's Word.

✳ **https://www.youtube.com/@DavidKBernardUPCI**

I have also enjoyed the history videos on YouTube by **Dr. Ryan Reeves, who teaches at Gordon Conwell Theological Seminary** and has published an amazing collection of Church History videos on YouTube. I believe he is a Trinitarian and an excellent historian. None of his videos were specifically used in this book, but I have watched/listened to almost all of his videos and quite a few more than once. His extensive work has enriched my understanding of numerous topics in church history.

✳ **https://www.youtube.com/@RyanReevesM**

In the study and understanding of models, and how models can control our thinking and even deceive us, I have really enjoyed the content from multiple YouTube channels. One of the best is **Soteriology101**.

Dr. Leighton Flowers, a Trinitarian, runs this amazing YouTube channel with content specifically on Biblical Thinking outside of the Calvinist worldview. He is not Apostolic, at least not yet, but because of His perspective on the Calvinist model, I wonder if He could be persuaded to realize how much the Trinity model has influenced His thinking and theology? Dr. Flowers, if you are reading this, there is more evidence for Pre-Destination in the Bible than for the Trinity (☺).

https://www.youtube.com/@Soteriology101

Lastly, I have generally enjoyed the articles on the Trinitarian website, **GotQuestions.org**. I generally prefer to cite authors I like and respect, even when I disagree with them on one or more points, and I have found the content on this website to be well written and to demonstrate a great love for the Bible and a general desire to be true to God's Word.

I have specifically referenced multiple videos throughout this book:

Does Christ have Two Natures?
https://www.gotquestions.org/Christ-two-natures.html

What does it mean that Jesus is the "firstborn" over Creation?
https://www.gotquestions.org/Jesus-first-born.html

What is the Logos?
https://www.gotquestions.org/what-is-the-Logos.html

Why did Jesus say, "Not my will, but yours be done"?
https://www.gotquestions.org/not-my-will-but-yours-be-done.html

APPENDIX 2 – EXPLANATIONS OF THE TRINITY

With a goal of fairness and accuracy, we will present several different summaries of the Trinity as presented by published and popular Trinitarians: one by Dr. James White and another by the popular Christian Apologist, Frank Turek, and a third by Jared Wilson.

I summarized Dr. White's explanation of the Trinity earlier in the book, but here is his full article from the Alpha & Omega Ministries website, where he is the director as well as a published author with over 20 books. I like a lot of Dr. White's materials and perspectives, even if He is strongly opposed to the Oneness Pentecostal position. He has debated David Bernard and remains firmly convinced that the Trinity is a Biblical or at least a Biblically compatible doctrine.

A Brief Definition of the Trinity
by Dr. James White

April 29, 1998, Published[58] on www.AOMin.org

I know that one of the most oft-repeated questions I have dealt with is, "How does one explain, or even understand, the doctrine of the Trinity?" Indeed, few topics are made such a football by various groups that,

---

[58] https://www.aomin.org/aoblog/theology-matters/a-brief-definition-of-the-trinity

normally, claim to be the "only" real religion, and who prey upon Christians as "convert fodder." Be that as it may, when the Christian is faced with a question regarding the Trinity, how might it best be explained?

For me, I know that simplifying the doctrine to its most basic elements has been very important and very useful. When we reduce the discussion to the three clear Biblical teachings that underlie the Trinity, we can move our discussion from the abstract to the concrete Biblical data, and can help those involved in false religions to recognize which of the Biblical teachings it is denying.

We must first remember that very few have a good idea of what the Trinity is in the first place – hence, accuracy in definition will be very important. The doctrine of the Trinity is simply that there is one eternal being of God – indivisible, infinite. This one being of God is shared by three co-equal, co-eternal persons, the Father, the Son, and the Spirit.

It is necessary here to distinguish between the terms "being" and "person." It would be a contradiction, obviously, to say that there are three beings within one being, or three persons within one person. So what is the difference? We clearly recognize the difference between being and person every day. We recognize *what* something is, yet we also recognize individuals within a classification. For example, we speak of the "being" of man—human being. A rock has "being"—the being of a rock, as does a cat, a dog, etc. Yet, we also know that there are personal attributes as well. That is, we recognize both "what" and "who" when we talk about a person.

The Bible tells us there are three classifications of personal beings—God, man, and angels. What is personality? The ability to have emotion, will, to express oneself. Rocks cannot speak. Cats cannot think of themselves over against others, and, say, work for the common good of "cat kind." Hence, we are saying that there is one eternal, infinite being of God, shared fully and completely by three persons, Father, Son, and Spirit. One *What*, three *Who's.*

NOTE: We are *not* saying that the Father is the Son, or the Son the Spirit, or the Spirit the Father. It is very common for people to misunderstand the doctrine as to mean that we are saying Jesus is the Father. The doctrine of the Trinity does not in any way say this!

The three Biblical doctrines that flow directly into the river that is the Trinity are as follows:

1) There is one and only one God, eternal, immutable.

2) There are three eternal Persons described in Scripture – the Father, the Son, and the Spirit. These Persons are never identified with one another – that is, they are carefully differentiated as Persons.

3) The Father, the Son, and the Spirit are identified as being fully deity—that is, the Bible teaches the Deity of Christ and the Deity of the Holy Spirit.

One could possibly represent this as follows:

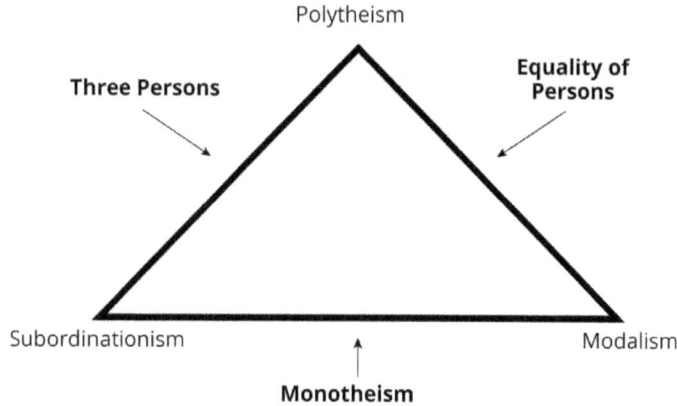

The three sides of the triangle represent the three Biblical doctrines, as labeled. When one denies any of these three teachings, the other two sides point to the result. Hence, if one denies that there are Three Persons, one is left with the two sides of Full Equality and One God, resulting in the "Oneness" teaching of the United Pentecostal Church and others. If one denies Fully Equality, one is left with Three Persons and One God, resulting in "subordinationism" as seen in Jehovah's Witnesses, the Way International, etc. (though to be perfectly accurate the Witnesses deny *all three* of the sides in some way—they deny Full Equality (i.e., Jesus is Michael the Archangel), Three Persons (the Holy Spirit is an impersonal, active "force" like electricity) and One

God (they say Jesus is "a god"—a lesser divinity than Yahweh; hence they are in reality not monotheists but henotheists). And, if one denies One God, one is left with polytheism, the belief in many gods, as seen clearly in the Mormon Church, the most polytheistic religion I have encountered.

Hopefully, these brief thoughts will be of help to you as you "grow in the grace and knowledge of our Lord Jesus Christ."

How Could Jesus Be God if He Didn't Know All Things - by Frank Turek

October 15th, 2019, YouTube Clip[59]

I believe this is a great attempt to show both the Trinity and the Dual-Nature of Jesus Christ by Frank Turek during a Question-and-Answer session at what appears to be a University Apologetics Presentation. Frank uses humor here to present the complications that the Trinity brings to the situation, but this is also a great overall summary.

He generally does a great job in his presentation of the Gospel and the existence of God and how the Bible is very compatible with observations from science and moral challenges, even if I disagree with his Trinitarian beliefs.

---

[59] https://youtu.be/R9FBLtOCCcc

Student Question:

In Mark 13:32, the Bible talks about Jesus not knowing the time or the hour when He would return. If Jesus didn't know that, how could He be divine?

Frank Turek's Answer (*edited for better readability, charts recreated to hopefully make this easier to follow*) :

In approaching this question, you need to first know that Jesus had two natures. If you look at a graphic of the Trinity, and there is no perfect illustration of the Trinity, but I believe this one does a pretty good job of it. Think of God in His divine nature like a triangle having three corners: Father, Son, and Holy Spirit.

God is comprised of three persons sharing one divine nature. Jesus is the second person of the Trinity. He also has a human nature. These two natures are not intermingled, but He has both. So, you asked the question, "How can Jesus be God when He did not know when He would return?"

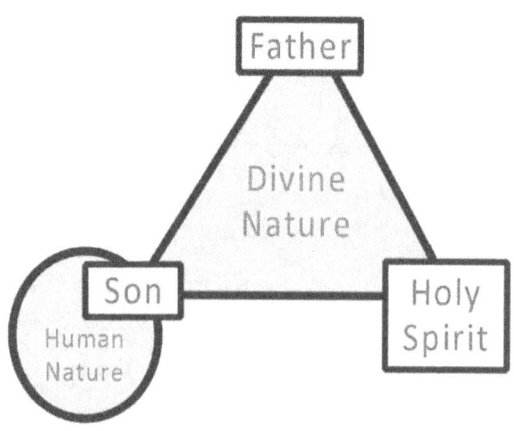

Whenever you ask a question about Jesus, you have to ask two questions. Why? Because He has two natures.

1. Did Jesus know when He was coming back?
   As God – Yes.
2. Did Jesus know when He was coming back?
   As man – No.

We can look at other examples...

1. Did Jesus get hungry? As God – No.
2. Did Jesus get hungry? As man – Yes.

1. Did Jesus get tired? As God – No.
2. Did Jesus get tired? As man – Yes.

So whenever you ask a question about Jesus, you have to ask two questions. You can also look at it this way, that God is "One What with Three Who's".

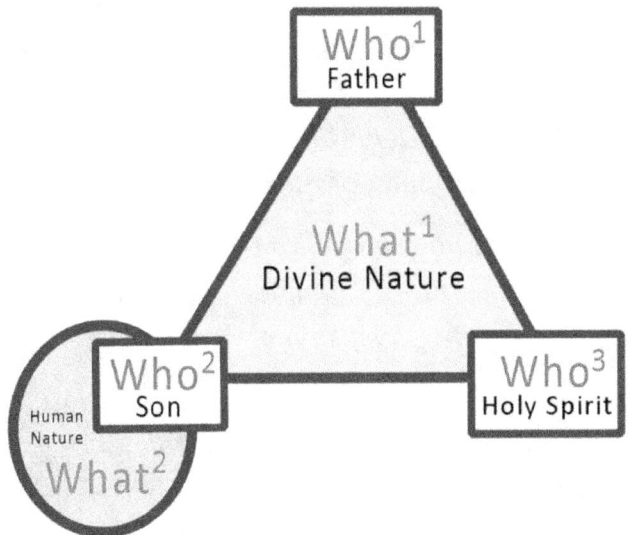

God is "One What with Three Who's":

- ✓ Who #1 – The Father
- ✓ Who #2 – The Son
- ✓ Who #3 – The Holy Spirit

But "Jesus is One Who with Two What's":

- ✓ What #1 – The Divine Nature
- ✓ What #2 – The Human Nature

"So whenever you ask a question about Who #2, you have to ask What What are you talking about. Are you talking about What #1 or What #2? If you get those mixed up, you will not know which Who will give you the right answer."

Author's note:
Obviously, this is meant to be a somewhat humorous portrayal, but also to legitimately answer a question combining the model of the Trinity with the Trinitarian understanding of the Dual Nature. Frank even calls it "Abbott and Costello Theology".

I recommend that you search for the video on YouTube, it is on the channel Cross Examined under the title, "How could Jesus be God if he didn't know all things"?

Apostolics would largely agree with the Dual-Nature part of this answer, but we would point out that once you have the Dual-Nature, you don't need the three Who's anymore to understand God and the Bible.

No Trinity, No Love by Jared Wilson

May 7th, 2016 article[60] on TheGospelCoalition.org

"The Beatles said all you need is love," Larry Norman sang. "Then they broke up."

Love is the thing we all know we need. And yet love is the thing we struggle so much to get right. We think of it largely in terms of feelings, of "being in love" or "falling in love," but feelings are fleeting. That kind of love certainly can't be all we need; it's so hard to maintain!

I remember some of the best love advice I ever got. It was right before my wedding, and my dad had taken me aside to encourage and pray for me. I jokingly said, "What if I fall out of love?" He returned my sarcasm, "Then you fall right back in!" My dad was really making the point that real love is not something you fall in and out of. It's intentional. It has movement.

I think of this every time I'm attending a wedding and 1 Corinthians 13 is read. Many couples automatically go to this great "love chapter" simply because it's all about love. But I don't think many are paying much attention to what it actually says. Because when things start getting difficult, when conflict pops up—as it inevitably must in close relationships—suddenly keeping no record of

---

[60] https://www.thegospelcoalition.org/article/no-trinity-no-love/

wrongs and hoping and bearing all things doesn't seem to make much sense.

The kind of love that's real, the kind of love Scripture actually teaches, the love that's higher and deeper and stronger than all our stupid pop songs and romance novels and chick flicks, is impossible to manufacture out of emotions and human ambition.

So how do we get it?

God is Love

The religious person will suggest that love comes from God. But Christianity teaches that God is himself love (1 John 4:8, 16). Love isn't God. But God is love. So what does it mean for God to be love?

It doesn't necessarily mean God is simply *loving*. Judaism and Islam, and Mormonism proclaim a God who loves. But when Christians teach that God *is himself love*, they're saying that real love itself has its origin and essence in God.

And this cannot be true unless God is a Trinity.

God is Triune

Think about it: A solitary god cannot be love. He may learn to love. He may yearn for love. But he cannot in himself be love, since love requires an object. Real love requires relationship. In the doctrine of the Trinity, we finally see how love is part of the fabric of creation;

it's essential to the eternal, need-nothing Creator. From eternity past, the Father and the Son and the Spirit have been in community, in relationship. They have loved each other. That loving relationship is bound up in the very nature of God himself.

If God were not a Trinity but merely a solitary divinity, he could neither be love nor be God.

So the Trinity isn't some weird religious aberration Christians have stupidly clung to. It's the answer to the deepest longing of the human heart. The Trinity answers history's oldest desire. It even clarifies the question. It makes us go deeper than sentimental notions and ethereal feelings, and elusive emotions. It puts us on solid ground with all this love stuff we've been chasing forever. We're all looking for love. Deep down, we all need it in ways we don't understand or even acknowledge. We search and search. We find glimpses, moments, tastes, and samples of love. We have genuine experiences of love. And yet nothing quite gets us outside of our own hurts, our own self-interest, our own sins. We need the realest love there is.

Ultimate Love

"Greater love has no one than this," Jesus said, "that someone lay down his life for his friends" (John 15:13). Sacrificial love is the ultimate love. Now imagine that the One who is Love himself sacrificed himself. Imagine that the eternal loving fellowship of the divine community sent out one of their own to die not just for their friends but for enemies. Why would this loving fellowship do this? To make the enemies friends, of course.

And this is precisely what God has done. The second person of the Trinity, the Son of God, takes on flesh and comes to die, that he who is true Love might show true love and give true love and transform by true love. That we might finally know true love. It's for this reason Fred Sanders declares, "Trinity and the gospel have the same shape! This is because the good news of salvation is ultimately that God opens his Trinitarian life to us."

This is the hope of all mankind—that the "fusty doctrine" of the Trinity would "come to life" by swallowing us up into the love God has enjoyed since before time began. C. S. Lewis, himself once an atheist, was right: "The thing that matters is being actually drawn into that three-personal life."

And when somebody trusts in the Jesus of Christianity, they are.

Author's note:
This kind of reasoning, using philosophy and beautiful word images, might work very well, if you are right about your underlying assumptions. Given the opportunity,

I would remind Jared Wilson that Colossians 2:2-10 specifically warns us against this approach in drawing us away from Jesus Christ.

I understand that we are made in God's image, and so to some degree, we can relate to God's desire to create, have relationships, and interact with soulful life, but I would be concerned about extending our understanding of God so far into areas where the Bible remains silent. How do you know that God needed something or someone to love in eternity past?

God has other basic attributes that could be used in the same line of reasoning to create doctrines that no Christian would find acceptable.

God is all-powerful → He must have something to exert power upon in eternity past, or it denies His omnipotence.

God is sovereign → He must have something to rule over from eternity past, or it violates His basic attribute of sovereignty.

God is omnipresent → Therefore, He must have a realm in which to exist and fill in eternity past or He is not everywhere.

These are typically considered necessary attributes in God's nature, but no one would agree to this application. We should be very careful about telling each other and God what God had to have to exist in eternity past.

APPENDIX 3 – A BRIEF HISTORY OF THE TRINITY

To understand the history of the Trinity, you need to learn about another model disagreement. Many Christians are aware that the word Trinity, as well as Triune, co-equal, co-eternal and eternally begotten are not found in the Bible. Few understand the history behind how this model became the dominant view.

The Common Model of the Trinity	The Historic Model of the Trinity
Believes that Paul and the Apostles were really Trinitarian but just didn't use the exact language of the Trinity in the Bible.	The core beliefs of the Trinity developed slowly over 350 years through multiple debates and conversations.

Both models believe in one God in three persons, the persons of God are co-equal, co-eternal. The Son is eternally begotten from the Father. Both believe these persons are clearly differentiated in scripture.

Believed mainly by attending members of Trinitarian churches, along with some ministers who haven't studied very much church history.	The official position of the Catholic Church and largely agreed upon by almost all serious students of Church History, both Trinitarian and otherwise.

If you haven't noticed the theme, this is your last chance in this book to discover that models control a lot of our thinking. You can learn a great deal about the reasoning behind a model by examining how it was developed. This doesn't always work, because you need valid source materials, and we also need to check our bias and the bias of our sources while examining the evidence.

For the Trinity, we have sufficient evidence to trace its development with confidence, but we still need to examine the models that were in the minds of the people writing centuries after Calvary. We also need to be careful to know that just because a written record survived, it doesn't mean it wasn't altered or even popular in its day, only that we still have it.

The assassination of Abraham Lincoln would have been recorded differently by a New York abolitionist compared to a Georgia slave-owner. A pro-slavery account and an anti-slavery account would likely record the details of his murder and the consequences much differently. One side might think President Lincoln ruined their lives, but some on the other side call him "The man that freed the slaves". As a fellow abolitionist, I am quite biased but recognize that accounts from both sides may contain both truth and embellishments. That's why you must be careful when examining historical documents and trying to determine what people originally believed in any given time period.

So, we should exercise some caution here.

When it comes to the Trinity, the first thing to note is that the Adjacency pattern in scripture is NOT the same thing as the Trinity[61]. The Trinity attempts to explain and understand Adjacency. The Oneness model also attempts to explain and understand all the Adjacency verses. The presence and repetition of Adjacency language in the centuries to follow DO NOT PROVE either model.

The question and point of the Trinity would be to explain the Adjacency. History tells us that the Trinity developed through several key stages from the early 150's through 400 [A.D.], and that we can see evidence of these crucial developments in multiple sources.

Let's take a look at this timeline, first in summary, then in detail with sources. All of this happens after the New Testament is completed, so this is all in the A.D. part of human history[62]. As a real Christian, I am not interested in rewriting history and labeling these years as A.C.E., which would be "After the Common Era". We know what event marks the common era — or I hope you know.

So, I will follow the traditional practice. B.C. is "Before Christ" and A.D. marks events "After Dat".

---

[61] See the Adjacency chapter in Part 2, if you missed this key point.

[62] One joy of writing your own book is that you can include jokes. A.D. is Anno Domini, Latin for "in the year of the Lord".

MILESTONES IN THE ADOPTION OF THE TRINITY

150 A.D.

Justin Martyr declares the Son is a separate divine being from the Father.

212 A.D.

Tertullian is the first to call God a Trinitas. Believes the Son is subordinate and created.

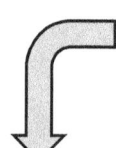

230 A.D.

Origen teaches that the three persons are co-equal and co-eternal.

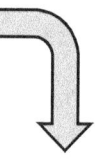

325 A.D.

Council of Nicaea rejects Arianism. Affirms the deity of the Son is same as the Father. The Son is begotten, not made.

381 A.D. **to ~400** A.D.

The Trinity language is finalized as official. The phrase "one God in three persons" is accepted as Catholic and doctrinal.

Some want to believe that Paul and the other Apostles were Trinitarian. They just didn't use the correct words to express their belief. This doesn't reflect what we see in historical documents. Christian scholars, both Protestant and Catholic, agree on this point. Here are just a few sources to confirm this:

> "Neither the word Trinity, nor the explicit doctrine appears in the New Testament, nor did Jesus and his followers intend to contradict the Shema in the Old Testament: 'Hear, O Israel, The Lord our God is one Lord' (Deuteronomy 6:4)." [63]

The New Schaff-Herzog Encyclopedia is well-respected as a reference from a Protestant, Reformation position. It makes this comment in its introduction to the Trinity:

> "[the Trinity] constitutes the distinctive characterization of Christianity as contrasted with Judaism and paganism, and is a modification of Christian monotheism." [64]

The Trinity is acknowledged as a "modification" of Christian monotheism. Apostolics reject this modification and choose to embrace Biblical language instead.

---

[63] Article on *The Trinity*, The New Encyclopedia Britannica, 1993 Edition, Volume 11 Micropedia, p.928.

[64] Article on *The Doctrine of the Trinity*, The New Schaff-Herzog Encyclopedia of Religious Knowledge, 1969, Volume 12, p.18.

In general, I highly recommend the New Bible Dictionary from Inter-Varsity Press. In its summary on the Trinity:

> *"The term 'Trinity' is not itself found in the Bible. It was first used by Tertullian at the close of the 2nd century, but received wide currency and formal elucidation only in the 4th and 5th centuries.*
>
> *Three affirmations are central to the historic doctrine of the Trinity. 1 – there is but one God. 2 – the Father, the Son, and the Spirit is each fully and eternally God. 3 – the Father, the Son and the Spirit is each a distinct person.*
>
> *Nowhere does the Bible explicitly teach this combination of assertions. It may, nevertheless, be claimed that the doctrine of the Trinity is a profoundly appropriate interpretation of the Biblical witness..."* [65]

I agree in part, it is an interpretation of the Bible, specifically a Catholic interpretation. As such, there is no reason for non-Catholics to embrace it or require others to agree with this model.

The New International Dictionary of New Testament Theology is highly regarded and includes details on the development of the Trinity over time. Zondervan publishes it in a three-volume set that may be more affordable than some of the resources listed here.

---

[65] Article on *The Trinity*, New Bible Dictionary, 1997, 3rd Edition, p.1209.

In its entry on "God", you will find the following:

> *"The New Testament does not contain the developed doctrine of the Trinity. ...primitive Christianity did not have an explicit doctrine of the Trinity such as was subsequently elaborated in the creeds of the early church."* [66]

The Scottish Bible scholar, James Hastings, describes the evolution of the Trinity in great detail in his 13-volume Encyclopedia of Religion and Ethics. We will visit his description further down, but he summarizes the Biblical perspective as follows:

> *"In the New Testament, we do not find the doctrine of the Trinity in anything like its developed form, not even in the Pauline and Johannine theology, although ample witness is borne to the religious experience from which the doctrine springs."* [67]

I hope it is clear that I am not cherry-picking quotes or pretending that these Trinitarians see zero basis for the Trinity in scripture. They see something that leads to the Trinity (which I call Adjacency), but they acknowledge that the Trinity itself is not declared directly in scripture.

---

[66] Article on *God*, The New Schaff-Herzog Encyclopedia of Religious Knowledge, 1969, Volume 12, p.18.

[67] Article on the *Trinity, The Development of the Doctrine*, Encyclopedia of Religion and Ethics, by James Hastings, 1921, Volume 12, p.458.

Of all the published views, the Catholic Church offers the most interesting perspective. They firmly believe in their authority to add to the Bible and modify doctrine. As such, they clearly state that the language and ideas of Trinity came about over time – they are, after all, the ones who claim to be the agents of this discovery. Catholic Church literature declares their understanding came not from the Bible, but as a "Divine revelation" from "God to man" through the church[68].

The account of the development of the Trinity, from official Catholic sources, is surprisingly candid and nuanced. The history of the Trinity is consistently portrayed as a bumpy process where the doctrine is clearly not found in scripture but took several centuries, and multiple arguments, to reach its current form.

> *"It is difficult, in the second half of the 20th century, to offer a clear, objective, and straightforward account of the revelation, doctrinal evolution, and theological elaboration of the mystery of the Trinity. Trinitarian discussion, [in] Roman Catholicism as well as other [denominations], presents a somewhat bumpy silhouette."* [69]

---

[68] Article on *Trinity, The Blessed*, The Catholic Encyclopedia, 1912, Volume 15, p.47.

[69] Article on *Trinity, Holy, Introduction*, New Catholic Encyclopedia, 1967, Volume 14, p.295.

This is far more honest and candid than how most Trinitarian Christians portray this doctrine. They assume the Trinity is clearly in the Bible, just that the exact words are missing. But the Catholic description of a "somewhat bumpy silhouette" feels more sincere and accurate.

The quote continues with this amazing disclaimer:

> "Two things have happened. There is the recognition on the part of exegetes and Biblical theologians, including a constantly growing number of Roman Catholics, that _one should not speak of Trinitarianism in the New Testament without serious qualification._"

What is this serious qualification?

> "There is also the closely parallel recognition on the part of historians of dogma and systematic theologians that _when one does speak of an unqualified Trinitarianism, one has moved from the period of Christian origins to, say, the last quadrant of the 4th century._ It was only then that what might be called the definitive Trinitarian dogma, 'one God in three Persons', became thoroughly assimilated into Christian life and thought."

Namely, that the Trinitarian position assumes a late 4th-century mindset, and pretending it was found at the beginning, in "Christian origins", is not historically accurate or valid.

I wish more Trinitarians knew a little church history and were this candid and accurate in their understanding of early church beliefs. I am sharing these sources and quotes here in the hopes that open-minded and interested students of the Bible and history could separate the Biblical perspective from the Catholic model for the Trinity.

Let's look at the progression to the Trinity in detail...

STEP 1 – DIVIDING THE FATHER AND THE SON

The Greek Apologists in the mid-100s took the first major step in the journey to the Trinity. James Hastings describes this as a transition of the "Trinity of experience" to the "Trinity of dogma".

"The story of the Trinity in ecclesiastical history is the story of the transition from the Trinity of experience, in which God is self-revealed as the Father or creator and Legislator, the Son or Redeemer, and the Spirit or Sanctifier, to the Trinity of dogma, in which the threefold self-disclosure of God is but the reflexion, as it were, of a threefold distinction within the divine Nature itself." [70]

I would describe this "Trinity of experience" as the Adjacency references discussed in this book. Yes, God

---

[70] Article on the *Trinity*, *The Development of the Doctrine*, Encyclopedia of Religion and Ethics, by James Hastings, 1921, Volume 12, p.459.

had revealed Himself in different ways. We agree. We do not agree or see where scripture demands or declares a permanent threefold distinction within God's divine nature. Hastings continues...

> "With the transition from the Trinity of experience to the Trinity of dogma, the theological statement tends to lose touch with the gracious figure of the historical Christ."

I wholeheartedly agree with Hastings' criticism that focusing on the Trinity takes away from the scriptural focus on Jesus. I will resist quoting Colossians 2:8-9 here, but we are warned in the Bible about philosophical speculations taking our focus away from Christ.

James Hastings identifies the influence of Justin Martyr and other Greek Apologists as the first step in the dogmatic development of the Trinity:

> "The formal identification of the pre-existent Christ (of the Pauline and Johannine theology) with the Logos of Greek philosophy. In the NT, the identification is in the practical rather than speculative interest, but _in Justin Martyr and the apologists, it may be regarded as the first step in the logical process_ whereby the historical figure of Jesus Christ was caught up into the purely speculative sphere."

The consensus is that prior to the Greek Apologists, the focus was largely on Christ and on continuing the language and pattern found in the New Testament itself.

> "With the Apostolic Fathers, Ignatius certainly, the <u>center of gravity in the Christian message had ever been Christ... They did no more than preserve the authentic rhythm of the New Testament</u>." [71]

I agree. The early Apostolic Fathers declared Jesus as the revelation of God, the "Sceptre of God", and the language used is very similar to that in the Bible.

However, the Greek Apologists, attempting to answer legitimate questions (such as "Why did Jesus pray?"), were the first to introduce language that fit their polytheistic world.

> "[It was understood that] the Word and Spirit are not to be separated from the unique Godhead of the Father. But why not? The Apologists at least attempt a reply. For Justin, the Godhead was very clearly a Triad, though it was Theophilus who first introduced this expression.
>
> For <u>Justin, the Word is no less than something numerically other in relation to the Father</u>." [72]

---

[71] Article on *Trinity, Holy, History of Doctrine to Constantinople I*, New Catholic Encyclopedia, 1967, Volume 14, p.296.

[72] Article on *Trinity*, p.296.

A couple of thoughts here.

I see no evidence that Justin believed in a "Triad". He focused on differentiating the Father and Son. Justin mentions hardly any specifics about the Spirit. He never calls God a Triad (or Trias). This is attributed to Theophilus. You can read more about Theophilus shortly, but no objective reader would call his quote a clear Trinity reference either.

The account above is typical of Trinitarian literature. It mentions Justin Martyr, but leaves out offensive details in Justin's presentation. Justin calls the Word something "numerically other" to the Father? You can describe it that way if you are desperate to make his contribution look acceptable and Christian. But in his *Dialogue with Trypho*, this is what Justin actually says about Jesus:

> "...there is said to be, <u>another God and Lord</u> subject to the Maker of all things; who is also called an Angel..."
>
> "He <u>who is said to have appeared to Abraham</u>, and to Jacob, and to Moses, and <u>who is called God, is distinct from Him who made all things, numerically,</u> I mean, not distinct in will." [73]

---

[73] *Dialogue with Trypho, Chapter 56,* Justin Martyr, 2015, Beloved Publishing p.63-65.

Serious church historians are aware of Justin's word choices, and some will openly admit that his views are "unacceptable" to modern Christian understanding.

Many Trinitarian historians ignore Justin's polytheistic language. They attempt to defend his words by claiming that he was trying to reach a pagan audience and to speak in ways that they could understand.

Introducing foreign and pagan words is the very problem that should bother you. He introduced pagan language and concepts instead of prioritizing the ideas and language of scripture.

Also, his polytheistic references just don't hold up to logical scrutiny. This book is called *Dialogue with Trypho*, a conversation, either real or imagined, where Justin is persuading a Jewish man named Trypho to believe in the identity and divinity of Jesus Christ. Claiming a plurality of Gods makes no sense when trying to reach a Jew. It violates the obvious Strict Monotheism of Judaism.

Whether Justin is aware of this fact or not, his teachings should not influence how Bible-believing Christians view the identity of Jesus. He clearly didn't understand even the Ten Commandments, yet he is recognized and cited in most historical literature as a pivotal figure on the road to the Trinity.

He is venerated as a saint in the Catholic and Orthodox churches today. I guess I should not be surprised...

Apparently, his numerous writings were popular, or grew popular later, although there is no record that he ever held a position in the church. As a Christian, Justin was an itinerant preacher based out of Ephesus, and he later moved to Rome, where he established a school of philosophy and continued to teach and defend his version of Christianity to a Roman audience. He likely influenced other Greek Apologists, attempting to bridge the gap between Biblical revelation and Greek philosophical ideas in their day.

Justin Martyr was likely the first, but not the only one, to describe Jesus as a second god. Other Greek Apologists, including Philo of Alexandria, also labeled Jesus as a deutero-theos (second god). We do not know if their writings were popular while they were alive or grew popular in the decades to follow. Most historical accounts of the development of the Trinity mention the Greek Apologists. Most mention Justin by name as a key figure in identifying the Son as separate from the Father.

The question in the 2nd century was whether God is one or two? To ask a different way, was Jesus the same deity as the Father or a separate divine being? The Holy Spirit, as the Spirit of God, or sometimes the Spirit of Christ, is mentioned, just as God's Spirit is mentioned in the Bible, but there is no discussion, question, or even mention of the Holy Spirit as a separate being, person, or separate God. There is no record of anything like the Trinity until the 3rd century (i.e. Tertullian around 213 A.D.).

We find another interesting confirmation of this focus on "two-ness" when we look at the hubbub regarding the heretical views of Marcion of Sinope. Sinope is a port city on the Black Sea, in modern-day northern Turkey. And Marcion taught some crazy stuff about Jesus and the God of the Old Testament. He was probably responsible for getting the rest of the Christian world to nail down the final list of canonical books in the New Testament.

Marcion rejected many normally accepted letters as authoritative and canonical. He recognized only ten Pauline epistles and his "special" edited version of the Gospel of Luke. The church world already had a fairly consistent list of which letters were legitimate and recognized as scripture. Marcion's weird ideas and writings likely caused others to firm up the list to avoid future nutty views.

We have none of Marcion's writings, but we get some sense of what happened through critiques by Iranaeus and Tertullian. The bias of the writers becomes a challenge in the next two centuries, but Iranaeus and Tertullian disagreed about almost everything. They were on opposite sides of the deutero-theos debate. Irenaeus rejected the idea that Jesus was a second god, because of his strong belief in the singular identity of God as one. Tertullian rejects Marcion from the opposite direction, in that Tertullian describes God as a Trinity for the first time, albeit very different from the 4th century version that dominates Christian thinking still today.

You can often get a more accurate portrayal when described by someone's critics, if there are multiple accounts, especially from different perspectives.

In this case, I want to point out that the controversies in the second century were on the question of whether God is one or two. Marcion believed in two Gods, or two divine beings. Irenaeus emphasizes belief in only one God, as one divine being, and so rejects Marcion's views.

Tertullian goes into much greater detail, repeatedly critiquing Marcion for belief in two deities. Tertullian is the first to suggest there are three in God, but in his conception, they are clearly not co-equal nor co-eternal. You really see this when you look at his questions and criticisms of Marcion:

> "How, therefore, can two great Supremes co-exist, when this is the attribute of the Supreme Being, to have no equal — an attribute which belongs to One alone, and can by no means exist in two?" [74]

> *"It follows, then, that if two gods are compared, as two kings and two supreme authorities, the concentration of authority must necessarily, according to the meaning of the comparison, be conceded to one of the two."* [75]

---

[74] *Against Marcion, the Five Books, Book 1, Chapter 3*, Tertullian, 2015, CreateSpace Publishing, p.11.

[75] *Against Marcion, the Five Books, Book 1, Chapter 4*, Tertullian, p.12.

There are dozens of references to two gods, two beings, throughout Tertullian's critique of Marcion, because that was the question of the day in the late 2nd century. No one, at that time, was arguing about or asking if God was three, or if there were three gods. Tertullian is writing in the early 3rd century, looking back on earlier views.

Considering that Tertullian believes in three divine beings within one God, it is hard not to wonder why we couldn't turn his own arguments against himself. Apostolics reading the following, are likely scratching their heads:

> *"But on what principle did Marcion confine his supreme powers to two? I would first ask, if there be two, why not more? Because if number be compatible with the substance of Deity, the richer you make it in number the better."*

> *"After two, multitude begins, now that one is exceeded. In short, we feel that reason herself expressly forbids the belief in more gods than one, because the self-same rule lays down one God and not two, which declares that God must be a Being to which, as the great Supreme, nothing is equal; and that Being to which nothing is equal must, moreover, be unique."* [76]

Hey Tertullian, I have some questions about your Trinity...

---

[76] *Against Marcion, the Five Books, Book 1, Chapter 5*, Tertullian, p.12-13.

Adding this just for fun, no extra charge...

Marcion's views appear quite bizarre. He really appeared to disdain the God of the Old Testament and favored his New Testament God, Jesus Christ. His conception of God rings with Gnostic tones, where the supreme God created in layers, making the Demiurge and others. Tertullian is mocking all of this, and I am not sure how accurate his depiction might be, but it does include this:

> *"Marcion suffers a manifest wrong from those persons who assume that he holds two gods, whereas he implies no less than nine, though he knows it not."* [77]

If Tertullian is right, Marcion and Benny Hinn have more in common than I would have guessed.

Back to the analysis... Prior to Tertullian in the early 200s, there is no mention of God as three, much less three persons. There was a contentious discussion on how Jesus could be God, mainly waged by the Greek Apologists. They used language that should be unacceptable to Bible-believing Christians. Their writings were popular, at least in Asia Minor and Alexandria. We don't have any confirmation from church leaders that these views were acceptable or popular among 2nd-century church fathers.

---

[77] *Against Marcion, the Five Books, Book 1, Chapter 15,* Tertullian, p.30. (If you don't get the joke, search online for 96s video "Benny Hinn 9")

STEP 2 – GOING FROM TWO TO THREE

Theophilus of Antioch is sometimes credited as the first to call God a "trias". Some claim this is Greek for Trinity, but others argue this is really the Greek word for "three". Note that "trinitas" is the Latin transliteration for Trinity, while the Latin word for three is "tres".

Nevertheless, it took roughly 150 years from Calvary for someone to maybe connect God to the number three, and it still isn't very Trinitarian. His second letter to Autolycus, around 180 [A.D.], includes the phrase:

> "The [trias] of God, His Word and His Wisdom." [78]

Some call this the first Trinity reference, but if you look at the context, it's a stretch, and a great example of twisting someone's words to fit a viewpoint. Most would agree that God, God's Word, and God's Wisdom are not the same thing as the Father, the Son, and the Holy Spirit.

But the stretch gets even weaker than this.

Theophilus is in the middle of a very symbolic and metaphoric description of how the six days of creation prove that the God of the Bible is superior to pagan deities. I don't necessarily disagree, but there is a lot of strange symbolism here, and I am not sure anyone would

---

[78] *Letters to Autolycus, Book II, Chapter 15, Of the Fourth Day,* Theophilus of Antioch, 2015, CreateSpace Publishing, p.29-30.

be convinced of this. I think it would help if you were high as giraffe ears while reading this next part. Buckle up. It gets a bit weird.

> *"...For the sun is a type of God, and the moon of man. And as the sun far surpasses the moon in power and glory, so far does God surpass man. And as the sun remains ever full, never becoming less, so does God always abide perfect, being full of all power, and understanding, and wisdom, and immortality, and all good. But the moon wanes monthly, and in a manner dies, being a type of man..."*
>
> *"...In like manner also the three days which were before the luminaries, are types of the [trias], of God, and His Word, and His wisdom. And the fourth is the type of man, who needs light, so there may be God, the Word, wisdom, man. Wherefore also on the fourth day the lights were made."*

Can we agree that this sounds nothing like the Trinity? Also, if the Sun is a type of God, why did it appear on the fourth day? Sorry, I was distracted by his terrible logic...

It takes extra work to check sources. It's so much easier to copy and paste a quote that sounds good. Even with the Internet, I still had to order books on Amazon and actually read, research, and use a highlighter.

Always check sources for yourself, including my sources. You need to determine which teachers and scholars are careful researchers who love the truth, and who are willing to fudge the "facts" to fit their model better.

I recommend that you follow this amazing principle from the New Testament:

1ˢᵗ Thessalonians 5:21 NKJV
Test all things; hold fast what is good.

In this world of increasingly biased reporting, with so few actually doing real research for themselves, please be careful who you trust and where you go to learn the truth. The Internet is becoming a toxic cesspool of bad ideas, and our schools are failing to teach people how to read, think, and logically analyze evidence. AI is only going to make it harder to separate historical facts from manufactured fiction. Learn to read critically, learn logic, and acquire actual physical books, and especially learn how to read and understand the Bible. I hope you will realize that the Bible deserves your trust and should be the sole authority in matters of doctrine.

Back to the analysis...

If Theophilus wasn't the first, then who gets the honor of being the first real Trinitarian? Could it be Tertullian from Carthage? Tertullian wrote extensively from his home base along the North African coast of the Mediterranean. He was also the first theologian to write in Latin and has been called the "Father of Latin Christianity".

Tertullian is most famous for being the first writer to clearly and directly call God a Trinity.

> *"While the mystery of the dispensation is still guarded, which distributes the Unity into a Trinity, placing in their order the three Persons— the Father, the Son, and the Holy Ghost: three, however, not in condition, but in degree; not in substance, but in form; not in power, but in aspect; yet of one substance, and of one condition, and of one power, inasmuch as He is one God."* [79]

Trinitarians, reading this account, may be excited to finally see words that sound like the language they hear in many denominal churches today. He definitely uses the word "Trinitas" in Latin, as well as the words for person and substance, the same words used in the formal definition of the Trinity towards the end of the 4th century.

Tertullian is the first to declare that God is both one and three at the same time, and he is careful in his word choices.

His conception of the Trinity attempts to embrace both a oneness and a threeness in God simultaneously. He clearly teaches distinct persons within one "monarchy" of God.

---

[79] *Against Praxaeus, Chapter 2*, Tertullian, 2012, Theophania Publishing, p.7.

> *"In like manner the Trinity, flowing down from the Father through intertwined and connected steps, does not at all disturb the Monarchy, while it at the same time guards the state of the Economy."* [80]

> *"Bear always in mind that this is the rule of faith which I profess; by it I testify that the Father, and the Son, and the Spirit are inseparable from each other, and so will you know in what sense this is said. Now, observe, my assertion is that the Father is one, and the Son one, and the Spirit one, and that They are distinct from Each Other."* [81]

For the Trinitarians reading this appendix and excited, you might want to stop reading here, because Tertullian does not believe in the modern Trinity.

He believes the Son was created at a moment in time, and that the 2nd person, at least, is subordinate and not equal to the Father. In Against Praxaeus, Tertullian states:

> *"For the Father is the entire substance, but the Son is a derivation and portion of the whole, as He Himself acknowledges: 'My Father is greater than I.'"* [82]

---

[80] *Against Praxaeus, Chapter 8*, Tertullian, p.23.

[81] *Against Praxaeus, Chapter 9*, Tertullian, p.24.

[82] *Against Praxaeus, Chapter 9*, Tertullian, p.24.

The Catholic analysis of Tertullian confirms this:

> *"In not a few areas of theology, Tertullian's views are, of course, completely unacceptable. Thus, for example, his teaching on the Trinity reveals a subordination of Son to Father that in the later crass form of Arianism the Church rejected as heretical."* [83]

Tertullian was later celebrated for his innovation and understanding regarding the Trinity. He wasn't well-received in His day. I can't imagine why. His famous work, Against Praxaeus (~ 213 [A.D.]), attacks the bishop of Rome.

Lacking writings from Praxaeus, it is difficult to know the details of his beliefs, but he apparently believed the Father and the Son were the same divine being, along the lines of Apostolic or Modalistic thinking. Tertullian accuses Praxaeus of what we now call "Patripassianism", the doctrine that the Father suffered on the Cross:

> *"He maintains that there is one only Lord, the Almighty Creator of the world... He says that the Father Himself came down into the Virgin, was Himself born of her, Himself suffered, indeed was Himself Jesus Christ."* [84]

---

[83] Article on *Tertullian*, New Catholic Encyclopedia, 2003, Volume 13, p.837.

[84] *Against Praxaeus, Chapter 1,* Tertullian, p.3.

My intention is to focus on the history of the Trinity, but if you are wondering, Apostolics may not have a clear answer on whether the Father suffered. God absolutely is one, and God begat and made a Son, and God was in that Son in the incarnation. Falling back on clear Biblical statements, we know that God purchased the church with His own blood (Acts 20:28) and that the LORD, Yahweh, was Himself, pierced (Zechariah 12:10). The Biblical presentation could indicate that the Father did, in fact, suffer, in and through the incarnation. Apostolics may be uncomfortable describing it in these words.

Tertullian brings us much closer to a Trinitarian mindset than any that came before him, but his views were innovative and not yet popular. Even the bishop of Rome, at this time, believed God was one person along the lines of Apostolic Oneness thinking.

Tertullian also got involved in Montanism around 207 A.D.. Although we still don't know what Montanus actually taught, we know it was condemned as heretical, and Tertullian's interest was enough to get him condemned as well. Tertullian may not have been formally excommunicated, but his Montanist loyalties are likely the thing that blocked him from sainthood in the Catholic church.

I suggest that Tertullian was responsible for important innovations in the development of the Trinity, but he was not the first true Trinitarian.

Origen Adamantius, a contemporary of Tertullian, puts the final pieces in place for belief in the modern Trinity. Tertullian called God three, but not co-equal or co-eternal. Origen is the first to reject subordination, and finally level the three persons up around 230 [A.D.].

> *"Now God's wisdom is the brightness of that light, not only in so far as it is light, but in so far as it is everlasting light. His wisdom is therefore an everlasting brightness, enduring eternally. If this point is fully understood, it is a clear proof that the Son's existence springs from the Father himself, yet not in time, nor from any other beginning except, as we have said, from God himself."* [85]
>
> *"For the Holy Spirit would never have been included in the Unity of the Trinity, that is, along with God the unchangeable Father and with his Son, unless He had always been the Holy Spirit."* [86]
>
> *"Nothing in the Trinity can be called greater or less."* [87]

Origen made other statements that sound like some Subordination was retained, so he is criticized by some as failing to be a true Trinitarian. It is difficult to sort this out, because Origen wrote prolifically and often appeals to symbols and metaphoric interpretations.

---

[85] *First Principles, Book 1, Chapter 2.11,* Origen Adamantius, 2013, Christian Classics, p.35.

[86] *First Principles, Book 1, Chapter 3.4,* Origen, p.43.

[87] *First Principles, Book1, Chapter 3.7,* Origen, p.47.

After deep-diving back into early church writings, I found Origen to be one of the most difficult authors to process and understand.

Origen was popular in his day, although I can see why many struggled to understand the ramifications of his writings. I am guessing that he was one of those people who was easier to understand in person, than in written word. He was invited to travel, teach, and preach, even before he was properly ordained into the church.

It is common to believe that Origen was kicked out of the church for his beliefs. I believed this for years, and finally, in the research for this book, did I discover the truth behind the claim. Origen was discipled in Alexandria, under the bishop Demetrious. Origen's bishop was likely incredibly jealous of his star pupil's rapid rise and increasing fame. He was receiving invitations to travel and teach to other bishops and even governing officials. Origen taught without Demetrious' permission, and Demetrious refused to ordain Origen as revenge. When another bishop ordained him anyways, that led to an official condemnation from Alexandria, but few cared.

His writings increased in popularity, and after Origen's death (around 253 [A.D.]), Pope Dionysius continued to promote his views.

Most accounts also mention the strange question of whether Origen castrated himself. He tutored multiple students as a young man. He also lived in the home of a wealthy Gnostic woman who became his patron. Eusebius records that Origen castrated himself, or maybe had someone assist in the task, in order to protect his reputation while teaching individuals alone.

The irony is found in Origen's tendency to interpret everything in the Bible as symbolic. He apparently took Matthew 19:12 as a literal instruction, a passage usually considered as figurative, and he decided to take action.

Eusebius, who celebrates Origen's life and generally praises him, includes the details of this self-mutilation in Origen's biography. Eusebius became bishop of Caesarea Maritima, the home of Origen after he left Alexandria. Not only was Eusebius privy to local accounts of Origen's life and his writings, but he also had little to gain in making salacious or derogatory statements about the local theological hero of Caesarea.

It is currently popular to revise all ancient accounts, and some don't believe Eusebius' narrative on this point, but there is no known historical reason to doubt it. As one who has surveyed enough of Origen's writings, I conclude that he was very intelligent but had some out-there ideas in his head, and I believe it is likely that Origen did what Eusebius claims.

I also recognize that it is a low blow to allow a man's past mistakes to besmirch their reputation when considering their lifetime achievements. I would like my work here to be considered well-reasoned and scholarly, and so I have decided to remove any mention of Origen's castration from my conclusions.

I think it is valid and reasonable to recognize that Origen is the first real Trinitarian around 230 [A.D.]. It took about 200 years after Calvary for someone to describe God as a Trinity of co-equal and co-eternal persons. As we will see in the next section, this position remains the minority view in the church for another 100 years.

STEP 3 – THE TRINITY GROWS IN POPULARITY

It took 200 years of discussion to reach the first genuine Trinitarian, but Origen is just one man, albeit an influential one. According to Tertullian and Origen, their views were still very much in the minority in their time.

Many have provided quotes showing that Tertullian called his opponents "the majority of believers". Origen describes simple belief in Jesus as God as "the great multitude" of believers in his day. I want to provide longer quotes in context so you can decide for yourself if this is an accurate description. Considering their bias against belief in a single God without plurality, acknowledging that they are in the minority is very likely an accurate assessment.

Tertullian, known for being critical of any who dare to disagree with him, offers this description of general Christian beliefs about the nature of God in Christ:

> *"The simple, indeed, (I will not call them unwise and unlearned,) who always constitute the majority of believers, are startled at the dispensation (of the Three in One), on the ground that their very rule of faith withdraws them from the world's plurality of gods to the one only true God; not understanding that, although He is the one only God, He must yet be believed in with His own οἰκονομία."* [88]

This final word, οἰκονομία, does not translate well into English, but can best be understood as "household management" or "administration", and was used by philosophers and theologians to describe God's divine plan. Tertullian believes there is a plurality within God's being, but acknowledges that most Christians, including Christian leadership, viewed God as one and reject any notion of a plurality within God.

Origen provides even more details about Christian viewpoints in his day. His comments are found in his *Commentary on the Gospel of John*, where he classifies believers into four distinct groups. His Trinitarian views, and how he views the Logos, are in the first group.

[88] *Against Praxaeus, Chapter 3*, Tertullian, 2012, Theophania Publishing, p.8.

I would happily include myself in his description of the second group who know nothing but Jesus.

> "Now it is possible that some may dislike what we have said, representing the Father as the one true God, but admitting other beings besides the true God, who have become gods having a share of God..."
>
> "In the same way, now, <u>some have faith in that Reason which was in the beginning and was with God</u> and was God; so did Hosea and Isaiah and Jeremiah and others who declared that the Word of the Lord, or the Logos, had come to them.
>
> A <u>second class are those who know nothing but Jesus Christ and Him crucified, considering that the Word made flesh is the whole Word</u>, and knowing only Christ after the flesh. <u>Such is the great multitude of those who are counted believers.</u>" [89]

Origen considers his views on the Logos being separate from God as strong enough that he is even willing to quote scripture to describe those who don't see it his way. That takes some courage... or stupidity, but I am happy to stick with 1st Corinthians 2:2 and Colossians 2:9 as my rallying cry. I am thrilled to know that this group is still the majority of believers 200 years after Calvary.

---

[89] *Commentary on John, Book 2, Chapter 3*, Origen Adamantius, 2014, Beloved Publishing, p.48, 50.

Origen categorizes believers into two more groups:

> *"A third class give themselves to logoi (discourses)*
> *having some part in the Logos which they consider*
> *superior to all other reason: these are they who follow*
> *the honorable and distinguished philosophical schools*
> *among the Greeks.*
>
> *A fourth class besides these are they who put their trust*
> *in corrupt and godless discourses, doing away with*
> *Providence, which is so manifest and almost visible, and*
> *who recognize another end for man to follow than the*
> *good."* [90]

Apparently, there was a group of Christians still swayed by the view of the Greek Apologists in this day. This is the third class, and I would guess they believed in two Gods, with Jesus as a deutero-theos, a second god, and I am happy to hear they are in the minority.

I am not sure what to do with this fourth class. They don't seem very interested in doctrine. Maybe they would like Joel Osteen's sermons.

From the early 200s into the early 300s, the doctrine of the Trinity likely grew more popular, but still wasn't in the majority, but the worst single event to befall the Christian church loomed on the horizon.

---

[90] *Commentary on John, Book 2, Chapter 3*, Origen, p.50.

The emperor of Rome, Constantine, started as pagan in his early life, before he unified the empire. He believed that the God of the Christians had given him a sign and a victory against his greatest foe. He negotiated the Edict of Milan in 313 A.D. with the two other ruling emperors of Rome (yes, it wasn't quite unified at this point). This Edict was a public declaration to enforce tolerance towards Christianity and protection from persecution.

Unfortunately, he doesn't stop there. Constantine increasingly makes Christianity the unofficial state religion of Rome. Wanting to unify the empire, he discovered that the Christian world was split on questions about the deity of Jesus.

It is likely that many still believed, as Origen described it, that Jesus was simply God. A new growing group, influenced by Arius of Cyrene (in modern-day Libya), believed that Jesus was a created and second God separate from God Almighty. The third group, likely increasing in number, believed in the Trinity model for God, one God comprised of three distinct persons.

Constantine wanted unity and ordered the church bishops to convene a council and settle the matter. They met in Nicaea in 325 A.D.. This community was less than 100 miles from the newly named Roman capital, Constantinople, in northwestern Turkey.

This was the first of what would become the Ecumenical Councils, where the bishops of the church would gather to rule on matters of doctrine or administration. Somewhere between 250 and 320 bishops attended the Council, and they met for several months from May to July of 325 A.D..

It is common for many to claim the Trinity was first accepted as doctrine at Nicaea, but that isn't accurate. Nicaea was really a trial of the views of Arius, and spoiler alert... they condemned his views as heretical. Nicaea was primarily about the relationship between God and the Son of God, Jesus Christ. The resulting creed affirmed that the Son was of the same divine substance as the Father. The Holy Spirit is not mentioned much in the original Nicene Creed. We find the simple statement, "I believe in the Holy Spirit", towards the end.

The original creed does include a specifically Trinitarian declaration of a pre-existent and eternal Son. Jesus is described as "begotten not made". This is likely the only direct statement in the original Nicene Creed that most Apostolic Oneness Christians would find clearly unacceptable and unbiblical. Otherwise, we might quibble with some of the word choices, but the rest is not terribly far from statements found in the Bible.

The confusion over the Trinity at Nicaea comes because a later Council changed the Nicene creed. They added more Trinitarian language, specifically affirming the relationship between the Holy Spirit and the Father and the Son. In the literature, this later version is called the Nicene-Constantinople Creed.

We do not know how many Oneness bishops were present or how many Trinitarian leaders attended Nicaea, only that the Arians were outnumbered and condemned. The road to the Trinity still has a few more speed bumps, and the Arian controversy is not over.

To be clear, the doctrines of Arius are absolutely unbiblical. In the modern age, this view mostly closely resembles the teachings of Charles Russell and the Jehovah's Witnesses. Although condemned at Nicaea, Arian bishops still actively served. Constantine, for instance, put off his baptism in the hopes that it would cover more of his sins. When he grew seriously ill, he was finally baptized. He had the Arian bishop Eusebius (a different Eusebius from earlier) baptize him in the Jordan River in the Spring of 337 A.D.. He died a few weeks later.

If you haven't figured it out yet, Constantine was a terrible Christian and a terrible influence on Christianity. He made it the state religion, driving pagan and secular leaders in the Roman Empire to "convert" to this new religion. They had very little intention of actually taking up their cross and following Jesus. Instead, Christianity became politically important and influential, and it is logical to assume this only increased opportunities for corruption, ego, and sin to make inroads into Christian leadership.

We have one final and clear piece of evidence that the Trinity was not yet the majority position after Nicaea.

Alexander and Athanasius, both of Alexandria, were two of the principal critics of Arianism at Nicaea. Alexander passed shortly after Nicaea, naming Athanasius as his choice as the next bishop.

Athanasius was a vigorous champion of the Trinity and vocal critic of Arianism. No matter the opposition, he would not stop campaigning on both issues. As a Detroit, Michigan resident, it is easy for me to smile and celebrate his nickname. In Latin, he was called Athanasius Contra Mundum (Athanasius Against the World).

He needed that energy and commitment, because the Arians were not done after Nicaea, and the Trinitarians were not yet in the clear majority. From my research, it appears this question split the Roman Catholic Church in the middle of the 4th century. Any other views became inconsequential, and bishops were highly encouraged to take a side. Depending on the region where they served, Arianism was either influential or strongly opposed. I suspect that whatever contingent of Oneness bishops present in the early 300s were increasingly silent and reducing in number as the debate raged.

Athanasius was not silent in championing the Trinity and attacking Arianism, but the Arians retained influence in multiple cities and with multiple emperors.

For his views on the Trinity and his writings against Arian doctrine, Athanasius was exiled five times. The first exile was in 335 [A.D.], and the last around 365 [A.D.]. If Trinitarian views dominated, Athanasius' struggle and multiple exiles would not have happened.

His writings and persistence throughout this period had an enormous impact on the final dismissal of Arian beliefs near the end of the 4th century. It is almost as if Arianism were left outside, knocking on the door, but no one would answer…

Athanasius was described by one historian as:

"The greatest champion of Catholic belief on the subject of the Incarnation that the Church has ever known and in his lifetime earned the characteristic title of 'Father of Orthodoxy', by which he has been distinguished ever since." [91]

The nature of the incarnation, and the arguments that followed, triggered massive division and strife in parts of the Roman Empire through the middle of the 4th century. The Trinity position continued to gain ground as the Arian view was finally defeated, and we reached the final step in the adoption of the Trinity as the official doctrine of the historic orthodox church.

---

[91] Article on *Athanasius, Saint*, The Catholic Encyclopedia, 1912, Volume 1.

STEP 4 – THE FINAL ADOPTION AS DOGMA

Before we talk about 381 A.D., we need to address the general corruption of church leadership in the 4th century. I am not talking about Bishops acting selfishly or personal attacks and grudges. We see that kind of behavior throughout the Bible and even in the New Testament between the Apostles. But need for unity, and leading of the Holy Spirit, outweighed differences of opinion. Acts 15 remains a beautiful example of how Spirit-led Christians should handle division.

We find a very different culture in Rome as early as 366 [A.D.]. After the death of Pope Liberius, the churches of Rome were split over the successor. The deacons and laity preferred a man named Ursinus as the next leader. The ruling class preferred Damasus as the next pope and bishop of Rome. There are multiple accounts claiming that Damasus ordered mercenaries to attack the supporters of Ursinus, leading to a multi-day massacre with over 130 Christians found dead in the Julian Basilica. On top of all this, there are also accounts of Damasus bribing government officials to exile his political opponents, and accusations of multiple incidents of adultery. He is described as a womanizer, with the memorable nickname, "the ladies' ear-scratcher".

All of this egregious violence, gross moral failure, and political maneuvering did not stop the bishops from declaring Damasus the true pope at a synod in 378 A.D..

A few have claimed that some of Damasus' accusations come from false propaganda from Arians who opposed him. I don't think any credible historian is trying to exonerate Damasus from his involvement in murdering over 100 of his rival's supporters.

Even if most of the accusations were false, it would still paint a picture of a "Christian" world in Rome where geopolitics and ego are in charge, and no one is even remotely trying to follow the Holy Spirit. By the time of Pope Damasus, how far had we fallen from the Biblical mandate, especially for church leadership?

Romans 14:16 NKJV
Therefore, do not let your good be spoken of as evil.

When presented with the gross moral failures of the historic church, whether in the 4th century or even the Middle Ages, some try to argue that this was the culture of a given time. "They were living in a much different world... You shouldn't judge them by current standards of conduct..." I vehemently reject any excuses for tolerating rampant sin among leaders of God's church, and I have zero respect for doctrinal statements from people who condoned or tolerated murder.

I have strong doubts that many church leaders in the later 4th century were even born again according to John 3:5. That being said, leaders who tolerate, permit, or even contribute to murder or other gross moral failures, if they have not repented, are definitely going to hell.

I see no reason to care about their doctrinal statements and theological positions. I don't care if it is the school of Catholic bishops in the 4th century tolerating murder, or John Calvin in Geneva, who ordered a man executed because he proposed baptism in Jesus' name.

I have zero respect for evil people parading themselves as valid Christian leaders. The same bishops who confirmed Damasus as pope, are the ones heading to Constantinople in 381 A.D.. If you think their opinions matter, I doubt we will see eye-to-eye on this, but at least you know where I stand.

After almost a century of division over the Arian controversy, and the increasing popularity of the Trinity doctrine, the bishops are convened by the Roman Emperor Theodosius the 1st to come to Constantinople and attempt to unify the Western and Eastern Church.

Apparently, there remained some strong Arian influences in the East, and a controversy was brewing over whether the next bishop of Constantinople might have Arian tendencies or not. A group attempted to claim the bishopric in a midnight ceremony, and were caught and driven off, and the emperor, as well as the pope, were consulted on what they should do to solve the matter.

The council was convened, and bishops began arriving at Constantinople. 36 bishops from a Semi-Arian position arrived. They were denied entry when they refused to affirm the Nicene Creed. So, you can get a sense of who controlled this council and how they intended to proceed. Damasus also provides an incredibly ironic instruction about the selection of the next bishop:

> *"Take care that a bishop who is above reproach is chosen for that see."* [92]

At least someone cares about the moral authority of a bishop, even if that someone is a known murderer… I laughed when I saw this request from a man called the Ladies' Ear Scratcher.

The bishops convened in 381 [A.D.]. This council was marked with controversy, and questions followed of its legitimacy as an Ecumenical Church Council. This triggered a synod the next year, by Damasus, to revise the outcomes. There is even some question of which major Council changed or approved the Nicene Creed to include additional language about the Holy Spirit. It might have happened at Constantinople, or at Ephesus,

---

[92] *Leaders of Iberean Christianity, 50-650* [A.D.], Joseph Marique, 1962, Saint Paul Publishing, p.59.

or at some other Synod, but by Chalcedon in 451 [A.D.], everyone agrees it was completed and correct. The legitimacy of Constantinople is also affirmed by later councils.

To be clear, almost everyone except the Arians, who were blocked from attending, affirms that the Trinity was made church dogma at 381 [A.D.]. I am only adding the wrinkles and speed bumps because I want to present an accurate picture of what happened, and I find all this church history quite fascinating.

No one published and serious about church history disputes any of the major points of this summary. The most controversial statement that I have made regards Origen's self-mutilation, and I am siding with the slim majority of scholars who agree that he likely did the deed. The rest of my claims in this summary are fairly benign and conservative by comparison.

It took about 350 years from Calvary for the Trinity to develop and be affirmed as the official doctrine of the church, and that road is a bumpy one of conversations and disputes as different factions argued over their beliefs about the deity of Jesus Christ. At first it was a question of whether Jesus was God or a second god. Then 200 years after Calvary, the initial idea of a Trinity is finally introduced. It takes another 150 years to officially become the doctrine of the church.

Constantinople at 381 ^A.D.^ is the best date for the official adoption of the Trinity, but it was really the work of three additional theologians that ended the discussion and cemented the Trinity as dogma for the next 15 centuries.

The Cappadocian Fathers were three theologians and church leaders who were recognized and respected by Eastern and Western churches, and their writings and influence, unified church beliefs entering the 5th century, especially regarding the doctrine of the Trinity.

- Basil the Great, Bishop of Caesarea
- Gregory, Bishop of Nyssa (and Basil's brother)
- Gregory, Patriarch of Constantinople

In their writings, they not only established Trinity in the church world, but also worked to bring Arian believers into Trinitarian alignment. They established the specific Greek formula of "one substance (ousia) in three persons (hypostasies)" as the established and specific definition of the Trinity in their day.

If you agree with this process, and the authority of the church leaders to develop and establish the Trinity in 381 A.D., but you are not Catholic, you have an immediate problem on the horizon.

At the very next church council, the Council of Ephesus, in 431 A.D., the Bishops met (in the Southwest of Modern Turkey) to respond to disputes as Mary worship (Mariology) was increasing in popularity in the church.

They met supposedly to condemn the doctrine that Mary be called the Theotokos (the God-bearer), but it feels foolish that they picked the Church of Mary, in Ephesus, to answer the question.

Spoiler alert, they didn't condemn the practice, but through some adroit politics among the 250 bishops who assembled, the church affirmed Mary as the "Mother of God" as she was officially titled of "Theotokos". This was commonly celebrated in the ancient world and is still celebrated in Catholic and Orthodox churches today. You can easily find iconography today, especially in the Greek Orthodox world, celebrating Mary as the Theotokos[93].

Protestant Christians who accept the decision to declare God as a Trinity, have a challenging question they seem to avoid. Protestants consistently affirm the Catholic language of the Trinity but also reject the idea that Mary is the God-bearer. Why should we listen to the bishops in 381 [A.D.], but then disregard their decision in 431 [A.D.]?

Apostolics have an easy and consistent answer for this. We only use scriptural language and declarations as

---

[93] *Icon of Mary as the Theotokos*, Metropolitan Church of the Presentation of the Lord in Thira, Greece, Photograph by Scott Lynn, 2025.

authoritative, so we disregard all these church councils as irrelevant in matters of doctrine. We just look at the Bible and Biblical language.

The Protestants want to claim they follow Sola Scriptura. When you ask about the Trinity, they pretend that this 4th century doctrine is Biblical, but none of the key terms and definitions are clearly declared in scripture. The Trinity contradicts multiple verses, while requiring a specific and careful interpretation of other passages.

STEP 5 – BUT WHY DID JESUS PRAY?

The church world started with legitimate questions in the 2nd century. Why did Jesus pray? Why did He talk about God and also claim divine prerogative and identity? Some called Jesus a second god and then argued through its ramifications. Later, Tertullian and Origen decided God is three, but it took another 150 years to agree on the belief and final language of the Trinity.

In the process of making each person co-equal, the church found itself back at one of the original questions. Why did Jesus pray? After all, if Jesus is divine, and co-equal with the Father, how and why would He participate in an activity of intrinsic submission? Prayer is a relational interaction from an inferior being to a superior one.

The development of the Trinity did not solve the original question. It just postponed the discussion into the

5th century. They decided that Jesus is truly divine and made His divinity more complicated than the Biblical narrative. Then, Catholic Church theologians begin wrestling with the question of His humanity:

- **Council of Chalcedon, in 451** ^{A.D.}, meeting near Constantinople – they rejected the teaching that Christ had one nature and declared that He has two natures in one person – human and divine.

- **2nd Council of Constantinople in 553** ^{A.D.} – apparently more precisely defines how Christ has two natures in a single person.

- **3rd Council of Constantinople in 680** ^{A.D.} – declares Christ has two wills – human and divine.

But if Jesus has two wills and two natures, then you can answer how and why He prayed, and the Trinity is irrelevant to the answer. He prayed as a man. His human will explains: "Not My will but Your's be done." And the Trinity contributes no clarity or value to this answer. It only adds confusion and unbiblical details.

The historic church argued for over 350 years to develop the language and ideas of the Trinity, and took 300 years to answer and agree on the dual-nature of Jesus Christ. Had they answered the dual-nature question first, they could have skipped the Trinity part, because it doesn't explain much or add anything but a confusing mystery to the Christian world.

FINAL THOUGHTS ON THE HISTORY OF THE TRINITY

I understand the sincere desire to validate Trinitarian belief to be as early and Biblical as possible. For many Christians, this false notion that the Church Fathers and maybe even the Apostles were Trinitarian feels much more reassuring. Instead, we have a Bible that fails to include any declarations that teach or affirm the specifics of the Trinity. Scripture also includes dozens of verses that disagree with the Trinity model. Then we have a 350-year bumpy road in church history for the development and acceptance of this doctrine.

If you are committed to the Trinity doctrine, you can find Adjacency references in scripture and in the writings of the Church Fathers. Then, you can tell yourself that this is proof of the Trinity. This is hardly objective or convincing.

For the rest of us, it feels like any mention of three things pertaining to God becomes evidence of the Trinity. This leads to out-of-context quotes, such as Theophilus of Antioch, as the first official declaration of the Trinity.

"The [Trias] of God, His Word and His Wisdom."

This becomes the extra-Biblical version of Selectaversitis. Picking and choosing factoids from history while ignoring evidence to the contrary. It feels about as honest as picking and choosing Bible verses while ignoring the pesky ones you don't like.

Then the Catholic church comes along with candid and historically accurate descriptions of the development of the Trinity. These are bitter pills for Protestant Trinitarians to swallow.

"Herein lies the difficulty. On one hand, it was the dogmatic formula "one God in three Persons" that would henceforth for more than 15 centuries structure and guide the Trinitarian essence of the Christian message, both in the 'profession of faith and in theological dialectic'.

On the other hand, the formula itself does not reflect the immediate consciousness of the period of origins; it was the product of 3 centuries of doctrinal development." [94]

I understand that a sincere Trinitarian wants their belief to be valid and shared by 19 or 20 centuries of Christian thinking, but that's just not true. Catholic and Protestant church historians agree that the Trinity "does not reflect the immediate consciousness" of the early church. In other words, this is not how Christians were thinking or talking about God in the first couple of centuries.

"But Scott", I can hear my Trinitarian friends say, "the first or second century Christians, really were Trinitarian. I can find them talking about God as our Father, and

---

[94] Article on *Trinity, Holy*, New Catholic Encyclopedia, 1967, Volume 14, p.295.

about the Son, and even the Holy Spirit." Apparently, you missed the main point of this entire book. Apostolics also believe that God is our Father, and that God has a Son, and God gave us His Spirit. This is Adjacency, and we all agree on that. We disagree on what it means, and on the specifics of how this works. The issue here is the specifics of the Trinity. Do we see evidence in the Bible, or even in early church history, of one God in three Persons?

The Bible says no. Church history reflects this reality, and the Catholic Church agrees with the Apostolic position.

> *"The formulation 'one God in three Persons' was not solidly established, certainly not fully assimilated into Christian life and its profession of faith, prior to the end of the 4th century. But it is precisely this formulation that has first claim to the title 'the Trinitarian dogma'.*
>
> *Among the Apostolic Fathers, there had been nothing even remotely approaching such a mentality or perspective."* [95]

Please read and reflect on that line in the quote above. "...nothing even remotely approaching such a mentality or perspective." Why would a Bible-believing Christian embrace such an idea? The better answer is to embrace Biblical language and the mighty God in Christ.

---

[95] Article on *Trinity, Holy*, New Catholic Encyclopedia, 1967, Volume 14, p.299.

APPENDIX 4 – THE COMMA JOHANNEUM

Other works cover the story of this interesting text much better. I only include a note here because I make a claim in this book, and this verse might be mistakenly brought up to counter the claim.

I argue several times and in several different ways that there isn't a single verse in the Bible that declares God is a Trinity or that God in His nature is somehow specifically "three". The Bible never says He is multiple persons, and we see no clear, declarative, ontological statement in scripture that shows three persons in Heaven.

There is one interesting line in the King James and New King James Bible that might seem to disagree with me:

> **1st John 5:7 NKJV**
> *For there are three that bear witness in heaven: the Father, the Word, and the Holy Spirit; and these three are one.*

This text has a crazy story and unique distinction. It is the only "verse" that has been removed from every modern translation. It did make it into the NKJV in honor of the KJV, but with a footnote declaring an issue:

> *"Only 4 or 5 very late manuscripts contain these words in Greek..."*

To be clear, this line "there are three that bear witness in heaven...Father... Word... Spirit... and these three are one" is NOT found in a single Greek manuscript of the Bible from the first 1,300+ years of Christianity. It did not exist in the Greek according to all the textual evidence we have. Even in the Latin Vulgate, this verse was NOT present in any Latin Bible in the first 500 years since Calvary. Based on clear and consistent evidence, it has been dropped from every modern translation, and this is the only verse for which this is true.

Except for people who don't know textual history and those in the King James Only Movement, this claim is not controversial. Almost all respected and published Trinitarian authors and scholars agree that this verse was not in the original Bible. It was likely added as a comment in a Latin Bible margin by a Catholic monk at some point. Maybe a century later, it was inserted into the Latin Vulgate. For that reason, this text has the nickname of the "**Comma Johanneum" or John's comment**, a note that started as a comment in the margins and eventually made it into the Catholic Bible.

There is a group, called the King James Only Movement, that strongly opposes any criticism of any passage in the KJV Bible. They believe and contend that this specific translation is a restoration of scripture in some unique and sacred way. As you might guess, the King James Only crowd strongly defends every verse in the KJV and dismisses any criticisms. Although I love and respect the

King James Translation and use both the KJV and NKJV frequently in my study and memorization, I do not believe it has a unique sacred role compared to other translations. It is great but not perfect.

While I am bringing up controversial ideas, here is something you won't hear many Pentecostals say. I am incredibly thankful that the Catholic Church believes they had the authority to declare new doctrines in addition to the Bible. This might surprise you, but my gratitude comes from a unique perspective. I think they are wrong, but because of their false belief in ongoing revelation, there is no evidence of systematic suppression or modification of the Bible by Catholic monks and leaders. Instead, we have this incredible wealth of manuscript evidence and copies giving us great confidence in the accuracy and reliability of God's Word.

I do believe and defend the position of inerrancy, contending that the original writings in the Bible were God-inspired and God has preserved His Word for us to know it without error. We can know God's Word accurately and with confidence regarding all areas of doctrine and application. Based upon extensive examples to the contrary, I do not contend that God magically prevented inaccurate translations or mistakes from happening. The evidence and data show that poor translations have clearly happened. You can know the difference and know which translations are better. It does require some homework, but inerrancy is not a promise that finding the truth will be easy-peasy, only that we can know God's Word if we pursue it diligently. Belief in inerrancy is not incompatible with the simple fact that a monk inserted a verse in the Latin Bible, and it made its way into a couple of Greek manuscripts, and unfortunately, into the King James Translation.

This might bother you. I was surprised, and it bothered me too when I first learned about this issue years ago. Almost all respected and published Trinitarian authors and scholars are in agreement that this verse was not in the original letter of 1st John. Apostolics are somewhat torn and divided on this verse, mainly because most are not aware of how much scholarship and knowledge we have about this. Many Apostolics agree it doesn't belong in the Bible. Others are uncomfortable suggesting that anything could be wrong with even a single verse in the King James Bible.

I have listened to Apostolic teachers make the case that this verse works in the Oneness model and even supports the Oneness position. I disagree. If you cannot see and acknowledge that 1st John 5:7 would support the Trinity model and be a problem for the Apostolic position, then your model as an Apostolic has blocked you from objectively reading and considering the words in this text.

1st John 5:7 in the King James is exactly the kind of declarative statement I would expect multiple times in scripture if the Trinity were actually true. Although a single verse is a terrible basis for an important doctrine, if this were in the Bible, then I could NOT credibly say "there isn't a single verse in the Bible that declares God is three". 1st John 5:7 would be a declarative statement and would be the best Biblical support for the Trinity if it were in the original epistle.

But it only shows up in Greek manuscripts in the 14th century, and all serious Trinitarian scholars are in complete agreement on this.

You might know that during the 3rd and 4th centuries, when the arguments about the Trinity were most active, there were letters and publications by leaders about this new doctrine of the Trinity. They often quoted Bible verses in their writings. This verse was never quoted. Not once. Because it did not yet exist. 1st John 5:7 is not found in our oldest Latin Bibles, going back to the 4th century. It first showed up in the Latin Vulgate in the 6th century, over 500 years after Calvary.

If you ever pick up a Catholic Bible or look up 1st John 5 online in a New Jerusalem Bible, you will find something like the following note at the bottom of the chapter.

"5:7 – The words in italics are not found in any of the early Greek manuscripts or translations, or in the best manuscripts of the Vulgate. They are almost universally regarded as a gloss."

If you look at the translation notes in other modern translations, you will find similar details:

1ˢᵗ John 5:8 NIV Footnotes

"*Late manuscripts of the Vulgate testify in heaven: the Father, the Word, and the Holy Spirit, and these three are one.* ⁸ *And there are three that testify on earth: the (not found in any Greek manuscript before the fourteenth century).*"

This might be shocking for some Christians to read. If you are concerned, you should know it isn't easy to "corrupt" the Bible. Erasmus and other textual experts knew these words were not in reputable manuscripts 500 years ago. This is not news to anyone who studies Biblical texts.

The story behind these words and their inclusion in the King James translation has been well understood for centuries. The Catholic textual expert, Desiderius Erasmus, began compiling the best New Testament Greek text starting in the late 1400s. Others in the Church noticed that 1ˢᵗ John 5:7 was missing from his published work in the first and second editions. He was asked to include it, but he had no Greek words for it since it was not present in any Greek manuscripts at the time. He refused to "make up Greek words" for this line and would only add it if they could produce a Greek manuscript with the verse in it. Someone in the Catholic Church was able to find a manuscript with the verse.

They called his bluff, and Erasmus included the extra words along with notes indicating his doubts about the authenticity of the passage. 1st John 5:7, with the words "the three that bear witness in heaven...", made it into his 3rd edition Greek New Testament, the *Novum Testamentum Omne*, published in 1521.

This was the Greek text used by William Tyndale in his translation work from 1522 to 1535, and it was also the basis for the King James translation in 1611. We have since learned that the Greek manuscripts with 1st John 5:7 were likely back-translations from Latin back to Greek. They were probably not fakes, or altered, but they were not original Greek manuscripts either. Erasmus was correct, the verse did not belong.

I understand the motivation for wanting these words in the Bible. If you believe that God is actually three in one, wouldn't it be better if it were declared at least once somewhere in the Scriptures? Although 1st John 5:7 doesn't say God is three persons or a Trinity, at least it gives the Trinitarian side one verse that connects God with the number three. As a Trinitarian, it must be frustrating that their side doesn't even get a single verse that directly declares any part of the Trinity doctrine. But this is a false insertion, and not original to the Bible.

The Bible doesn't contain a single credible verse that teaches that God is multiple persons or identified specifically with the number three. The emphasis in scripture is always on the one true God who speaks with one mind, one voice, and one will.

If this appendix is the first time you have heard about issues with 1st John 5:7, I suspect that you may need more evidence to settle your understanding of this interesting passage. I would strongly encourage you to look into it for yourself and not trust a single source, even if I hope I am careful and did my homework.

As mentioned earlier, I have a 1st Thessalonians 5:21 mentality of "Test all things, hold on to the good". I strongly encourage you to look up sources and verses and put the Bible and the facts first and your models second. That really is the main point of this entire book.

I really like it when we have an opportunity, wherever possible, to verify a claim or a source for ourselves. It is one of my favorite ways to check if someone is presenting factual and accurate information. I often check sources and quotes where I can, and you would be stunned at how often they are incorrect or taken out of context.

If you want an interesting confirmation that the Comma Johanneum is an inserted text, you can look at Martin Luther's 1545 Bible, which was translated from the 1st Edition of Erasmus' Greek New Testament. We know it was the 1st Edition, because we still have Luther's copy of Erasmus' *Novum Testamentum Omne*. I viewed it personally when I visited Wittenberg, Germany, in 2019.

Even if you don't speak German, which I do not, you can find the Luther 1545 Bible online and find 1st John 5. It is available at www.BibleGateway.com and other websites.

Copy the verses from 1st John 5:5 to 5:9 and paste them into an online German to English translator, and you won't find the words from the Comma Johanneum in Luther's Bible as well.

Martin Luther's copy of the New Testament
Greek codex (published 1516) by Erasmus.
On display in Luther's House on the 3rd floor.

These words from 1st John 5:7 are not found in a Greek manuscript before the 14th century, and they were also not found in the Latin Vulgate in the 4th and 5th centuries. There is zero evidence that this verse was in the original letter of 1st John. That's why it is the only verse that has been removed from every modern Bible translation.

Appendix 4 – The Comma Johanneum

APPENDIX 5 – ANOTHER REASON TO TRUST THE BIBLE

These thoughts are deep enough that you might need to cinch down your thinking cap a bit to follow this. If you are willing, I believe it's worth the journey. The stuff to follow is contemplative on my part and really deserves additional research and evaluation. Since it is not central to this book, but a logical application of models and specifically the Apostolic model, it is left here in the appendix for your consideration.

FIRST, A LITTLE BACKGROUND....

We live in an age where most academic Christians have a "low" view of scripture. They regard the Bible as containing some words from God, somehow, along with myth and human philosophy and accumulated wisdom mixed in. Many don't believe the Gospels were written by the stated authors, or as Bart Ehrman presents it, the teachings of Jesus were handed down for decades, maybe longer, and Jesus' miracles and even deity were mythologized over time and then finally recorded far from the original eyewitness testimony.

In essence, many modern Christian scholars believe the New Testament lies in how it describes itself. These are NOT eyewitness testimonies but embellishments and myths. In a similar "evolution", many believe that the key doctrines of scripture, such as the Trinity, took time to evolve in the midst of Greek philosophical ideas, and so the Bible and Christian doctrine are often viewed as a mix of ancient ideas, evolving over centuries. It is common to believe Christian thought incorporated pagan philosophical influences from the Egyptian deities, Babylonian religion, as well as Platonic and Socratic thinking from the Greeks.

I think the development of the Trinity certainly does match this pattern of combining Biblical ideas with secular worldviews and philosophy. The Trinity is very compatible with Plato's ideas and the Greek conception of the demiurge. Many Christians and the Catholic church have let secular thinking into their theology. I can see their point, when they claim that some beliefs are influenced by secular and pagan sources.

Other times, this kind of thinking strikes me as bizarre. I've read articles and books where the author ponders something like John's use of "Logos" to describe the plan of God. The author sometimes seems incapable of giving the simplest answer for a given verse, that God inspired these words and this verse because it is true and from God.

This reminds me of attempts to dismiss Old Testament miracles through unimpressive naturalistic answers. I have read explanations such as:

"You can believe in the Red Sea crossing because it really was the 'Reed Sea', a shallow body of water at the north end of the Red Sea where sometimes the tide and winds combined to expose land beneath... They likely crossed on

that land, and that's how this 'miracle' actually happened when the wind and tides combined at just the right moment..."

Or... I can believe in God, who made everything, and parting the water isn't terribly difficult for Him. And I can believe in His Word, which uses certain terms and language to supernaturally convey meaning and purpose to us without diluting it and dismissing it because of the influences of Greek philosophers and worldly experts.

The low view of scripture is the popular view in the vast majority of seminaries and Bible colleges in America, and this view dominates in many Christian denominations, especially in America and Europe.

Apostolics (and a few other Christian groups, to be fair) hold to a "high" view of scripture, where the Bible is inerrant. We believe the original writings were God-breathed and inspired, and that we can know the Word of God in all areas of doctrine and significance without error.

This view, the high view of scripture, is still taught in a few seminaries, but is often mocked and definitely represents a tiny minority among recognized Christian scholars and institutions in the modern world.

BACKGROUND DOWNLOAD COMPLETE...

That's the necessary background for the hopefully deep thoughts to follow. Buckle up.

When we actually examine the Apostolic model and the way the scriptures consistently portray the incarnation and even salvation, we are struck with an amazing pattern that does NOT remotely fit the "low" view of scripture that is so popular in seminaries today.

Instead, the consistency of language and preservation of the Apostolic model, by people and institutions who do NOT subscribe to the model, becomes an astounding confirmation of the integrity of God's Word.

When you think about it, multiple core doctrines of the Apostolic model have been consistently and clearly preserved by a religious culture and power that did NOT agree with these teachings.

This is remarkable.

- ✓ The Son in the Bible is firstborn, begotten, and made. This teaching was preserved by an institution that has believed, for over 1,600 years, that the Son is not firstborn but eternal. He is not begotten but "eternally begotten", and yet the Word still says the opposite of what the Catholic Church declares. Remarkable.

✓ The Catholic church craves a picture of the Trinity in scripture, yet you never find God the Son at the right hand of "the Father". Instead, we find Jesus, specifically as our human high-priest, and He is next to "God" in this figurative Adjacency picture that does not match the Trinity. Yet the word choices of this scriptural portrayal are preserved in every single account in scripture with consistent language. Remarkable.

✓ The Catholic church and most protestants believe that Jesus is the 2nd person of a Triune being, and yet the Bible faithfully describes Him as the image of the invisible God, the fullness of deity bodily, and the express image of God's single person or nature. The church preserved these words even though they portray Jesus in a way that does not match their views. Remarkable.

✓ The Catholic Church doesn't baptize (because baptism means immersion or dipping) but instead sprinkles in the titles of the Trinity. Almost all Protestants also baptize or sprinkle in the titles of the Trinity. Yet the Bible faithfully records every baptism with details as being done in the name of Jesus. This record has been preserved for over 1,600 years by churches that don't agree with the book of Acts' baptism fulfillment. Remarkable.

✓ The New Birth pattern was also preserved. The Catholic church teaches that you were saved through obedience and fulfillment of the sacraments of the church, yet they preserved a Biblical record that consistently teaches Salvation as a New Birth of water and Spirit. The Biblical examples of salvation don't even remotely match what has been taught by most churches for over 1,600 years. Remarkable.

The consistency of these doctrines was maintained NOT by its adherents but by its opponents. It wasn't the Apostolics that preserved these words in the Bible, but the Catholic church that does NOT believe them. This demonstrates and destroys a couple of very interesting ideas.

This pattern strongly demonstrates the integrity of God's Word as something that transcends culture and worldview. This is not a religion that came from Greek philosophy or Canaanite culture, Egyptian idolatry, or Babylonian influences. It doesn't reflect Greek influences in the 2nd and 3rd centuries or other worldviews. The Bible, instead, transcends them all to a greater domain than human philosophy can explain.

Bart Ehrman's explanation of the "myth of Jesus" and His deity needing time to build is utterly destroyed. First, by the consistent language of scripture shouting out the deity of Jesus repeatedly in the Old Testament and throughout the New Testament. And second, by the complete repudiation of Greek demiurge thinking that was present in the writings of the 2nd and 3rd centuries. These pagan and Gnostic influences are completely missing from the Bible, and the consistency of the Apostolic model in scripture profoundly validates the transcendent nature of God's word!

This pattern also demolishes the "evolution of God" hypothesis that our understanding of God evolved, and therefore the text continued to change and evolve as leaders refined their understanding and theology. When we look at history from Rome forward, we see pagan and Gnostic ideas taking root, such as plurality in God, holy water, praying to Mary and statues, and celibacy in the priesthood. These kinds of doctrines increased through the Catholic Church and Holy Roman Empire, while the text remained consistent in rejecting pagan ideas and even calling some of these doctrines specifically demonic.

As a thought experiment, pause for a moment and consider the likelihood of the following scenario...

As Gnosticism increasingly influenced the church, and church leaders were elevated as more "Spiritual" than the unwashed masses, they eventually wore special clothes to designate their unique status. Over the centuries, celibacy in the ministry grew more common and was encouraged and finally codified as official church doctrine. The Catholic church could have easily issued commands to "update" or "cleanse" the following verses from the Bible, but they didn't...

1st Timohty 3:1-4 NKJV

This is a faithful saying: If a man desires the position of a bishop, he desires a good work. *²A bishop then must be blameless, the husband of one wife, temperate, sober-minded...* *⁴one who rules his own house well, having his children in submission with all reverence.*

1st Timohty 4:1-3 NKJV

Now the Spirit expressly says that in latter times some will depart from the faith, giving heed to deceiving spirits and doctrines of demons, ²speaking lies in hypocrisy, having their own conscience seared with a hot iron, ³forbidding to marry, and commanding to abstain from foods which God created...

And this is just one example, but a fairly glaring one, where the Catholic teaching directly disagrees with scripture, even to the point of the Bible calling the practice of forbidding to marry as "demonic".

And this is just one example among many of Catholic doctrines not supported by Scripture and even in opposition to the Bible. The Trinity, the veneration of Mary, holy water, celibacy of the priesthood, kissing the Pope's foot, veneration of statues, the immaculate conception and assumption of Mary, purgatory, limbo, the purchase of indulgences, the list just keeps going...

Yet there is no evidence of a systematic attempt to whitewash or change any major doctrines in the Bible.

The Bible, instead, preserves a pure and beautiful message of one God and Biblical love and freedom to choose Jesus, who is the fullness of deity in the flesh, even while corrupt philosophical ideas crept into Christianity in the 3rd and 4th centuries and onwards. The Bible does not reflect an "evolution of God" pattern but a pattern of transcendent thought, sublime wisdom, and revelation, even while the church shifted further away from Biblical truth.

It got so bad, they outlawed the Bible from general availability, but it never occurred to them to change the Bible to match their corrupt doctrine. Clearly, God was at work through incredibly flawed and broken vessels, and God preserved His transcendent Word.

The basic premise of scripture is that God inspired this work. The consistent description and language of the Apostolic model and its preservation by people who don't even agree with the model, powerfully support two simple conclusions:

1) This is truly God's Word, inspired by God.

2) God has preserved His Word in the midst of a world and through institutions that didn't even believe the core details they were preserving!

The Oneness Apostolic message of the mighty God in Christ was preserved by a corrupted and Trinitarian church world that doesn't truly believe all of God was in Jesus. Yet we still have all these beautiful verses declaring the true identity of Jesus Christ.

The Pentecostal New Birth doctrine was preserved by a church that doesn't believe in immersion baptism in Jesus' name or the infilling of the Holy Ghost as a distinct supernatural experience. Yet we still have all these wonderful declarations and examples of Biblical salvation.

God's Word was preserved by an institution that didn't teach these fundamental doctrines. God provided the evidence such that we can know these truths with confidence. This is not man-made religion, but God inspired, transcendent, revealed truth.

Maybe the broader Christian world wouldn't have such a "low" view of scripture if they actually followed Biblical teaching on the identity of Jesus, as well as the Biblical pattern of a New Birth of water and Spirit. Since so many church groups don't follow the plain statements of scripture, is it any wonder that they eventually concluded the Bible was somehow the problem and not their theological models?

These ideas need to be developed further... But ponder how stupendous and unlikely these results would be without God orchestrating the process.

Truly, this is God's plan, and He has preserved His Word that we may know Him.

Thank you for taking this journey with me. I pray and trust that you learned something, and that God's Word has increased in stature and influence in your life from this book.

The Express Image became far more ambitious than the book I intended to write. It poured out of me, most of it in less than 2 months of early morning and evening writing sessions. It largely wrote itself. I had to research and write a couple chapters more carefully, including Firstborn, Begotten, and Logos, as well as carefully checking sources for Appendix 3, but the rest came together quickly. I give God the glory for the true parts. My limited thinking caused any of the flawed parts.

It is my hope and prayer, for both of us, that we continue to evaluate our models for God and the world we live in to make them more accurate and effective, such that we can do more to honor God and fulfill His calling on each of our lives.

In His Service,

About the Author

Scott Lynn is a Christian, Bible Teacher, Apostolic Church Planter, and Pastor in the Metro Detroit Area. Scott and Kendra, along with their teen daughters, Meredith and Kelsey, moved back to Metro Detroit in 2016 to establish a Spirit-filled, Apostolic church with the support and blessing of the Michigan District of the UPCI and later the Metro Detroit District of the UPCI. They were assisted with training and financial support from North American Missions, the church planting ministry of the United Pentecostal Church International.

Scott was born again in 1992 at Apostolic Faith Church in Ypsilanti, Michigan, pastored by William Nix. Although growing up in New Jersey, He loved church here so much, he moved to Michigan for the church and enrolled at Eastern Michigan University.

He received his Bachelor's of Science in Computer Science in 1995 with high honors and his Bachelor's of Theology from Indiana Bible College with high honors in 2000. He completed a third Bachelor's degree in the Natural Sciences with high honors back at EMU in 2001. He has done extensive graduate coursework in both computer science and the natural sciences, including classwork in physics, astronomy, biology, geology, and climatology.

This education may have uniquely helped Scott tackle this book. The world of computer science attempts to build models to track multiple aspects of the real world, whether it is a database tracking customer sales or a monitoring system that tracks a warehouse conveyor system. Scott has built systems to model multiple real-world environments. Then, in the natural sciences, especially in graduate school, Scott was exposed to numerous examples of models being argued, built, and refined as scientists learned about the universe, gravity, cellular structure, chemical processes, and DNA. The building of a new model, and the dismantling of a flawed model, both took time and a lot of convincing. Even when the data was incredibly clear, scientists tended to get stuck in their models. Formally studying theology, computers, and the natural sciences provided a unique vantage point to see how people get blinded by the models that control their thinking.

Scott married Kendra Roberts (now Kendra Lynn) in 2000, and they served in ministry together at several churches, helping in youth ministry, young adults, outreach, and discipleship. Kendra is an anointed worship leader and teaches youth Bible classes and personal Bible studies. Their daughters, Meredith and Kelsey, have both finished college and love serving in the "family business" as they call it. Meredith plays piano, sings, teaches Sunday school, and is a computer programmer. Kelsey plays drums, sings, helps manage our church, along with being a professional illustrator (she created multiple graphics for this book), book reviewer & future bookstore owner.

Scott is passionate about teaching the Bible and has taught Bible classes and personal Bible studies since the mid-1990s. He became an instructor at Purpose Institute in 2010 and has taught theology classes on a variety of topics at three different PI campuses in the past dozen years. He has been writing Bible study materials since 2010. This is his first book.

Visit their church website: **www.FamilyApostolic.org**. You can find free Bible studies on salvation, speaking in tongues, and other topics as well as Scott's allegory on the Incarnation, called *The Beggar King*.